Growing Up with Science

Growing Up with Science
Developing Early Understanding of Science

Edited by
Kjell Härnqvist and Arnold Burgen

Jessica Kingsley Publishers
London and Bristol, Pennsylvania
and

Academia Europaea

First published in the United Kingdom in 1997 by
Jessica Kingsley Publishers Ltd
116 Pentonville Road
London N1 9JB, England
and
1900 Frost Road, Suite 101
Bristol, PA 19007, U S A

Library of Congress Cataloging in Publication Data

A CIP catalogue record for this book is available from
the Library of Congress

British Library Cataloguing in Publication Data

A CIP catalogue record for this book is available from the British Library

ISBN 1-85302 449-X

Printed and Bound in Great Britain by
Athenaeum Press, Gateshead, Tyne and Wear

Contents

Preface

This book is the outcome of a workshop on early science education arranged by the *Academia Europaea*. Previous activities in education by the *Academia* have appeared as *Schooling in Modern European Society*, edited by Torsten Husén (1992) and the *Goals and Purposes of Higher Education in the 21st Century*, edited by Arnold Burgen (Jessica Kingsley, 1996).

This workshop can be regarded as a sequel to the chapter on challenges for science education in the first of those books. When planning the workshop preliminary discussions had led to the conclusion that the really important questions concerned the way in which the way of thinking scientifically is introduced into education. Most of the earlier discussion about science education has concerned better teaching in high school, making science more relevant and overcoming the barrier imposed by resistance to mathematics. We see a need to consider how to tackle scientific literacy from the beginning of education in the primary school, and even in the pre-school period, so that at every stage of education asking questions about life and the physical world is regarded as important, as is the means by which answers to these questions are obtained.

Planning for the workshop had the following aims:

o   to examine ways of improving science education for children from the earliest years

o   to discuss the kinds of scientific understanding, skills and attitudes that can be introduced early in education

o   to suggest the changes needed in European pre-school and primary school education.

These aims cover a very broad area – from basic developmental psychology, to pedagogics with practical examples from current practice, to implementation and evaluation.

With minor exceptions this book follows the order of presentation at the workshop. In the Introduction Arnold Burgen discusses some of the reasons why an improvement in science education is so pressing. Ann Brown and her colleagues and Stella Vosniadou discuss the learning and understanding of young children against a background of developmental psychology. Then Paul Black, Ingrid Pramling and Wynne Harlen consider the pedagogical issues from their particular viewpoints.

1

Next, three special aspects of science education; Patricia Murphy on gender differences, Naama Sabar on the importance and difficulties in teacher education, and Goéry Delacôte on media support. The third set of papers present different practical approaches to early science education. Kees Both from the Jenaplan schools in the Netherlands, Rena Barker, Anne Lea and Gustav Helldén on their experiences in England, Norway and Sweden.

Finally we have three comprehensive contributions; from Wynne Harlen on evaluation, Peter Kelly on policy implementation and Janet Tuomi on an American approach to setting up national standards.

The organisers of the workshop and of this published record are grateful to The Bank of Sweden Tercentenary Foundation which has provided generous financial support and to the City and University of Göteborg for their warm hospitality at the workshop which was held at the University on 12–14 October 1995.

We hope that the interaction at the workshop together with this volume will stimulate interest in early science education and contribute to its improvement.

References

Burgen, A. (ed) (1996) *Goals and Purposes of Higher Education in the 21st Century*. London: Jessica Kingsley Publishers.

Husén, T. (ed) (1992) *Schooling in Modern European Society*. Oxford: Pergamon Press.

Introduction

Arnold Burgen

We are living in a period of very rapid growth in scientific knowledge, much of which is quickly utilised in the creation of new technology. Science and technology are in the present day the greatest factors in changing the way we live. They have also made the world very small, so that we no longer live in the confined world of our town, region, or country isolated from what is happening in the rest of the globe. We are on the threshold of a further leap in communication which has been called the 'Information Revolution'.

It would seem self-evident that understanding how science works and feeds into technology should be a fundamental requirement of education; furthermore, those who grow up with little understanding of science may feel excluded and become disaffected.

However, the understanding of science is not intuitive, and many of the findings of science oppose long-held and cherished beliefs. For instance, the account of the creation of the world including man and all living creatures some six thousand years ago in a period of eight days, as related in the Old Testament, is not compatible with the powerful evidence that man is a product of evolution and has a close genetic relationship not just to the primates but to all vertebrates and even has very many common genetic features with plants and microorganisms. Nor is it compatible with the well-established age of the Earth of several billion years. It was natural for man to feel that the Earth was centre of the universe, and the realisation that it is just a rather small speck in one galaxy out of many others is a chastening view of his importance and his world. The changes wrought by science have made the nature of our life more uncertain and apt to change rapidly. It is often suggested that science is dehumanising in that it reduces the understanding of nature to such simplified and abstract ideas (reductionism) that it becomes out of touch with human life. This may be apparent in some physics, but one can hardly apply the same stricture to biology, which helps us to understand ourselves and cannot avoid emphasising just how complex living things and the phenomena of life are. In any case science itself is an

extraordinary expression of the power of human thought and inge-
nuity.

The scientific view of the world and of objects within it has arisen
by the application of a complex of observation, theory and experiment, seeking always to find a better understanding of the problem
under study. Due to its progressive nature, in which new findings are
continually added, the explanations offered by science are not fixed
but subject to refinement. Sometimes a previous explanation is
shown to be adequate only within certain limitations. This is the case
with Newtonian mechanics which remains perfectly adequate to
describe the 'ordinary' world but breaks down when the conditions
are extreme in temperature, pressure or scale, when relativity theory
becomes necessary. Sometimes old explanations are superseded, as
was the case with the humoral explanation of those diseases found
to be due to infecting micro-organisms. However, it was later realised that the ability of micro-organisms to cause those diseases did
also depend on humoral factors, the antibodies and cellular responses that are the body's defences against them. Since science is
always seeking to improve understanding, this may mean abandon-
ing old ideas which are no longer adequate to provide a satisfactory
explanation of all the available facts. However, this is no reason to
reject scientific explanation as so prone to error as to be useless.
Indeed, science has advanced so far today that many of the explanations offered are unlikely to be greatly changed. An exception is in
those areas of science where our understanding is still at a rather
early stage, such as the very complex operation of the human nerv-
ous system or the mechanisms of development of organisms.

There are many common misunderstandings about the nature of
science, one of which is that it is simply concerned with collecting
facts. Facts are of course necessary but only as the raw material, the
essence of science is the seeking of understanding of how these
'facts' came about, how things and beings are constructed and how
they came to be so. This understanding gradually extends to the
more complex, such as human behaviour individually and in society.
The better one's understanding of the real nature of things, the better
one is able to evaluate claims of the supernatural, of national or racial
superiority, or the effectiveness of new remedies for disease or society. The ability to make rational judgements is needed by all people
in society whether or not they will themselves be engaged in scientific activity. It can very reasonably be said that to drive an automobile you do not need to understand the theory of the internal
combustion engine, but if someone claims to have made an engine
that needs no fuel, or even one that uses fuel with one hundred per
cent efficiency, you do need to know that this is impossible because

it is *scientifically* impossible. In making this judgement it is helpful to understand why it is that some motions such as the rotation of the Earth or the vibration of molecules can continue without change and do not need any external energy, as much as to understand why in the case of the automobile energy is required to overcome friction and the resistance of the air: this is all explained in Newton's first law and similar examples could be drawn from other areas of technology.

A problem with scientific explanation is that it often provides a way of expressing relationships in a compressed form which allows excellent predictions to be made without also providing a tangible understanding of how they happen. When Newton introduced the inverse square law that described with great accuracy the motions of the Earth and the planets, his opponents protested that the nature of gravity was not defined and that the notion of action at a distance was absurd – in fact, these problems still exist and bother us.

If we accept that some knowledge of science should be part of the education of every child, we need to think how best to provide that education. How early in the education process can science be introduced? We know that, in general, the earlier certain subjects are introduced the better they are assimilated; for instance this is well attested in the teaching of a second language. However, we need to establish how well the child is able to comprehend abstract ideas at an early age. Our deliberations will also need to consider which aspects of science are best suited for teaching to young children and how they should be taught. We should try to inculcate the logical approach to understanding that is characteristic of science with ideas and examples carefully selected to provide the grasp of important principles which will help the child grow into a good citizen able to deal critically with new propositions encountered throughout life. This must clearly be the aim.

Putting this into practice is not at all straightforward, as will be all too apparent from the articles in this volume. What is early? The conclusion reached by most of those who have considered this question, is that kindergarten is the ideal starting point, since we are all aware that children start asking 'scientific' questions about themselves, about animals and plants and the world about them at a very early age and there is evidence that we are influenced throughout life by some of the attitudes acquired very early. This raises the questions of how to find time for this in the curriculum, how to integrate it with other aspects of kindergarten activities, and how to make sure that kindergarten teachers have some understanding of the nature of science and hence have the confidence to deal with the children's questions. Motivation needs to be provided, perhaps to some extent through making science into a pleasurable game that is fun; however that will not be enough – as the explanations become more testing they must invoke the sheer pleasure of *understanding*.

The *Academia Europaea*, founded in 1988, is an international, non-governmental association of individual scholars and scientists, aiming to promote learning, education and research. It currently has 1650 members from 34 countries. It covers a wide range of disciplines including the physical sciences and technology, the biological sciences and medicine, the humanities, the social and cognitive sciences, economics and law.

CHAPTER 1

The Development of Science Learning Abilities in Children[1]

Ann L. Brown, Joseph C. Campione,
Kathleen E. Metz and Doris B. Ash

Children as Learners

In this chapter we will trace briefly the set of constraints, both positive and negative, said to influence learning in young children. The four major classes of negative constraints we will discuss are: (1) universal novice constraints, or the lack of general knowledge with which to reason; (2) processing constraints due to limited capacity; (3) limitations due to strategic ignorance; and (4) lack of certain forms of metacognitive knowledge and control. We argue that although these constraints suggest limitations to the young child as learner, closer examination of the past 30 years of research reveals far greater capabilities in the young than previously were supposed.

A fifth so-called 'constraint' would be better served by a more positive definition such as predisposition to learn because the term, constraint on learning, has often been used to refer to biological constraints that predispose organisms to learn certain things more readily than others (Brown, 1990; Carey and Gelman, 1991).

The second section of this chapter consists of a discussion of the influence of Piagetian theory on the design of science education and science standards in Europe and America.

In the third section, we illustrate some of the strengths and weaknesses of young children's learning of science in urban classroom settings. Like many developmental psychologists, we no longer think that it is optimal to rely exclusively on the study of children's learning in a vacuum, i.e., through some highly stylized set of laboratory tasks designed to capture certain aspects of thought, although we still rely

1   The research and preparation of this manuscript were supported by grants from the Andrew W. Mellon, James S. McDonnell and Spencer Foundations, and by grant HD-06864 from the National Institute of Child Health and Human Development, US.

on such measures as part of our protocol. Rather, we now look at learning within complex disciplinary fields, such as biology, studied over long periods of time via sustained effort. Therefore, in the final section of this chapter, we concentrate on general principles of young children's learning situated within our own programme of research designed to foster primary school children's learning of science. We will concentrate on two types of learning: the set that includes metacognition, intentional learning and reflective thought, and the set that includes positive biases to learn privileged classes of information more readily than others. In keeping with the focus of this volume, we will concentrate on the developing understanding of science, notably biology.

Impediments to Children's Learning

Universal Novices

Quite reasonably, it has always been assumed that young children are less effective learners than their older counterparts. The fact that the first five years represent an enormous growth of linguistic and conceptual competence has not allayed that opinion. And it is certainly the case that because of a general lack of expertise children can be characterized as 'universal novices' (Brown and DeLoache, 1978). They suffer from ignorance, i.e., lack of knowledge within which to reason, but not, as we shall see, stupidity or the inability to reason within knowledge fields they do understand (Chi, 1978; Goswami and Brown, 1989, 1990).

Learning Capacity and Strategic Endeavours

When background knowledge is controlled, as when no student 'has' it, it is undoubtedly the case that the older student outperforms the younger. This is true in a wide variety of situations that require deliberate intentional learning. Experimental work in the latter part of this century has provided several reasons for the young child's difficulty in situations that require effortful learning. Initially, it was thought that the child just had less *learning or memory capacity per se*, but during the 1970s it became clear that what children lack is not capacity *per se*, but the ability to make *strategic use of the capacity they have* (Brown, 1975; Chi, 1976, 1978). Trained to use a variety of strategies, such as classifying, organizing, summarizing, etc., children could improve their learning performance dramatically. But there was a catch: when left to their own devices, when there was no teacher, instructor or experimenter present to prompt them, there was little evidence of continued use (maintenance) or flexible deployment (transfer) of these strategies (Brown, 1978; Campione and Brown, 1977).

Metacognition

On further investigation it was found that children's failure to make use of their strategic repertoire was predominantly due to lack of understanding: they had little insight into their own ability to learn intentionally. This was regarded as a *metacognitive* problem: children do not use a whole variety of learning strategies because they do not know much about the art of remembering; they fail to appreciate the constraints of limited human memory capacity, nor do they know how to alleviate this by the employment of strategies and tactics. Furthermore, they know little about *monitoring* their own activities, i.e., they do not think to plan, orchestrate, oversee or revise their own efforts at intentional learning (Brown *et al.* 1983).

As with the case of strategic limitations, metacognitive lacunae were initially overstated. Under certain situations, very young children can be found to be strategic and monitor their performance successfully (Brown and DeLoache, 1978; Brown et al. 1983). It all depends on what is counted as metacognition. This term has been used to refer to widely different levels of cognitive activity, ranging from simple forms of planning and self-regulation that even toddlers can indulge in readily, up through complex reflective practices including the reflective abstraction that was the epitome of formal operations in Piagetian theory. The term has also been used to refer to the child's epistemology, or her knowledge of the nature of knowing and learning itself. Obviously, these types of knowing have different developmental trajectories. And we have argued previously that the term metacognition, used in such a multiplicity of meanings, loses its explanatory value (Brown et al. 1983). In this chapter we will concentrate on intentional learning coupled with reflection, the type of behaviour required for the learning of school science.

Predisposition to Learn in Privileged Domains

Up until now we have concentrated on children's learning difficulties. Another branch of developmental psychology has turned in the other direction, looking at positive biases to learning certain privileged classes of information readily, and early in life (Carey and Gelman, 1991; Hirschfeld and Gelman, 1994). There is a growing body of evidence that young children attend selectively to certain sources of information rather than others; they are said to be constrained or predisposed to learn rapidly in certain domains. To give but one example, infants learn rapidly about what makes objects and people move. Young children show an early understanding that animate objects can move themselves and hence obey what Gelman (1990) calls the innards principle of mechanism; in contrast, inanimate objects obey the external-agent principle; they cannot move themselves, but must be propelled into action by an external force. Because infants preferentially attend to an object's pattern of motion (Bertenthal *et al*. 1985), their initial cut on the world leads them to learn rapidly that inanimate objects need to be pushed, pulled or propelled into movement, whereas animate objects do not.

In addition to early precocity concerning animate objects, infants know a great deal about the properties of inanimate objects (Baillargeon, Spelke and Wasserman, 1985; Gibson and Spelke, 1983). Object perception in infancy appears to be guided by a coherent set of conceptions about the physical world: that objects cannot act on each other at a distance; that an object cannot pass through the space occupied by another; that movement must be externally caused; that once set in motion, the path of motion has certain predictable properties, etc. (Carey and Spelke, 1994).

In brief, there are three essential interrelated parts to a predisposition to learn/constraints theory that could have important implications for how a child learns science. Fundamental to learning is a search for cause, for determinism and mechanism. Children assume (implicitly) that events are caused and that it is their job to uncover potential mechanisms. Second, that which determines an event and delimits potential mechanisms is different for animate and inanimate objects. Third, these initial biases constrain what is selected from the range of available perceptual inputs to form the basis of emergent categories. Of the many sensations to which children are sensitive, they learn most rapidly about those constrained by core concepts (Medin and Ortony, 1989), guiding skeletal principles (Gelman, 1986, 1990) or theories of the world (Carey, 1985). This early differentiation between properties of the natural and artificial kind provides the basis for growing knowledge about biological and physical causality. In a later section we will stress the advantage of capitalizing on our growing understanding of children's natural precocity to learn about biological causality when designing environments in which they must learn about biological phenomena.

Despite these biases that make some learning easy, we still must consider the fact that not all learning is privileged in this way. The child may come endowed with predispositions to learn about certain kinds of things over others. But she still has to learn more about them, and she still has to learn about the others. Luckily, by seven or eight years of age, human beings are starting to be fairly efficient general-purpose learning machines. With experience the child becomes able to learn almost anything by will, effort, skill and strategy. It just so happens that in the early years the child does not have to work so hard to acquire the fundamentals (Brown, 1990). Thus early kinds of knowledge provide entry points to science that we would ignore at our cost; the job of science education is to recognize and refine these forms of knowing into formal scientific knowledge.

Piagetian Theory and Children's Science Learning[2]

In a recent paper (Brown, Metz and Campione, 1996), we discussed some construals of Piaget's theory that have had an important impact on the design of grade (primary) school education in the US and to some extent in Europe. Dating back to the science reform movement of the 1960s, the predominant interpretation of Piagetian theory was to postulate constraints on what it is that children can reasonably be expected to learn and understand (for a more extensive treatment of this argument, see Metz, 1995). A simplistic interpretation of Piagetian theory led to a consistent underestimation of young students' capabilities. This slant on Piagetian theory encouraged sensitivity to what children of a certain age *cannot* do because they have not yet reached a certain stage of cognitive operations. An alternative view is to emphasize what children can do readily and efficiently given their early scientific curiosity (Piaget, 1952, 1954) and their predisposition to learn certain classes of information pertinent to science (Carey and Gelman, 1991).

Following this negative constraints position, it became received wisdom that: (1) observation, measuring, ordering and categorizing constitute appropriate science objectives for the young grade school child, since these are core intellectual strengths of the concrete operational period; (2) science should be presented in a 'hands on' manner to primary children, who are capable of reasoning only about the concrete and manipulable; and (3) 'true' scientific inquiry should be postponed until adolescence when students become hypothetical-deductive thinkers who grasp the logic of experimental design.

In this chapter we discuss several primary reasons why young children are thought incapable of sustained scientific reasoning. These are a subset of those discussed in Brown *et al.* (1996). These include: (1) misunderstanding what concrete refers to in concrete operations; (2) undue emphasis on decontextualized skills; (3) regarding the child as lacking the scientific method; (4) ignoring the

---

2   Portions of this section are drawn from Brown, Metz and Campione (1996) and Metz (1995).

child's epistemology; (5) underestimation of the child as theorist; (6) decontextualization of second-order thought; and (7) devaluation of the role of people and powerful artifacts in scaffolding thought.

The Meaning of Concrete in Concrete Operations

The widespread belief that science for young children should be hands-on, dealing with the concrete and the manipulable, was reborn and strengthened by an interpretation of Piaget's notion of the concrete-operational child. But let us reconsider Piaget's view. Piaget viewed concrete-operational thought as concrete in the sense that the child's mental operations are applied to some aspect of external reality, *either physically present or mentally represented*. Piaget assumed that either tangible objects or their mental representations play a key role in the child's reasoning at the period of concrete operations. Piaget argued that, 'absent objects are replaced by more or less vivid representations, which are tantamount to reality' (Piaget, 1968, p. 62). Whereas the formal operational thinker can reason on the basis of any referent – real, symbolic or arbitrary – the concrete thinker is restricted to operations on objects or their mental representations that are 'tantamount to reality'. But note the term *mental representation*. It is a limiting view of concrete to restrict its meaning to the directly touchable and manipulable, although the touchable and manipulable do, of course, have the advantage for adults and children alike.

Decontextualized Skills at the Expense of Knowledge Base Factors

American science educators were primarily influenced by Piaget's structural period, where he was concerned with how an *epistemic subject* acted; Piaget's focus was not on individual children acting *in situ*, but rather on the general structures underlying the thought of the universal child. This interest led to a concentration on the logical operations of concrete thought: conservation, seriation, classification, etc. Children were asked to classify and seriate, but classify what, seriate what? Children's classifications in typical Piagetian-based curricula are formed apart from any purpose beyond 'putting together the things that go together'. But observation and classification each presume a purpose, a goal, a situation or a realm of inquiry.

The emphasis in early science on description and organization of the directly perceptible, *decontextualized from purpose*, is problematic from the viewpoint of both developmental psychology and the philosophy of science (Popper, 1972; Shapere, 1966). Scientific descriptions can only be derived and evaluated in relation to a *context of inquiry*. Young children can be asked to collect rocks and formulate their own systems of classification, but without a focus for that inquiry any internally consistent taxonomy is as good as any other (colour, size, sharpness, hardness, etc.), but the scientific knowledge that may result is minimal. It is precisely because the softness to hardness continuum of rocks is one indicator of crystal structure that scientists choose this form of seriation (Metz, 1995).

Wellman and Gelman (1988) give many examples of pre-schoolers' classification in terms of non-obvious deep structure. Indeed, they argue that without knowledge, focus and purpose, the classification task becomes absurd:

'...when we ask children simply which objects belong together, we are neglecting the deeper question of whether the grouped objects form a motivated category, and what the consequences are of having such a category'.
(Wellman and Gelman, 1988, p.116)

The influence of what one knows on how one might observe and classify is a problem of knowledge and purpose, as well as logical reasoning. Children are 'universal novices' (Brown and DeLoache, 1978); they know a lot less about a good many areas. If the child is not privy to the deep structure in a domain, she has no basis upon which to reason, no recourse but to fall back on surface features as the basis of classification (Brown, 1989). Consider classical analogy. Although Piaget believed that the ability to solve formal analogies of the form A:B:C:D was part of formal operational thought, studies of this ability typically confound knowledge and reasoning. When the child fully understands the basis of the analogy (e.g., simple causality: cutting, breaking, wetting), even preschool children can achieve success on such problems (Goswami and Brown, 1989).

Many would argue that the ability to categorize is present from the first year of life (Ross, 1980): what changes with age and knowledge is the basis of that categorization. This is also true of the development from naive to expert reasoning in adults (Chi, Feltovich and Glaser, 1981). And there are historical precedents. For example, in his history of biological thinking, Earnst Mayr (1982) described the history of biological taxonomies from Aristotle through the medieval alchemists to Linnaeus and beyond. All entertained stable, reliable classifications that the authors could reason with and justify; what changed with time was not reasoning ability but the accumulation of scientific knowledge that forced restructuring of categories, often leading to problems of incommensurability (Kuhn, 1962) between the old and new ways of thinking.

Children Lack the Scientific Method

When directly tested, often on arid decontextualized tasks, young children certainly evidence shortcomings in their use of the traditional scientific method. Children's experiments are typically inadequately designed to enable definitive conclusions (Dunbar and Klahr, 1989; Schauble and Glaser, 1990). They ignore disconfirming evidence (Dunbar and Klahr, 1989; Kuhn, Amsel and O'Loughlin 1988), lose track of experimental outcomes (Schauble, 1990; Siegler and Liebert, 1975) and entertain goals that are more engineering-like than scientific (Schauble, Klopfer and Raghavan, 1991). All are, however, also true of everyday thinking by lay people (Bartlett, 1958), and are more true of scientists than we would like to imagine (Medawar, 1982).

However, the coordination of theory and evidence central to scientific inquiry *is* problematic for children. Children have difficulty seeking and valuing negative evidence. Indeed, when accumulating evidence is at war with a favoured theory, they will select out fragments of evidence that can still be seen as supportive (Kuhn, Schauble and Garcia-Mila, 1992).

These observations to some extent support Inhelder and Piaget's (1958) claim that scientific reasoning is a feature of formal operational thought. Prior to this stage, children lack the ability to guide their experimentation and constrain their pattern of inference rigorously because they, '...lack a systematic method, notably the procedure of varying a single factor at a time while holding the others constant' (Inhelder and Piaget, 1958, p. 226). Without the power of combinatorial thought, propositional logic or hypothetical-deductive reasoning, the young child's experimentation cannot be systematic, nor can her 'experimental proof' be adequate. However, in hospitable settings the child as scientist emerges much earlier than was once supposed.

The Child as Epistemologist

One place to look for children's growing competence in the use of the scientific method is to inquire into their knowledge of what science means and what it means to learn science. Piaget, not particularly interested until his later years in learning *per se*, obviously had very little to say about the child's theory of learning. It was not until more recent research that we have seen interest in the child's theory of mind (Astington, Harris and Olson, 1988). Piaget's approach has been called anti epistemological in the deep sense (Gopnik and Wellman, 1994). But of central importance to our understanding of what the child is like as a scientist at any one point is what she thinks science is.

Smith, Hennessy and Carey (1994) distinguish between non-interpretation and interpretation frameworks concerning knowledge. A *non-interpretive* framework is one in which knowledge is regarded as unproblematic. By this view knowledge consists of facts and information which are observable, are acquired piece by piece, accumulate and become more accurate and complete over time. An *interpretive* framework involves a network of interrelated core concepts that cohere and mutually support each other. The core concepts, though resistant to change, are modifiable if anomalies arise and a more fruitful explanatory framework presents itself. At any one time the core concepts of the explanatory framework guide the selection of relevant problems to test, the generation of specific causal hypotheses and the interpretation of relevant data.

A similar 'developmental' sequence can be taken from the work of Kuhn (1992). She describes a four-stage progression in epistemological beliefs: (1) a *pre-absolutist stance* when what is said is what is true; (2) an *absolutist position* in which knowledge is seen as gradually accumulating towards a certain truth and any anomalies are resolved by appeal to fact or authority; (3) a *multipliestic epistemology* that involves a multiple perspective stance (there is more than one way of looking at the world); and (4) an *evaluative epistemology* in which all opinions are not equal and knowledge is understood as not in stasis but as evolving through the process of judgement, evaluation and argument.

Although the interpretive framework (Smith *et al.* 1994) and the evaluative epistemology (Kuhn, 1992) appear to be more mature, and indeed do represent higher-order ways of thinking, they should not be regarded as completely age-related. Witness the interpretive framework in action in children's attempts to make blocks balance (Karmiloff-Smith and Inhelder, 1974/5). Indeed, in many cases when a microgenetic approach is taken, children evidence a great deal more maturity than one would have supposed if snapshots of competence across age were our only data base.

Piaget paid little attention to the growth of children's epistemological stance, and we are only just beginning to see studies of children's conscious access to their theory of mind and its properties (Gopnik and Wellman, 1994) or how children think about themselves as learners (Ellery and Brown, work in progress; Smith *et al.* 1994). But once again when we look we see far more early competence than was previously supposed: competence that must be expanded upon, practised and improved. Consider just the following two examples from children talking about science learning:

[Child, age 7] Learning science is like finding pieces of a puzzle and trying to find the ones that last and the ones that are important. Then we put all the pieces together and make a bigger piece. Then we ask more questions – if this bigger piece makes sense. Then we ask our friends, our tutors (older students), and books and things, and make changes. Science goes on forever – we make changes, we make bigger pieces – we ask more questions. (Brown and Ellery, work in progress)

[Child, age 11] Science is made up of people's ideas. Some ideas are simple like facts (the earth is the third planet from the sun) and some ideas are more complicated (the theory of gravity that keeps the earth in orbit around the sun). All science ideas are based on someone's understanding of what they are trying to explain. Different people see things from different perspectives and choose to describe the same thing differently (like the theory of gravity by Newton and the theory of gravity by Einstein).

Learning in science is much more than repeating different people's perspectives. As I said, learning in science is trying to understand different perspectives – my own perspective, other people's perspective, and the science community's perspective. (Smith *et al.* 1994)

The Child as Theorist

Despite obvious limitations to the child's understanding of the scientific method, one should not overlook the child's emergence as theorist, as well as epistemologist. Many developmental psychologists believe that children entertain theories, just as do mature scientists. Children's theories may be incomplete, or just plain wrong, but they are theories. We find the following claims about children's theories, starting with Karmiloff-Smith and Inhelder's (1974) classic block-balancing task, and including more recent work on areas as diverse as: (1) theories of mind (Gopnik, 1993; Wellman, 1990); (2) astronomy (Brewer and Samarapungavan, 1991); and (3) physics (Smith, Carey and Wiser, 1985). Children's theories at their best:

o transcend the concrete and directly perceptible

o are internally consistent from the child's perspective

o involve attempts to integrate different sources of information

o lead to predictions

o reach towards a unified theory to account for all events

o   reject non-confirmation as due to errors of procedure

o   are sometimes available to verbalization, i.e., the child can
     talk about their understandings as well as act on them

o   support revision due to counter-evidence, experimentation
     and simplicity considerations

(Gopnik, 1993; Karmiloff-Smith and Inhelder, 1974; Wellman,
1990).

Second-Order Thought and Reflection

If children lack complete control of the scientific method, but also
entertain defensible *and* consistent, although sometimes inadequate,
theories of both learning *and* science, where then do we look for the
source of the difficulty students have in studying science? In fact a
great deal of work is left to be done, as we shall see in the next
section. One area where maturity of thought is implicated is in the
ability to take one's own thinking, experimentation and hypothesis
as an object of thought. This is the area Piaget referred to as reflective
abstraction.

The *sine qua non* of scientific reasoning and formal operations is
second-order or reflective thought. Early on, Inhelder and Piaget
argued that, '...the child has no powers of reflection, no second-order thoughts which deal critically with his own thinking' (Inhelder
and Piaget, 1958, p. 340). Because of this inability, concrete operational children cannot think systematically. Because they cannot
think systematically, they cannot construct scientific theories:

> [The concrete operational child's] spontaneous thinking may be
> more or less systematic (at first only to a small degree, later, much
> more so); but it is the observer who sees the system from outside,
> while the child is not aware of it since he never thinks about his own
> thought.... No theory can be built without such reflection.
> (Inhelder and Piaget, 1958, pp.339–40)

Mental experimentation, which is most closely associated with
Piaget's concept of reflected abstraction, is an enduring candidate for
late-developing thought:

> Finally, at the third level (from eleven to twelve years) which is that
> of reflected abstraction (conscious products of reflexive abstraction)
> the situation is modified in that [consciousness] begins to be ex-
> tended in a reflexion of the thought itself – This means that the
> subject has become capable of theorizing and no longer only of
> 'concrete,' although logically structured, reasoning. The reason for

this is the child's new power of elaborating operations on operations – he thereby becomes capable of varying the factors in his experiments, of envisaging the various models that might explain a phenomenon, and of checking the latter through actual experimentation.
(Piaget, 1976, pp.352–353)

At the end of his writing life, Piaget reconsidered to some extent his theory of children's conceptualization of action. This occurred predominantly in his work on the difference between *success* and *understanding* (Piaget, 1976, 1978). Piaget considered children's learning about a variety of construction tasks, such as building bridges between mountains strong enough to support vehicles where the solution was to use counterweights, etc. Young children, from about four to six years of age, focused on *trying to succeed*, working to attain the specified effect within the physical system. In contrast, older children (7–8 years) tried both to succeed and to *understand*. Conceptualization of why the physical system behaved as it did was as important as attaining the goal. The older children formed anticipations of the outcome of new design experiments, detected what went wrong and began to grasp the relations involved in the apparatus. The monitoring involved in self-regulation during a 'trying to succeed' episode differs from that involved in a 'search for understanding' stance. The characteristics that Piaget attributed to the four to six age group would support rudimentary learning about physical phenomena, albeit within an engineering-like frame. The characteristics that Piaget attributed to the seven- or eight-year-old's independent design efforts and causal explorations manifest important aspects of scientific inquiry. In microgenetic studies such as those of Karmiloff-Smith and Inhelder (1974), children pass from trying to succeed to trying to understand, not over chronological age but over short periods of time that allow learning to occur. Metacognition admits of degrees. Learning takes time, but is not always strictly age-related.

Another argument that may temper a position that 'formal operations' is always late-developing is that Piaget's theory was developed to explain performance on a finite set of tasks involving combinatorial reasoning. Changing the task environment might give one a different picture of competence; a similar point was made by Johnson-Laird (1985) with regard to the development of formal logic.

The argument in short is that one needs to consider the situation in which thinking occurs, not just thinking in the abstract. And, in fact, at the end of his career, Piaget came to view his earlier model of the development of children's thinking, particularly formal operations, as flawed because it failed to capture the essential role of the situation in influencing and constraining the direction and form of children's thinking. In other words, Piaget began to appreciate the extent to which context and semantics constrain reasoning (Metz, 1995).

Underestimation of the Role of People and Conflict in Scientific Discovery

Notwithstanding this later speculation, Piaget has been criticized for underestimating the degree to which the development of scientific knowledge is a social activity. This point is made forcibly in Harre's (1983) description of the making of scientific experiments and Dunbar's (1994) and Ochs's (1995) studies of the day-to-day activities of practising scientists. Although Piaget did recognize the power of social interaction in the development of thought, the study of social adaptation was outside the scope of his already ambitious research agenda. This agenda was taken up primarily by followers of Vygotsky.

In summary, a consideration of Piaget's total opus leads to a more optimistic picture of the grade school child as scientist. First, young children come predisposed to learn certain classes of information relevant to science, notably conceptions of physical and biological causality. Second, young children are able to identify variables, determine cause, and develop and refine theories. Third, when familiar situations and well-developed knowledge are the domain of inquiry, children's reasoning is much more sophisticated. It is often difficult to sort out deficiencies of scientific reasoning *per se* from inadequacies in domain-specific knowledge (Brown, 1990). Fourth, by concentrating on reflective abstraction Piaget underestimated the importance of less rigorous but valuable metacognitive activities such as planning, monitoring, self-regulation and revision, and even the origins of the ability to talk about science and hence to learn from talk (Lempke, 1990). Fifth, Piaget paid little attention to children's epistemology, their growing understanding of what learning and doing science is. Sixth, as Piaget came to realize, the hypothesis testing of children (Tschirgi, 1980) and, indeed, most adults (Johnson-Laird, 1985) does not accord well with the extensional logical model of Piaget's structural period, but rather reflects a natural inductive logic. Such logic is constructed in everyday situations where the child manipulates variables with the goal of conserving some desired effect and eliminating the undesirable. And seventh, Piaget himself came to question the model of the genesis of logical-mathematical structures from which the purported limitation to young children's scientific thinking is principally derived.

On the other hand, grade school children have a lot to learn. They have less experience within which to reason. Their epistemological stance, although often more mature than one might suppose, needs continual exercise if it is to mature, exercise that is rarely given in traditional classroom exercises. Often young children's competence is fleeting and fragile, what is known in a particular situation is not used flexibly in another. Formal logical operations are rarely in their grasp even fleetingly – in short, there is a long way to go. But understanding early competence so that one can build upon strength is a better metaphor for science education than one that emphasizes only what children cannot do. The glass half-full is a more positive metaphor than the glass half-empty.

The Design of Grade School Curricula

A simplified analysis of science education for the young highlights two major activities. One consists of having students study science texts, similar in many ways to standard reading texts, where the task is to learn *about* science. The second, a keystone of more formal curricula, involves children in hands-on activities through which children are led to *do* science.

The majority of science texts, especially for the very young, again seriously underestimate children's abilities and do little to enhance them. In brief there are four major drawbacks to these texts:

1. *Assumed developmental sequence.* Skills are introduced from basic to more advanced according to a simplistic assumed developmental sequence. For example, a child might be required to categorize shapes and colours in grade 1, animals by habitats in grade 4, and vertebrates and invertebrates in grade 8. There is no rationale given for why shapes and colours prepare students for more advanced categorization, nor even a mention of the fact that this is why the young children are playing sorting games. Thus the younger the children, the weaker the rationale for activities and the more fragmented the curriculum.

2. *Pseudo-narrative style.* The texts are often narrative rather than expository. They contain 'stories', often written in 'Disney-land' style, with animals personified in such a way that it is difficult for children to distinguish fact from fiction.

3. *Lack of cumulative reference.* There is a striking lack of cumulative reference (volcanoes following magnets, following a unit on whales, etc.). This lack of coherent themes or underlying principles all but precludes systematic knowledge-building

based on example, analogy, principle, or theme or theory; it does not encourage sustained effort after meaning.

4. *Causal explanation.* Equally problematic, presumably in order to conform to outmoded readability formulae that demand simple sentence structures, causal explanations are omitted, or are at best left enigmatic. This positively encourages a concentration on facts (what happens?) rather than generative understanding (why does it happen, how does it happen? etc.). We would like to emphasize here the developmental point. Many of the science curricula and science standards designed for the very young seem to make only passing contact with what we know about young children's learning. The assignment of content area to a specific age seems at best to be based on experience and success at teaching this kind of knowledge to that age of child, and at worst to be haphazard or even ill-informed. Too often practising scientists or science educators, experienced at teaching science to selected students of 16 years and above, imagine what precursors of the science they will teach would be useful to have developed in the young. As grade school teachers, almost by definition, are not science experts they are rarely called to the table in these discussions. As a result, grade school science curricula are rarely aligned to the young children's biases to learn certain kinds of information. Hands-on activities that are often ingenious are rarely tied together thematically or in such a way as to permit sustained inquiry and sustained reflection. The sheer number of concepts that must be mastered during the grade school years, according to a variety of new science standards both in America and Europe, do not allow sustained inquiry.

We prefer instead a concentration on a few 'lithe and beautiful and immensely generative' ideas (Bruner, 1969), rather than piecemeal coverage of many more areas. Immensely generative foundational ideas are few, and the idea behind education is to point children in the right direction so that they may discover and rediscover these ideas continuously. This is Bruner's (1969) idea of a spiralling curriculum. Central themes are introduced by the teacher early and revisited often at deeper and deeper levels of understanding.

Coupled with an introduction to these recurrent foundational themes should be reasoning activities that foster habits of mind by which children are encouraged to extrapolate, refine and use these underlying themes so that they can discover new theories for themselves. As Bruner argued, education:

...should be an invitation to generalize, to extrapolate, to make a tentative intuitive leap, even to build a tentative theory. The leap from mere learning to using what one has learned in thinking is an essential step in the use of the mind. Indeed, plausible guessing, the use of the heuristic hunch, the best employment of necessarily insufficient evidence – these are the activities in which the child needs practice and guidance. They are among the great antidotes to passivity.

(Bruner, 1969, p.124)

A concentration on a few pivotal ideas that are revisited in ever-deepening understanding, about which one reasons and queries, would be our candidate for early science activity.

Fostering a Community of Young Science Learners[3]

In this section we will describe some initial attempts to turn urban grade school classes into science learning communities. The programme, known as the 'fostering a community of learners' (FCL) project, involves 6- to 12-year-old minority students in urban grade school settings. We cannot describe the programme in detail because of space limitations; the reader is referred to Brown (1992, 1994) and Brown and Campione (1996) for details. Here we will concentrate on the main philosophy and the science 'curriculum' that is practised.

Philosophy

In his extremely generous review of FCL, Jerry Bruner (1996) discusses four general principles on which the programme is based: agency, reflection, collaboration and culture.

> The first of these is the idea of *agency*: taking more control of your own mental activity. The second is *reflection*: not simply 'learning in the raw' but making what you learn make sense, understanding it. The third is *collaboration*: sharing the resources of the mix of human beings involved in teaching and learning. Mind is inside the head, but it is also with others. And the fourth is *culture*, the way of life and thought that we construct, negotiate, institutionalize, and finally (after it's all settled) end up by calling 'reality' to comfort ourselves.
>
> (Bruner, 1996, p.87)

The means by which we set up this metacognitive culture of learning is summarized in Figure 1.1. At its simplest level, there are three key parts to the process. Students engage in independent and group *research* on some aspect of a topic of inquiry, mastery of which is

---

3   Parts of this section are adapted from Brown and Campione (1996).

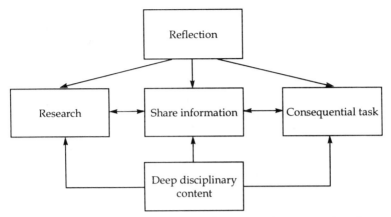

Figure 1.1 *Schematic representation of fostering the community of learners*

ultimately the responsibility of all members of the class. This requires that they *share* their expertise with their classmates. This sharing is further motivated by some *consequential task* or activity that demands that all students have learned about all aspects of the joint topic. This consequential task can be as traditional as a test or quiz, or some non-traditional activity such as designing a biopark to protect an endangered species. These three key activities – (1) research, (2) in *order* to share information, (3) *in order* to perform a consequential task – are all overseen and coordinated by self-conscious reflection on the part of all members of the community. In addition, the research–share–perform cycles of FCL cannot be carried out in a vacuum. All rely on the fact that the participants are trying to understand *deep disciplinary content* (Shulman, 1986).

To make Figure 1.1 concrete, let us consider a second-grade class (seven-year-olds) just beginning FCL activities. Children are engaged in research on animal survival mechanisms. They begin their research sharing a common piece of information. They read a well-written, beautifully illustrated children's book such as *The Tree of Life*, by Barbara Bash (1989), in which the theme is animal/habitat interdependence. Individual students then adopt an animal or plant mentioned in the book. With help from their colleagues, they write and illustrate a paragraph on why their animal is dependent on the tree of life (the baobab tree), and why the baobab tree is in turn dependent on the animal or plant. They post their illustrated text on a large mural of the tree for all the class to see and share. Although individually prepared, the tree and all its inhabitants belong to the community. Children can describe to an array of visitors why their animal or plant is dependent on the tree and vice versa. Over time they become able to describe not only their own choice, but also those of their classmates. The class owns the tree and the lives that depend on it.

The research process is then expanded as students build on their emerging knowledge by exploring common features that have surfaced; the big idea underlying their research is that of animal/habitat interdependence. Six research groups are formed and begin working concurrently. Their chosen subtopics are: (1) defence mechanisms; (2) predator/prey relations; (3) protection from the elements; (4) reproductive strategies; (5) communication; and (6) food chains. Children in each research group write and illustrate booklets about their subtopic. Periodically, the groups gather together in a whole class format and talk about their progress. Opportunistically during the unit, and always at the end of the unit, the students divide up into 'jigsaw' (Aronson, 1978) teaching groups. Each teaching group consists of one designated member of each of the research groups. These designated members have the responsibility of teaching the remaining members of the group about their research topic in order to complete the consequential task, in this case to design an animal of the future that has evolved a solution to the six research group questions – reproductive strategies, protection from the elements, etc. Thus, in each teaching group someone knows about predator/prey relations, someone can talk wisely on the strengths and weaknesses of possible methods of communication, and so forth. All pieces are needed to complete the puzzle, to design the 'complete animal', hence 'jigsaw'.

The Role of Expertise

Benchmark Lessons

Grade school teachers are rarely subject area specialists, and this has been true in most of our FCL classrooms. Given this fact of life, FCL has adopted the procedure of providing a subject area specialist who works with teachers to develop units and subtopics, to select a variety of research materials and artefacts, and to deliver occasional guest lectures called 'benchmark lessons'. These benchmark lessons serve several important functions. First, at the beginning of a unit of study, the benchmark lesson serves to introduce the class to the big ideas and deep principles that they will be studying. Second, benchmarks occur when the classroom teacher feels the class is ready to progress towards higher levels of abstraction. The adult leads the students to look for higher-order relations, encouraging the class to pool its expertise in a novel conceptualization of the topic. For example, if they have discovered the notion of energy and amount of food eaten, the expert might lead them towards the biological concept of metabolic rate. Third, in benchmark lessons, the teacher or expert models thinking and self-reflection concerning how a pupil would go about finding out about a topic, or how she might reason with the information given, or not given, as in the case of reasoning on the basis of incomplete information (Bruner, 1969; Collins and Stevens, 1982). Fourth, a simple but imperative type of benchmark lesson is when the adult teacher asks the group to summarize what is known and what still needs to be discovered, thereby helping students set new learning goals to guide the next stage of inquiry.

Children Teaching Children
Children as well as adults enrich the system by contributing their particular expertise. After a year or so in the programme, FCL students have considerable expertise themselves, both concerning the domain and concerning learning and teaching. Therefore, cross-age teaching becomes an important support for FCL. FCL uses cross-age teaching, both face-to-face and via electronic mail (see below), and also uses older students as discussion leaders. Cross-age teaching not only increases the knowledge capital of the community, but it also provides students with invaluable opportunities to talk about learning. We agree with Bruner (1972) that the higher goal of tutoring is the building of community. Cross-age teaching gives students responsibility and purpose, and reinforces collaborative structures throughout the school. The use of older children to assist the research efforts of their younger colleagues: (1) contributes to the self-esteem of the older students; (2) provides individualized attention to the younger students; (3) helps relieve the teaching burden on the classroom teacher; and (4) contributes to the building of a sharing community.

On-Line Consultation
Face-to-face communication is not the only way of building expertise, as FCL classrooms have the benefit of wider experience via electronic mail. Both teachers' and students' expectations concerning excellence, or what it means to learn and understand, may be limited if the only standards are local. Experts coaching via electronic mail provide FCL with an essential resource, freeing teachers from the sole burden of knowledge guardian and allowing the community to extend in ever-widening circles of expertise.

Face-to-face and on-line experts are not merely providers of much-needed information, they act as role models of thinking, wondering, querying and making inferences on the basis of incomplete knowledge. Extending the learning community beyond the classroom walls to form virtual communities across time and space not only enriches the knowledge base available to students, but also exposes them to models of reasoning and reflection about the learning process itself (Brown, Ellery and Campione, in press; Campione, Brown and Jay, 1992).

A Metacognitive Environment: the Importance of Reflection and Discussion

The research–share–consequential task scheme is subsumed under the overarching concept of reflection. FCL is historically and intentionally a metacognitive environment. The classroom talk in FCL is largely metacognitive: 'Do I understand?', 'That doesn't make sense', 'They [the audience] can't understand X without Y', and so forth.

Discussion is essential to the FCL classroom in which we explicitly aim to simulate the active exchange and reciprocity of a dialogue. Our classrooms are intentionally designed to foster interpretive communities of discourse (Fish, 1980). FCL encourages newcomers to adopt the discourse structure, goals, values and belief systems of a community of research practices. Ideas are seeded in discussion and migrate throughout the community via mutual appropriation and negotiated meaning (Vygotsky, 1978). Sometimes they lie fallow, and sometimes they bloom. The FCL community relies on the development of a discourse genre in which constructive discussion, questioning, querying, and criticism are the mode rather than the exception. In time these reflective activities become internalized as autocriticism (Binet, 1909) and self-reflective practices (Brown, 1978) and foster the child's growing theory of mind.

The FCL Curriculum

Disciplinary Content

Although initially designed as a thinking curriculum (Resnick and Resnick, 1992), FCL has always relied heavily on disciplinary content units of sufficient rigor to sustain in-depth research over substantial periods of time. One cannot expect students to invest intellectual curiosity and disciplined inquiry on trivia; there must be a challenge; there must be room to explore, to delve deeply, to understand at ever-deepening levels of complexity. Of central importance to the theme of this volume is the development of the science content about which the children are asked to reason and reflect. In FCL, we have concentrated primarily on environmental science. We will end by describing the actual and the ideal.

The Actual

FCL does not involve a curriculum in the usual sense because the students are partially responsible for designing their own. Our curriculum teams, consisting of teachers and domain area experts, guide the development of central themes to be revisited over time. To support the 'discovery' of these themes, the classrooms are rich with human resources, such as visiting experts, older tutors and electronic mail. The classrooms are also provided with a selection of artefacts: books, videos, hands-on experiments, newspapers, periodicals, and so forth that the students can use in the service of their research.

A main tenet is that an FCL unit should lead students to conduct research, read, write and think about a compelling deep theme at a developmentally appropriate level. It is precisely because we know something about the development of children's theories of biology (Carey, 1985) that we initially selected the biological underpinnings of environmental science as our focus. The idea is to understand children's emergent theories about biology and lead them gradually towards deep principles of the discipline, such as interdependence, biodiversity, adaptation and evolution.

Although we believe it to be somewhat romantic to think of young children entering the community of practice of adult academic disciplines (Brown, Collins and Duguid, 1989), awareness of the deep principles of academic disciplines should enable us to design intellectual practices for the young that are stepping stones to mature understanding, or at least are not glaringly inconsistent with the end goal. For example, in the domain of ecology and environmental science, we realize that contemporary understanding of the underlying biology would necessitate a ready familiarity with biochemistry and genetics that is not within the grasp of young students. Instead of watering down such content to a strange mixture of the biological and the biochemical, as textbooks for the young often do, we invite young students into the world of 19th century naturalists, scientists who also lacked modern knowledge of biochemistry and genetics. The idea is that by the time students *are* introduced to contemporary disciplinary knowledge, they will have developed a thirst for that knowledge, as indeed has been the case historically.

Practically speaking this means that as we revisit, for example, the topic of endangered species across the grades, we gradually reach towards increasingly sophisticated disciplinary understanding. We refer to this as a *developmental corridor*. Children remain in the programme for several years, during which time they delve more deeply into the underlying principles of the domain. Second, fourth, sixth and eighth graders may be working on extinction, endangered and rebounding populations, assisted populations, selective breeding, etc.; and all will be guided by the basic disciplinary principles of interdependence and adaptation. However, different levels of sophistication will be expected at each age, a spiralling curriculum (Bruner, 1969) if you will. Topics are not just revisited willy-nilly at various ages at some unspecified level of sophistication, but each revisit is based on a deepening knowledge of that topic, critically dependent on past experience and on the developing knowledge base of the child. It matters what the underlying principles are at, say, kindergarten and grade two; it matters that the sixth-grade students have experienced the fourth-grade curriculum.

We take seriously the fact that an understanding of the growth of children's thinking in a domain should serve as the basis for setting age-appropriate goals. As we learn more about children's knowledge and theories about the biological and physical world (Hirschfeld and Gelman, 1994), we can be more precise about designing age-sensitive curricula. It is for these reasons that in our environmental science/biology strand we seek guidance from developmental psychology concerning students' evolving biological understanding (Carey, 1985; Hatano and Inagaki, 1987; Keil, 1992; Wellman and Gelman, 1988). We know that by age 6, children can fruitfully investigate the concept of living things (alive/not alive/dead, natural thing/artefact, etc.), a topic of great interest that they refine over a period of years. It is not until approximately age 10 that they begin to assimilate plants into this category (Carey, 1985), and perhaps not even then (Hatano and Inagaki, 1987). By second grade we begin to address animal/habitat mutuality and interdependence. Sixth graders examine biodiversity and the effect of broad versus narrow niches on endangerment. By eighth grade the effect of variation in the gene pool on adaptation and survival is not too complex a topic. Whereas second graders begin to consider adaptation and habitats in a simple way, sixth graders can distinguish structural, functional and behavioural adaptations, biotic and abiotic interdependence, and so forth.

A similar developmental guideline governs our approach to reasoning within the domain. For example, we initially permit teleological reasoning (Keil, 1992) and an overreliance on causality in general, but we then press for an increasingly more sophisticated consideration of chance, probability and randomness (Metz, 1996). Personification as analogy (Carey, 1985) is a powerful, if limited, reasoning strategy used by the young (and by the old, for that matter). It supports inductive reasoning and helps children to distinguish between natural kinds and artefacts (Gelman and Markman, 1986). We allow children to reason on this basis, putting off until later discussion of the limitations of this way of thinking.

It is of no small theoretical interest to developmental psychologists that by deliberately aligning instruction to the child's developing theories about biology, we face a theoretical and practical issue about developmental sensitivity. A great deal of our knowledge of young children's theories of the biological and physical world have been provided by developmental psychologists. True to the tradition of this discipline, cross-sectional data are taken from children divorced from the culture in which they are developing, a culture that includes school. We know a great deal about what the average (usually upper middle class) child knows about what is alive or not alive at age 5, 8, 10, etc. What is not known, however, is the influence of instruction on these developmental milestones. If we target children's developmental theories as the essence of instruction, what will change developmentally and what will be resistant to such change?

We have introduced the term *developmental corridor* to capture the notion that units of FCL should be revisited at ever-increasing levels of complexity. This allows us to ask whether, after four or five years in the programme, sixth graders will be capable of performing at much more mature levels of reasoning, capable of acquiring and using domain knowledge of considerably greater complexity than that of sixth graders in the programme for the first time. In a very fundamental sense, to the degree FCL is successful, we should be mapping a moving target. Units once thought suitable for sixth graders will now be found more appropriate for fourth grade, and so on. Of considerable theoretical interest to developmental psychologists, and of practical interest to the designers of science curricula, are answers to the question: what, if any, forms of knowledge and process are immutable in the face of carefully tailored instruction?

To give just a flavour of the kinds of results one can glean from this approach we present two concrete examples. The first is a study of change in the second grade classroom described previously (Walker and Brown, work in progress), and the second is a case study of one child's acquisition of a more mature notion of adaptation (additional results can be found in Brown [1992] and Brown and Campione [1994]).

Children in the second-grade classroom were required to design an animal of the future that conformed to a habitat and incorporated methods of meeting the design criteria researched by the different groups: reproductive methods, defence mechanisms, means of communication, etc. We scored the proportion of biological solutions mentioned and the constraining links between solutions. By 'constraining links' we mean that if an animal were endowed with webbed feet to fit a swamp-like environment, other, related design features would follow – e.g., webbed feet, beak, long legs, lays eggs, eats fish and waterborne insects, camouflages in reeds – that is, a coherent picture akin to something like a marsh bird. Children could, however, include no links, i.e., all of their six solutions could be independent. And this is indeed what happened in our first iteration when a new (to the project) teacher did an FCL unit for just three months. Although the children did provide five or six design solutions as required, those solutions were independent of each other.

To check whether this was typical developmentally, we then conducted a cross-sectional study where children *not* in FCL were asked to complete the same task after experience with only two similar tasks, to design an animal to fit a specified habitat or design a habitat to fit a given, unfamiliar animal. These data, taken from children in grades 2, 4, 6 and 8, are shown in Figure 1.2. The cross-sectional data confirmed our original microgenetic data: second graders did not provide coherent, interrelated linkages in their design of animal survival mechanisms, whereas older children did so to a much greater extent. Although at no age did the children link all

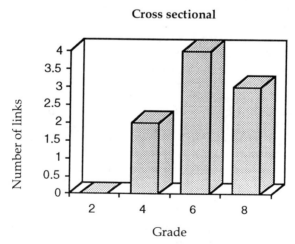

Cross sectional

Figure 1.2 Number of biological links produced by children across grades

six possible solutions, there was an improvement in age even in the relatively untutored.

But we did not stop there. We conducted a year-long intervention with second graders and found that they did manage some linkages, usually concerning the food chain and predator/prey relationships. Finally, in our third replication, the now experienced teacher reinforced the children's request that they design the habitats carefully *first* and then design the animal of the future to fit that habitat. This resulted in a major improvement in the number of habitat-constrained linkages, with children here performing as well as sixth to eighth graders. These data are shown in Figure 1.3.

Microgenetic

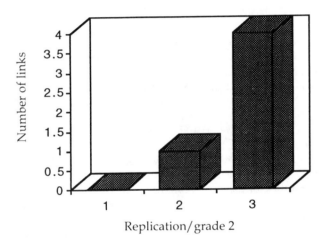

Figure 1.3 Number of links produced by successive cohorts of second-grade students

Examples of animals of the future from the first versus third replication are the Junkyard Wolf and the Ripple Green (students' names):

The Junkyard Wolf

Are animal of the future lives in the junk yard. It is a amnnore [omnivore]. The babies come out of the side of the mother. It's a scavenger. It camouflages by changing colors and by standing very still. This animal is nocturnal. It has large elephant feet so that it can stomp on the junk to find food.

It communicates by hitting its tail against the [abandoned] cars. The shell protects it from the elements. The animals defense mechanisms are playing dead and ducking its head into its shell. When it needs to fight, it uses its tail. It has a spiked tail.

It eats plants and meat. It eats peoples' scraps and animals that come in. It has a lobster snapper on the back with cheese on it. When the rat sees the cheese it gets caught up in the snapper and the food digests in its stomach. It can also eat things with its mouth.

(Second-grade students, replication one, no spell check.)

In contrast, the Ripple Green involves adaptations that cohere. Once the habitat was designed, the other design criteria were 'adapted' to that habitat:

The Ripple Green

The description of ripple green is much like the description of an alligator and crocodile. The animal's name is ripple green because it is green and it has ripples all over its body. It is a reptile. It's a medium sized animal. Ripple green has webbed feet to help it swim in the swamp. It has a long tail to help it defend itself. The animal has two scents. It also has sharp teeth to help it carry its food and tear its food apart. One scent is to attract a mate and the other scent is to scare its enemies away.

The animal's habitat is in the swamps of Florida. The ripple green lives in mixed water [salt and fresh]. In the habitat there are plants, reptiles, birds, fish, amphibians and insects which sometimes can be alligators, frogs, crocodiles, big birds, tall grass, fish, sand and water.

The mother builds the nest high up in the grass so the snakes won't eat the eggs. The mother lays fourteen eggs every summer. It takes three to seven days for the babies to hatch depending on the weather. The mother lays green eggs. The eggs are green so they can camouflage into the grass. Camouflaging protects the eggs. The mother stays with the eggs, close to the edge of the water. She stays close to the swamp in order to get food and water for herself. The mother brings the eggs water to keep them cool. If the eggs get too hot, they will hatch too early and the babies will die. Once the eggs are hatched, the babies stay with their mother for three weeks. After three weeks, the babies are on their own.

Ripple Green communicates with a sweet smelling scent to attract a mate. The scent comes out the back of the tail. They mate once a year in the spring. It sprays a strong smelling scent to communicate to warn other ripple greens that danger is near.

The Ripple Green is a plant and meat eater or you can say an omnivore. It camouflages the same color as the swamp and has ripples just like the swamp. It quietly swims behind its prey, such as a fish, and then eats the fish. It also eats the grass that is around the swamp.

Since the animal is a reptile, it is a cold blooded animal. It protects itself from the heat by going into the water when it's hot. If the animal gets cold it goes into the tall grass to get cool. It goes on land to get warm.

The animal defends itself by camouflaging. This way it confused its predators, like the alligator and the crocodile. It also uses its long tail to hit its enemy. It can also spray a scent to scare its enemies away.

We think the Ripple Green will probably be endangered because of the polluting in the swamp. When the swamp is polluted and the Ripple Green goes under the water, it won't be able to breathe. When people throw trash and other things into the swamp the Ripple Green thinks it is food and eats it. This will cause the ripple green to get lung cancer. We hope the Ripple Green will survive.

(Second-grade students, replication three, spell check available.)

We see a similar development of adaptational coherence in an older child, Malia (age 11), over a period of approximately four-and-a-half months in which she makes steps towards the development of what Ash (1995) calls the adaptationist stance. Children have a predisposition to form a functionalist or design perspective as they analyse the world around them. Things exist for a purpose; forms are for certain functions. Indeed, children have been described as unduly teleological (Ash, 1995; Keil, 1994; Kelemen, 1996). Ash and Brown (1995) have argued that children bootstrap more mature understandings of adaptation by capitalizing on these early biases. They progress from an expectation that biological structures have identifiable functions towards a broader, more holistic adaptationist view. From an early understanding of functional reasoning of isolated attributes – that sharp teeth are for tearing, keen eyes for hunting and long legs for running – they progress gradually to correlating sets of form/function relations into coherent structures: the teeth, eyes and legs are adapted to a certain mode of life, in this case a predatory one. Adaptationist reasoning is 'functional reasoning plus' (Ash and Brown, 1996). It is not equivalent to mature thinking biologically, but it is not discordant with it (Ash, 1995). It is just another stepping stone towards evolutionary thinking.

Malia is studying sea otters. She begins with a good understanding of form/function (that fur is for warmth) but her understanding of individual adaptations is not linked coherently, they are isolated facts: 'I know the sea otter has one million hairs per inch...it keeps it warm'. She then discovers some notion of environmental constraints: '...their habitat is mainly kelp and water. They need fur because of the water temperature and stuff. If the fur is thin, what do you expect – hot weather – if the fur is thick, cold'.

She then goes on to discover the special feature of otter fur; it contains air bubbles that are needed because the animal has no blubber. This leads to a decision about insulation: '...the fur is an advantage 'cause it keeps it warm, but it would be better off if it had blubber'. She adds next that otters need to eat at least 20 per cent of their body weight each day, '...because they have no blubber and need energy'. She begins to consider the biological principle of high metabolic needs and metabolic rate.

After more time spent studying the otter, Malia begins to correlate several different adaptations. She uses the fur/air bubbles/no blubber link to explain the declining population of southern versus northern populations – the northern populations migrated south and are less well adapted to the warmer waters (an inference). She begins to note the lack of fur on the paws and the need to keep them dry because of this lack of fur. She adds the delicate structure of the claws and their tool use capabilities. Gradually, she builds up a coherent picture of correlated attributes that includes repeated mention of the need for fur and air bubbles because of the cold water, with the fact that there is no blubber leading to high metabolic needs. Finally, she shows understanding of a coherent picture: that the otter's many diverse adaptations are to its particular constraining environment: its streamlined shape, flexible spine, large lungs, dry paws, mating habits, feeding habits, etc. all enable the otter to survive in a kelp forest. Malia ends her research talking in terms of constellations of characteristics. This experience is a stepping stone that will enable her to seek a rationale for selection and genetic diversity in populations. It sets the stage for another step along the way to evolutionary thinking (Ash, 1995; Ash and Brown, 1996).

Conclusions

The Ideal

Although we have made considerable headway in aligning our understanding of children's growing biological knowledge and the design of a 'biology curriculum' for grade school children, we still have a long way to go. Quite simply, we need a great deal more research in both domains. Ideally, we seek a developmental trajectory that grows in stepping stones towards mature thinking that would look something like Figure 1.4.

Given knowledge of the early biases as children enter school, we can build upon, extend and refine this knowledge until we reach blocks to continuing refinement. For example, R. Gelman and Williams (in press) argue that rational number is just such a block to the gradual build-up of knowledge based on the child's core concept of number. The concepts of randomness and chance, and the notion of population versus sample, appear to be an equal problem for the development of biological thought. We need to recognize children's conceptions that are fruitful errors, ones that are not mature understandings but which, if carefully harnessed, would lead towards more mature understanding, as in the example of Malia's stepping stones towards adaptationist reasoning. Fruitful errors are distinct from misconceptions that lead in the wrong direction and will impede the growth of scientific thinking unless replaced. Finally, we need to look at the hallmarks of the mature science as received wisdom undergoing change to a relativist/evaluative position which adds the essential notion of narrative invention (Bruner, 1996; Medawar, 1982) to a student's understanding of science.

We need such a progression in science *and* in the student's understanding of learning and reasoning about science. The field of devel-

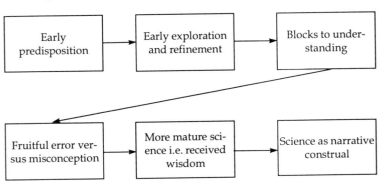

Figure 1.4. Schematic representation of the development of science understanding in children

opmental psychology is moving slowly but surely in that direction. Harnessing that knowledge in the service of the design of science environments for the young is an activity that holds promise for the future. It will take thoughtful collaboration between domain area specialists, science educators, psychologists, grade school teachers and, yes, students for us to reach these desired goals.

References

Aronson, E. (1978) *The Jigsaw Classroom*. Beverly Hills, CA: Sage.

Ash, D. (1995) From functional reasoning to an adaptationist stance: children's transition toward deep biology. Unpublished PhD dissertation, Berkeley: University of California.

Ash, D. and Brown, A.L. (1995) Otter fur and delayed implantation: children's guided transition from form–function reasoning towards an adaptationist stance. Paper presented at the meetings of the American Educational Research Association, San Francisco.

Ash, D. and Brown, A.L. (1996) Thematic continuities guide shifts in biological reasoning: children's transition towards deep principles of evolution. Paper presented at the meetings of the American Educational Research Association, New York.

Astington, J.W., Harris, P.L. and Olson, D.R. (1988) *Developing Theories of Mind*. New York: Cambridge University Press.

Baillargeon, R., Spelke, E.S. and Wasserman, S. (1985) 'Object permanence in five-month-old infants.' *Cognition 20*, 191–208.

Bartlett, F.C. (1958) *Thinking: An Experimental and Social Study*. New York: Basic Books.

Bash, B. (1989) *Tree of Life: The World of the Baobab*. San Francisco: Sierra Club Books, Little Brown Co.

Bertenthal, B.I., Profitt, D.R., Spetner, N. and Thomas, M.A. (1985) 'The development of infant sensitivity to biomedical motion.' *Child Development 56*, 531–543.

Binet, A. (1909) *Les Ideés Modernes sur les Enfants*. Paris: Ernest Flammarion.

Brewer, W. and Samarapungavan, A. (1991) 'Children's theories versus scientific theories: differences in reasoning or differences in knowledge?' In R.R. Hoffman and D.S. Palermo (eds) *Cognition and the Symbolic Processes: Applied and Ecological Perspectives*. Hillsdale, NJ: Erlbaum.

Brown, A.L. (1975) 'The development of memory: knowing, knowing about knowing, and knowing how to know.' In H.W. Reese (ed) *Advances in Child Development and Behavior 10*, 103–152. New York: Academic Press.

Brown, A.L. (1978) 'Knowing when, where, and how to remember: a problem of metacognition.' In R. Glaser (ed) *Advances in Instructional Psychology 1*, 77–165. Hillsdale, NJ: Erlbaum.

Brown, A.L. (1989) 'Analogical learning and transfer: what develops?' In S.Vosniadou and A. Ortony (eds) *Similarity and Analogical Reasoning*. Cambridge: Cambridge University Press, pp 369–412.

Brown, A.L. (1990) 'Domain-specific principles affect learning and transfer in children.' *Cognitive Science 14*, 107–133.

Brown, A.L. (1992) 'Design experiments: theoretical and methodological challenges in creating complex interventions in classroom settings.' *The Journal of the Learning Sciences 2*, 2, 141–178.

Brown, A.L. (1994) 'The advancement of learning.' *Educational Researcher 23*, 4–12.

Brown, A.L. and DeLoache, J.S. (1978) 'Skills, plans, and self-regulation.' In R.S. Siegler (ed) *Children's Thinking: What Develops?* Hillsdale, NJ: Erlbaum.

Brown, A.L., Bransford, J.D., Ferrara, R.A. and Campione, J.C. (1983) 'Learning, remembering, and understanding.' In J.H. Flavell and E.M. Markman (eds) *Handbook of Child Psychology (4th ed.) Cognitive Development Vol.3*, 77–166. New York: Wiley.

Brown, A.L., and Campione, J.C. (1994) 'Guided discovery in a community of learners.' In K. McGilly (ed) *Classroom Lessons: Integrating Cognitive Theory and Classroom Practice.* Cambridge, MA: MIT Press/Bradford Books, 229–270.

Brown, A.L. and Campione, J.C. (1996) 'Psychological theory and the design of innovative learning environments: on procedures, principles, and systems.' In L. Schauble and R. Glaser (eds) *Contributions of Instructional Innovation to Understanding Learning.* Hillsdale, NJ: Erlbaum.

Brown, A.L., Metz, K.E. and Campione, J.C. (1996) 'Social interaction and individual understanding in a community of learners: the influence of Piaget and Vygotsky.' In J. Voneche (ed) *The Social Genesis of Thought: Piaget and Vygotsky.* Geneva, Switzerland: Cahiers de la Fondation (Archives Jean Piaget).

Brown, A.L., Ellery, S. and Campione, J.C. (in press) 'Creating zones of proximal development electronically.' In J.G. Greeno and S. Goldman (eds) *Thinking Practices: A Symposium in Mathematics and Science Education.* Hillsdale, NJ: Erlbaum.

Brown, J.S., Collins, A. and Duguid, P. (1989) 'Situated cognition and the culture of learning.' *Educational Researcher 18*, 32–42.

Bruner, J.S. (1969) *On Knowing: Essays for the Left Hand.* Cambridge, MA: Harvard University Press, 21.

Bruner, J.S. (1972) 'Nature and uses of immaturity.' *American Psychologist 27*, 687–708.

Bruner, J.S. (1996) *The Culture of Education.* Cambridge, MA: Harvard University Press.

Campione, J.C. and Brown, A.L. (1977) 'Memory and metamemory development in educable retarded children.' In R.V. Kail, Jr. and J.W. Hagen (eds) *Perspectives on the Development of Memory and Cognition*, 367–406. Hillsdale, NJ: Erlbaum.

Campione, J.C., Brown, A.L. and Jay, M. (1992) 'Computers in a community of learners.' In E. DeCorte, M. Linn, H. Mandl, and L. Verschaffel (eds) *Computer-Based Learning Environments and Problem Solving.* NATO ASI Series F: Computer and Systems Science, 84, 163–192. Berlin: Springer-Verlag.

Carey, S. (1985) *Conceptual Change in Childhood.* Cambridge, MA: Bradford Books, MIT Press.

Carey, S. and Gelman, R. (1991) *The Epigenesis of Mind: Essay on biology and cognition.* Hillsdale, NJ: Erlbaum.

Carey, S. and Spelke, E. (1994) 'Domain-specific knowledge and conceptual change.' In L.A. Hirschfeld and S.A. Gelman (eds) *Mapping the Mind: Domain Specificity in Cognition and Culture*. Cambridge, MA: Cambridge University Press.

Chi, M.T.H. (1976) 'Short-term memory limitations in children: capacity or processing deficits?' *Memory and Cognition 4*, 559–572.

Chi, M.T.H. 1978) 'Knowledge structures and memory development.' In R.S. Siegler (ed) *Children's Thinking: What Develops?*, 73–96. Hillsdale, NJ: Erlbaum.

Chi, M.T.H., Feltovich, P.J. and Glaser, R. (1981) 'Categorization and representation of physics problems by experts and novices.' *Cognitive Science 5*, 121–152.

Collins, A. and Stevens, A. (1982) 'Goals and strategies of inquiry teachers.' In R. Glaser (ed) *Advances in Instructional Psychology 2*, 65–119. Hillsdale, NJ: Erlbaum.

Dunbar, K. (1994) 'How scientists really reason: scientific reasoning in real-world laboratories.' In R.J. Sternberg and J. Davidson (eds) *Mechanisms of Insight*. Cambridge, MA: MIT Press.

Dunbar, K. and Klahr, D. (1989) 'Developmental differences in scientific discovery strategies.' In D. Klahr and K. Kotovsky (eds) *Complex Information Processing: The Impact of Herbert A. Simon*, 109–144. Hillsdale, NJ: Erlbaum.

Ellery, S. and Brown, A.L. Work in progress.

Fish, S. (1980) *Is there a Text in this Class? The Authority of Interpretive Communities*. Cambridge, MA: Harvard University Press.

Gelman, R. (1986) First principles for structuring acquisition. Presidential Address to Division 7 of the American Psychological Association, Washington, D.C., August.

Gelman, R. (1990) 'First principles organize attention to and learning about relevant data: number and the animate–inanimate distinction as examples.' *Cognitive Science 14*, 79–106.

Gelman, R. and Williams, E.M. (in press) 'Enabling constraints for cognitive development and learning: a domain-specific epigenetic theory.' In D. Kuhn and R. Siegler (eds) *Cognition, Perception, and Language, Vol. 2*. W. Damon (ed) *Handbook of Child Psychology, Vol. 5*.

Gelman, S.A and Campione, J.C. (1994) 'Guided discovery in a community of learners.' In K.McGilly (ed) *Classroom Lessons: Integrating Cognitive Theory and Classroom Practice*. Cambridge, MA: MIT Press/Bradford Books.

Gelman, S.A and Markman, E.M. (1996) 'Categories and induction in young children.' *Cognition 23*, 183–209.

Gibson, E.J. and Spelke, E.S. (1983) 'The development of perception.' In J.H. Flavell and E.M. Markman (eds) *Handbook of Child Psychology, (4th ed.) Vol. 3, Cognitive Development*, 1–76. New York: Wiley.

Gopnik, A. (1993) 'Theories and illusions. Author's response to open peer commentary.' *Behavioral and Brain Sciences 16*, 90–100.

Gopnik, A. and Wellman, H.M. (1994) 'The theory theory.' In L.A. Hirschfeld and S.A. Gelman (eds) *Mapping the Mind: Domain Specificity in Cognition and Culture*. Cambridge, MA: Cambridge University Press.

Goswami, U. and Brown, A.L. (1989) 'Melting chocolate and melting snowmen: analogical reasoning and causal relations.' *Cognition 35*, 69–95.

Goswami, U. and Brown, A.L. (1990) 'Higher-order structure and relational reasoning: contrasting analogical and thematic relations.' *Cognition 36*, 207–226.

Harre, R. (1983) *Great Scientific Experiments: Twenty Experiments that Changed our View of the World*. New York: Oxford University Press.

Hatano, G. and Inagaki, K. (1987) 'Everyday biology and school biology: how do they interact?' *The Newsletter of the Laboratory of Comparative Human Cognition 9*, 120–128.

Hirschfeld, L.A. and Gelman, S.A. (1994) *Mapping the Mind: Domain Specificity in Cognition and Culture*. Cambridge, MA: Cambridge University Press.

Inhelder, B. and Piaget, J. (1958) *The Growth of Logical Thinking from Childhood to Adolescence*. New York: Basic Books. Translated by E.A. Lunzer and D. Papert.

Johnson-Laird, P.M. (1985) 'Logical thinking: does it occur in daily life? Can it be taught?' In S. Chipman, J. Segal and R. Glaser (eds) *Thinking and Learning Skills: Research and Open Questions Vol. 2*, 293–318. Hillsdale, NJ: Erlbaum.

Karmiloff-Smith, A. and Inhelder, B. (1974/5) 'If you want to get ahead, get a theory.' *Cognition 3*, 195–212.

Keil, F.C. (1992) 'The origins of autonomous biology.' In M.R. Gunnan and M. Maratsos (eds) *Minnesota Symposium on Child Psychology: Modularity and Constraints on Language and Cognition*. Hillsdale, NJ: Erlbaum.

Keil, F.C. (1994) 'The birth and nurturance of concepts by domains: the origins of concepts of living things.' In L.A. Hirschfeld and S.A. Gelman (eds) *Mapping the Mind: Domain Specificity in Cognition and Culture*. Cambridge, MA: Cambridge University Press.

Kelemen, D.A. (1996) The nature and development of the teleological stance. Unpublished PhD dissertation, University of Arizona.

Kuhn, D. (1992) 'Piaget's child as scientist.' In H. Beilin and P. Pufall (eds) *Piaget's Theory: Prospects and Possibilities*. Hillsdale, NJ: Erlbaum, 185–208.

Kuhn, D., Amsel, E. and O'Loughlin, M. (1988) *The Development of Scientific Thinking Skills*. New York: Academic Press.

Kuhn, D., Schauble, L. and Garcia-Mila, M. (1992) 'Cross-domain development of scientific reasoning.' *Cognition and Instruction 9*, 285–327.

Kuhn, T.S. (1962) *The Structure of Scientific Revolutions*. Chicago: University of Chicago Press.

Lempke, J.L. (1990) *Talking Science: Language, Learning, and Values*. Norwood, NJ: Ablex.

Mayr, E. (1982) *The Growth of Biological Thought*. Cambridge, MA: Harvard University Press.

Medawar, P. (1982) *Pluto's Republic*. Oxford: Oxford University Press.

Medin, D. and Ortony, A. (1989) 'Comments on part I: psychological essentialism.' In S. Vosniadou and A. Ortony (eds) *Similarity and Analogical Reasoning*. Cambridge, MA: Cambridge University Press.

Metz, K.E. (1995) 'Reassessment of developmental constraints on children's science instruction.' *Review of Educational Research 65*, 93–127.

Metz, K.E. (1996) Children's and adults' interpretation of random phenomena: developmental and non-developmental aspects of the construction of chance. Unpublished manuscript, University of California, Riverside.

Ochs, E. (1995) Scientists in action. Paper presented at the National Academy of Education meetings, Harvard University.

Piaget, J. (1952) *The Origins of Intelligence in Children*, M. Cook, Trans. New York: Norton (original work published in 1936).

Piaget, J. (1954) *The Construction of Reality in the Child*, M. Cook, Trans. New York: Basic Books (original work published in 1937).

Piaget, J. (1968) 'The mental development of the child.' In D. Elkind (ed) *Six Psychological Studies*, 3–37. New York: Vintage Books.

Piaget, J. (1976) *The Grasp of Consciousness*. Cambridge, MA: Harvard University Press.

Piaget, J. (1978) *Success and Understanding*. Cambridge, MA: Harvard University Press.

Popper, K.S. (1972) *Conjectures and Refutations: The Growth of Scientific Knowledge, 4th edition*. London: Rutledge and Kegan Paul.

Resnick, L.B. and Resnick, D.P. (1992) 'Assessing the thinking curriculum: new tools for educational reform.' In B.R. Gifford and M.C. O'Connor (eds) *Future Assessment: Changing Views of Aptitude, Achievement and Instruction*. Boston: Academic Press.

Ross, G. (1980) 'Categorization in 1- to 2-year-olds.' *Developmental Psychology 16*, 391–396.

Schauble, L. (1990) 'Belief revision in children: the role of prior knowledge and strategies for generating knowledge.' *Journal of Experimental Psychology 49*, 31–57.

Schauble, L. and Glaser, R. (1990) 'Scientific thinking in children and adults.' *Human Development 21*, 9–27.

Schauble, L., Klopfer, L.E. and Raghavan, K. (1991) 'Students' transition from an engineering model to a science model of experimentation.' *Journal of Research in Science Teaching 28*, 859–882.

Shapere, D. (1966) 'Meaning and scientific change.' In R.G. Colodny (ed) *Mind and Cosmos: Essays in Contemporary Science and Philosophy, Vol. 3*, 41–85. University of Pittsburgh Series in the Philosophy of Science.

Shulman, L.S. (1986) 'Those who understand teach: knowledge growth in teaching.' *Educational Researcher 15*, 4–14.

Siegler, R.S. and Liebert, R.M. (1975) 'Acquisition of formal scientific reasoning by 10- and 13-year olds.' *Developmental Psychology 11*, 401–412.

Smith, C., Carey, S. and Wiser, M. (1985) 'On differentiation: a case study of the development of the concepts of size, weight, and density.' *Cognition 21*, 177–233.

Smith, C., Hennessy, G. and Carey, S. (1994) Children's knowledge about science. Paper presented at the J. S. McDonnell Foundation meetings, Vanderbilt University.

Tschirgi, J.E. (1980) 'Sensible reasoning: a hypothesis about hypotheses.' *Child Development 51*, 1–10.

Vygotsky, L.S. (1978) *Mind in Society: The Development of Higher Psychological Processes* (M. Cole, V. John-Steiner, S. Scribner, and E. Souberman, Eds. and Trans.). Cambridge, MA: Harvard University Press.

Walker, J. and Brown, A.L. Work in progress.

Wellman, H.M. (1990) *The Child's Theory of Mind*. Cambridge, MA: Harvard University Press.

Wellman, H.M. and Gelman, S. (1988) 'Children's understanding of the nonobvious.' In R.J. Sternberg (ed) *Advances in the Psychology of Human Intelligence 4*, 99–135. Hillsdale, NJ: Erlbaum.

CHAPTER 2

On the Development of the Understanding of Abstract Ideas

Stella Vosniadou

Introduction

When 'The development of the understanding of abstract ideas' was suggested as a possible title of this chapter by the organizers of the workshop 'Growing up with science' my first inclination was to change it. The term 'abstract ideas' made me particularly uncomfortable because many psychological findings in the last years have questioned the validity of describing human thinking as abstract. Upon second thoughts, however, I decided to keep the title and make it an opportunity to discuss my difficulties with the notion of abstract ideas in the process of describing my theoretical commitments and assumptions. This chapter starts by trying to elucidate the meaning of abstract ideas, continues by describing a theoretical framework within which one can understand the development of knowledge acquisition in science, and ends by drawing some implications for science instruction.

Theoretical Framework

The notion of abstract ideas can take different meanings depending on the theoretical framework one adopts. In the empiricist tradition, which is the first that comes to mind when one hears the term, abstract ideas form out of simple ideas following the laws of association. According to Locke, for example, simple ideas are not fictions or fancies but the natural and regular productions of things, whereas abstract ideas are not intended to be copies of anything but are combinations of ideas which the mind by its free choice puts together without considering any connection they have in nature (Locke, 1956).

Many science educators and researchers adopt a basic empiricist approach to describe the process of learning science. They give a

Growing Up with Science

great deal of importance to experience and consider that learning is mostly a matter of enriching existing knowledge and improving the processes of learning. According to this approach, science learning proceeds along a continuum where ideas become more general, more abstract and more widely applicable as a result of increased experiences. What this implies for instruction is that we should provide children with more experiences and with opportunities to understand the process of doing science.

The development of abstract ideas has been interpreted differently by Piaget (1970). Piaget has also given a great deal of attention to experience, but he has claimed that the process of developing more abstract conceptual structures depends on the constructive activity of the learner and not on the passive association of ideas. Piaget has chosen to provide a structural account of the intellect in terms of a mathematical model. According to this model, the process of intellectual development proceeds through a series of stages each of which is characterized by a different psychological structure. In infancy, intellectual structures take the form of organized patterns of behaviour in the form of concrete action schemes. These structures acquire representational status during the preschool years and develop into operational structures (described in terms of groupings based on the mathematical notion of sets and their combinations) at approximately the age when children go to school. The last stage of intellectual development, formal operational thought, is supposed to appear during adolescence and is characterized by the ability to engage in prepositional reasoning, to entertain and systematically evaluate hypotheses, etc.

Piaget considers this global restructuring to be the product of the natural spontaneous process of intellectual development and not of explicit learning. The implications of this approach for instruction is that we should encourage the constructive activity of the learner and provide experiences which may be interpreted differently at different stages but which, by the time students reach adolescence, will be transformed into scientific learning and understanding.

The theoretical framework described here to explain the process of learning science differs in important ways from the global restructuring and enrichment approaches previously described. This framework, which I have called 'domain-specific restructuring', focuses on the process of knowledge acquisition in specific domains and describes learning as a process that requires the significant reorganization of existing knowledge structures and not only their enrichment.

More specifically, the argument is made that the human mind has evolved specialized mechanisms to pick up information from the physical world that make it possible to develop what we may call a naive framework theory of the physical world,[1] that develops early on in infancy and allows the child to operate in the everyday physical environment. While this early competence forms the necessary foundations for further learning to occur, it may also hinder the acquisition of scientific knowledge in the physical sciences. This happens because scientific explanations of phenomena often violate fundamental principles of naive physics which are confirmed by our everyday experience. Some of these principles are, for example, the belief that unsupported objects fall 'down', or that moving objects will stop moving if their movement is not continuously sustained by a causal agent. For this reason, learning science requires the radical reorganization of the knowledge base and the creation of new qualitative representations. After all, the historical development of the physical sciences has also been characterized by revolutionary theory changes which have restructured our representations of the physical world.

Domain-specific restructuring is different from the global restructuring described by Piaget not only because it focuses on knowledge acquisition in specific subject matter areas but also because it assumes that this process is the outcome of learning and instruction. It also differs from previous approaches in proposing that the kind of instruction that promotes the learning of science should be guided by a different system of beliefs regarding the development of abstract ideas than that implicit in the empiricist and Piagetian frameworks. Recently, a series of findings in psychology have made researchers very aware of the situated nature of human cognition, of the fact that human thinking is highly influenced by the nature of the particular tasks we undertake to do, of the context in which they occur, and of the tools and artefacts that we use. The work of psychologists such as Wason and Johnson-Laird (1972), or Tversky and Kahnenman (1974) has shown that individuals are more likely to succeed at thinking tasks that contain familiar elements and allow the ready construction and manipulation of mental models. It has also been shown that individuals do not reach decisions in a way that is logically consistent and which obeys the laws of probability. In other words, it appears that 'abstract thinking' has relatively limited applicability to how humans reason.

---

1 The term 'theory' is used to denote a relational, explanatory structure, not an explicit, well-formed theory that is subject to conscious awareness and hypothesis testing. It is not assumed that children have metaconceptual awareness of the presuppositions and beliefs that comprise what we refer to as a framework theory.

Some recent approaches to the problem of knowledge acquisition, known as situativity theory, claim that knowledge is an activity that is fundamentally inseparable from the activities in which it is developed and deployed, and that humans and their interactions with the world can be understood only by observing them within real contexts. (e.g., Brown, Collins and Duguid, 1989; Lave, 1988). Although I do not agree with extreme positions of situativity theory, I think it is necessary to take into consideration the situational and cultural variables that influence the knowledge acquisition process. What this implies for instruction is that learning science needs to be supported by a culture where science becomes part of the everyday reality of students, through TV programmes, books, science museums and contacts with practising scientists. In order to make science learning easier, we need to understand how to make abstract ideas 'concrete' and meaningful by relating them to authentic experiences and scientific practices in the culture.

The Process of Learning Science

A great deal of information has been accumulated on how students learn science. Most researchers would agree on the following three conclusions about this process:

(1) *Science learning is difficult.* Even after many years of science instruction, students still seem to have difficulty understanding science concepts. This applies even to the students who are supposed to perform above average in terms of test scores and teacher evaluations. For example, diSessa (1982) has shown that students at the Massachusetts Institute of Technology who had at least one year of physics at college level still had a great deal of difficulty understanding Newton's laws and seemed to operate in ways more consistent with an Aristotelian theory of physics.

(2) *Science learning is characterized by misconceptions.* Misconceptions have been noted in practically all subject areas of science. Hundreds of misconceptions, enough to fill out tens of volumes, have been reported in the literature. Some examples of such misconceptions follow. Kempton (1987) has shown that many adults use a folk theory in dealing with home heating thermostats. These individuals hold a 'valve theory' according to which the thermostat is supposed to control the rate of heat flow. Thus they believe that the higher a thermostat is set, the more heat will flow and the faster the house will heat up. In the area of light, many individuals believe that their eyes

perceive objects directly and that colour is a property of the objects themselves (Anderson and Smith, 1986). In addition, it appears that young children believe that the currently perceived colour is a property of the object itself, even when they have seen the experimenter change the object's apparent colour with a colour filter (e.g., Flavell, Green and Flavell, 1986). Finally, some novices in the area of electricity believe that a switch is like the trigger of a gun; it sends an impulse to a battery to trigger current flow from the battery to a lightbulb (Collins and Stevens, 1984).

Research conducted in my laboratory has revealed several misconceptions that elementary school children form regarding the shape of the Earth and the explanation of the day/night cycle (Vosniadou and Brewer, 1992, 1994). Figure 2.1 shows the range of mental representations of the shape of the earth obtained by elementary school children in a study conducted in the United States.

As can be seen, some children believe that the earth is shaped like a flat rectangle or a disc, is supported by ground below and covered by the sky above its top. Other children think that the earth is a hollow sphere with people living on flat ground deep inside it, or a flattened sphere with people living on its flat top and bottom. Some other children form the interesting model of the dual earth, according to which there are two earths: a flat one on which people live and a spherical one that is a planet up in the sky. These representations of the earth are not rare. In fact, only 23 of the 60 children that participated in this study (mostly fifth graders) had formed the culturally accepted model of the spherical earth. This finding has been confirmed by a series of cross-cultural studies that investigated the concept of the earth in children from India, Greece, and Samoa (Vosniadou, 1994a).

(3)*Science learning is inert.* The term 'inert knowledge' has been used by Bereiter (1984) and Bransford *et al.* (1989) to describe the problem of knowing something but failing to use it when it is relevant. Inert knowledge is considered to be knowledge accessible only in a restricted set of situations although, potentially, it could apply to many more. Science knowledge is often inert in the sense that students learn how to solve science problems at school but fail to apply this knowledge to explain physical phenomena outside of school (diSessa, 1982).

Most researchers would agree on the above-mentioned descriptions of the process of learning science. Despite this agreement, the interpretations made of these difficulties differ. Some researchers think that science learning is difficult because students have limited expe-

Mental models of the Earth

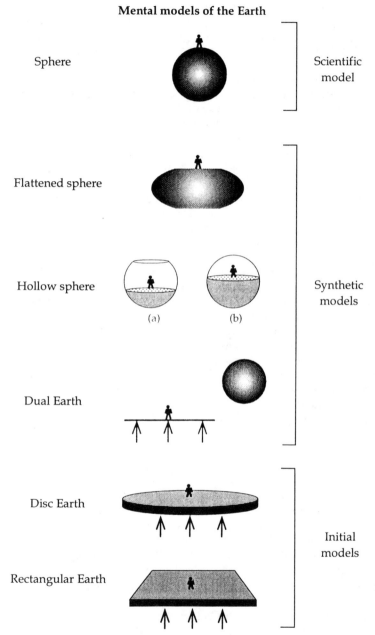

Figure 2.1

riences and/or because they do not know how to interpret the limited experiences they have. They claim that children do not know how to test hypotheses, accept explanations that should be rejected on the basis of the available evidence, base their explanations on what they perceive through their senses and not on the logic of things, or do not even see the need to explain why things happen (see, e.g., Harlen, this volume).

Other researchers believe that novices' thinking is based on superficial interpretations of physical reality which may be able to explain a limited set of situations but which do not constitute a coherent and systematic theory. According to this view, learning science is basically a process of organizing this 'knowledge in pieces' into more complex and systematic knowledge structures governed by the laws and principles of physics (diSessa, 1993).

I find a great deal of truth in the explanations mentioned above. There is no doubt that students base their explanations on everyday experiences which are by definition limited, that they need to develop better procedures for testing and evaluating hypotheses, and that the thinking of the expert is more coherent, more systematic and more closely linked to the laws and principles of physics. On the other hand, children's thinking does not appear to be quite as limited as suggested above. Vosniadou and Brewer (1994) found that 38 out of the 60 elementary school children they examined provided well-defined explanations of the day/night cycle. These explanations were empirically accurate, in the sense that they were consistent with the empirical evidence expected to be within their range. In addition to being sensitive to issues of empirical accuracy, the children seemed to show sensitivity to issues of logical consistency and of simplicity in their explanations.

In previous work (see Vosniadou 1994b) I argued that limitations in experiences and in logical thinking cannot fully explain the phenomena of misconceptions and of inert knowledge which are observed not only in elementary school students but in high school and college students as well. In order to explain the above-mentioned phenomena, we need a theory of learning not only as a process of enriching existing knowledge but of revising and restructuring this knowledge.

Let us consider, for example, the previously mentioned misconceptions found in elementary school children's representations of the shape of the earth. Even very young children are now exposed to considerable information regarding the spherical shape of the earth through children's books, TV programmes, discussions with parents, globes, etc. In our studies in the United States (e.g. Vosniadou & Brewer 1992) we had to go as far as testing three-year-olds to find children who had not been exposed to this information. Many four-year-old children already knew something about the spherical shape of the earth. It is therefore difficult to claim that children's misconceptions about the shape of the earth result from limited experiences or even from limitations in logical thinking. The explanation of misconceptions and of inert knowledge I have provided in my work is that they are caused by students' attempts to deal with incompatible pieces of information, some of them stemming from everyday experience and some coming from the surrounding culture, often in the form of science instruction in the schools.

We will start with misconceptions first. If we look carefully at the misconceptions of the earth presented in Figure 2.1, we can see that they can be explained as students' attempts to synthesize the information received from the culture, according to which the earth is a sphere, with the belief (stemming from everyday experience) that the earth is flat and that people live on the top of this flat ground. For example, the children who form the model of the hollow sphere seem to understand that the shape of the earth is spherical, but they believe that people live on flat ground inside the earth. On the other hand, the children who form the model of the flattened sphere think that the earth is spherical but also a little flat on the top and maybe the bottom where the people live. The children who form the dual earth model think that there are two earths: a round one which is up in the sky and which has all the characteristics of the adult model, and a flat one on which people live.

All misconceptions regarding the shape of the earth encountered in the American sample as well as the Indian, Greek and Samoan samples in our studies (Vosniadou, 1994a) can be explained as attempts on the part of the children to synthesize two inconsistent pieces of information: the information they receive usually from instruction according to which the earth is a sphere, and the information they receive from their everyday experiences.

Now, we can all understand how children may form an initial representation of the earth as a flat, physical object supported by ground underneath, with the people living on its top and solar objects, such as the Moon and the Sun, located above its top. Our studies of preschool children's ideas about the earth do indeed confirm the hypothesis that children start with this simple mental representation. The question is: why do children not change their flat earth representation to the representation of a spherical earth when we tell them so and when we show them a globe?

My answer to this question is that the representation of the earth as a flat, physical object is not a simple belief but a complex construction supported by a whole system of observations, beliefs and presuppositions, that form a relatively coherent and systematic explanatory system. Figure 2.2 shows a pictorial representation of some of the beliefs and presuppositions that underlie the mental representation of a flat, supported earth which I assume to be the first representation that children form.

I cannot go into detail here about this explanatory system, which is described in detail in previous work (see Vosniadou, 1994b). The important point to make for the purpose of this chapter is that the representation of a flat earth is based on fundamental presuppositions about the physical world, such as the organization of space in terms of the directions of up and down and the presupposition that unsupported objects fall 'down', which are not addressed by the instruction usually provided. When we tell children that the earth is round like a globe, we do not explain to them how it is possible for the earth to be round and flat at the same time or how it is possible for people to live on the 'sides' and 'bottom' of this flat globe without falling.

The above-mentioned examples clearly show that the mechanism of adding information onto what you know can produce a misconception if the two pieces of information are incompatible, as in the case of children who try to add the information that the earth is spherical and flat at the same time. Sometimes, and this is very often the case in the learning of science, the understanding of a scientific explanation needs a more fundamental restructuring of the knowledge base – the revision of fundamental presuppositions and beliefs – before the additive mechanisms can work. In other words, *in order to explain the formation of misconceptions we need a conception of learning not solely as a process of enriching existing knowledge but also as a process of revising and reorganizing existing knowledge.*

This type of explanation also applies to inert knowledge. One of the reasons why information acquired in school settings is inert and therefore not utilized in real life is because it is very different to, and incompatible with, existing explanations based on everyday experience, to the extent that students do not realize that the two belong to the same category.

The suggested analysis is confirmed not only in the case of astronomy but in many other subject-matter areas of physics. Our studies of the process of conceptual change in mechanics and thermal physics (Ioannides and Vosniadou, 1991; Vosniadou, 1994b; Vosniadou and Kempner, 1993), show that the successive mental models of force and of heat constructed by elementary and high school students can be explained as students' attempts to reconcile the information they receive from instruction with certain basic presuppositions and beliefs about the nature of the physical world. For example, in the area

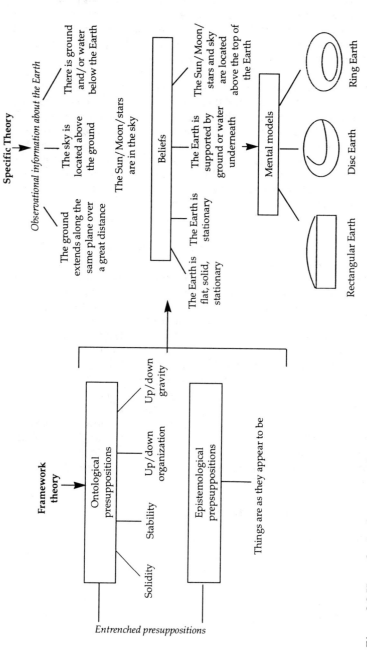

Figure 2.2 Hypothesized conceptual structure underlying children's initial models of the earth

of mechanics children construct an initial concept of force according to which force is a property of objects that feel heavy. This 'internal' force appears to represent the potential these objects have to react to other objects with which they come into contact. It is also central in explaining the motion of inanimate objects. In the ontology of the young child, the natural state of inanimate objects is that of rest, while the motion of inanimate objects is a phenomenon that needs to be explained, usually in terms of a causal agent. This causal agent is the force of another object.

The initial concept of force is very different from the way the linguistic term 'force' is currently interpreted by the scientific community. In Newtonian physics, force is not an internal property of objects but a process that explains changes in the kinetic state of physical objects. In the framework of the accepted view, motion is a natural state that does not need to be explained. What needs to be explained are changes in kinetic state.

The process of understanding the meaning implicit in the scientific concept of force is usually a slow and gradual affair, likely to give rise to misconceptions. It appears that students gradually differentiate the concept of weight from the concept of force and replace the notion of an internal force with the notion of an acquired force (an impetus) that is a property of the objects that move. Thus despite important changes in the concept of force that occur with development, certain entrenched presuppositions of the framework theory, such as that force is a kind of property of objects (that move or may not move) and that the motion of physical objects requires an explanation, continue to remain in place in the conceptual system of high school or even university students, despite the fact that these students have been exposed to systematic instruction in Newtonian mechanics.

Designing Instruction to Facilitate the Learning of Science in the Early Years

The first step in teaching science to young children is to provide them with an environment rich in new experiences and opportunities to observe interesting phenomena and to encourage them to try to make sense of these experiences. As children grow they need to be introduced to a deeper qualitative understanding of selected subject-matter areas in science. This qualitative understanding can provide the necessary foundations for the more systematic approaches to science to follow later on. The domain-specific restructuring interpretation of the process of learning science which was outlined above has specific recommendations to make for science instruction in the elementary school years, about curricula, about instruction, and about teacher education.

Curricula for Elementary Science

The finding that the understanding of science concepts and explanations is a difficult and time-consuming affair, likely to give rise to misconceptions, calls for a reconsideration of current decisions regarding the breadth of coverage of the curriculum in science education. It may be more profitable to design instruction that focuses on the deep exploration and understanding of a few, key concepts in one subject-matter area rather than cover a great deal of material in a superficial way. For example, the science curriculum for the fifth grade in Greece includes short units on mechanics, thermodynamics, energy, the particulate nature of matter and the processes of life. This approach encourages the casual memorization of facts, does not develop the qualitative understanding of science concepts, and is very likely to lead to logical incoherence and misconceptions. It also makes teachers very anxious about covering all the material, with the result that not enough attention is paid to what students actually understand.

Research in the learning of science has also shown that the concepts that comprise a subject-matter area have a relational structure that influences their order of acquisition. This structure needs to be taken into consideration when designing curricula and instruction. For example, in the subject-matter area of astronomy, students understand the spherical shape of the earth only after they have acquired an elementary notion of gravity. Explanations of the day/night cycle on the basis of the earth's axis of rotation cannot be understood before students know not only that the earth is a rotating sphere but also that the Moon revolves around the earth. Otherwise they form misconceptions such as that the Sun and the Moon are stationary at opposite sides of an up/down rotating earth (Vosniadou and Brewer, 1994). Similarly, a scientific explanation of the seasons only occurs in students who have formed a mental model of a heliocentric solar system, know the relative sizes of the earth, the Sun, and the Moon, and understand the scientific explanation of the day/night cycle. As Saddler's studies with Harvard undergraduates show, very few college students understand how the seasons occur, despite the fact that this is a piece of science included in the elementary school curriculum in the United States (Sadler 1987).

At present, such findings are not taken into consideration in the design of science curricula. A detailed investigation of the astronomy units in four leading science series in the United States (e.g. Vosniadou, 1991), as well as an examination of the national curricula for teaching astronomy to elementary school children in Greece, shows that many concepts are introduced in a sequence that does not provide students with all the information necessary for understanding them.

As mentioned earlier, the kind of instruction that elementary school students typically receive regarding the shape of the earth involves a simple statement that the earth is 'round like a ball', sometimes accompanied by a class demonstration of a rotating globe. In this type of instruction, teachers do not explain to students how it is possible for the earth to be spherical when it appears to be flat, or how it is possible for people to live on the 'sides' and 'bottom' of this sphere without falling 'down'. I have not found a single reference to the notion of gravity associated with astronomy instruction in the elementary-school grades. This is because gravity is considered to belong to the subject-matter area of mechanics and not of astronomy. It is obvious that this type of instruction does not address students' presuppositions, and therefore does not provide them with the information they need in order to construct an appropriate representation of the earth as a sphere.

Instructional Strategies and Interventions

The realization that students do not come to school as empty vessels, but have beliefs and presuppositions about the way the physical world operates that are difficult to change, has important implications for the design of science instruction. Teachers need to be informed about how students see the physical world and must learn to take their points of view into consideration when they design lessons. Instructional interventions need to be designed to: (1) make students aware of their implicit beliefs and presuppositions; (2) provide the necessary experiences so that students will understand the limitations of their explanations and be motivated to change them; and (3) support science instruction in the school with science-related activities that take place outside the school.

Facilitating Metaconceptual Awareness

Although children seem to be relatively good interpreters of their everyday experience, they do not seem to be aware of the explanatory frameworks they have constructed. They do not appear to know that their explanations of physical phenomena are hypotheses that can be subjected to experimentation and falsification. Their explanations remain implicit and tacit. Lack of metaconceptual awareness of this sort prevents children from questioning their prior knowledge and encourages the assimilation of new information to existing conceptual structures. This type of assimilatory activity seems to form the basis for the creation of synthetic models and misconceptions, and lies at the root of the surface inconsistency so commonly observed in students' reasoning.

To help students increase their metaconceptual awareness, it is necessary to create learning environments that facilitate group discussion and the verbal expression of ideas. Recently technology-supported learning environments have been constructed that make it easier for students to express their internal representations of phenomena and compare them with those of others. Such activities may be time-consuming, but they are important for ensuring that students become aware of what they know and understand what they need to learn.

It is important to emphasize here that science learning does not only mean that a student acquires a different explanatory system than the layman's; it also means a more flexible conceptual system, a system that makes it easier to adopt different perspectives and different points of view. What brings about this cognitive flexibility (and this is an important area for future research) is, in my opinion, increased metaconceptual awareness. It is difficult, if not impossible, to understand other points of view if you do not even recognize what your own point of view is. Increased awareness of one's own beliefs and presuppositions is a necessary step in the process of understanding the presuppositions and beliefs of others and probably the first step in the process of conceptual change.

Providing the Necessary Experiences

Students often do not see the need to change their beliefs and presuppositions because these provide good explanations of their everyday experiences, function adequately in the everyday world, and are tied to years of confirmation. In order to persuade students to invest the substantial effort required to become science-literate, and to re-examine their initial explanations of physical phenomena, it is necessary to provide them with additional experiences (in the form of systematic observations or the results of hands-on experiments), that prove to them that the explanations they have constructed are in need of revision. If we want these experiences to be useful in the process of belief revision we need to carefully select them so that they are theoretically relevant. It is not the case that any new experiences will do the job.

To make this problem even worse, there is a serious communication problem associated with science learning. The semantics of terms such as heat, force, weight, etc., are completely different in everyday language and in scientific language. This becomes the source of errors and misunderstandings that could perhaps have been avoided if different linguistic terms were used in the science vocabulary. Educators need to be more sensitive to the linguistic difficulties associated with the learning of science concepts and discuss them with their students.

Cultural Support for Science Learning

This brings us to the third and very important point that has to do with cultural support for science learning. Although scientific explanations are the ones our culture supports, they have not yet filtered down to everyday culture. Whatever science learning takes place in school, it is not really supported outside the school, except in cases where children have scientifically literate parents who provide them with books, take them to science parks and museums, and talk to them about science. It is important that science becomes more a part of everyday reality through TV programmes, popularized books, science museums for children, etc. than is currently the case.

Teachers and Teacher Education

Many elementary school teachers are often insecure about teaching science because they lack both the necessary knowledge of science and the relevant methods and pedagogic skills appropriate for science teaching (see Harlen, Chapter 5 this volume). My experience in Greece is that teachers try to deal with their insecurity about science by avoiding practical work, relying extensively on the provided books which are read in the classroom, and by not encouraging discussion. In the United States I have observed many teachers who do a great deal of process-oriented science in the classroom but do not provide the necessary conceptual understanding.

In order to be able to design learning environments for science along the lines described above, we need teachers who are much better trained in both science and pedagogy. This is difficult to achieve under the current situation, given the breadth of the curricula and the lack of specific instructions about how children learn. The teaching of science could, however, become easier and less anxiety provoking to teachers if we were to concentrate our curricula on a few key subject-matter areas and make them the focus for teaching science to elementary school children. Teams of researchers and teachers can then work together to first of all find out how children learn in the selected subject-matter areas, and then, based on the research results, design good books, good teaching methods and good teachers' education programmes. In this way we may have a better chance of providing a solid introduction to science to most children that will not make them scared of science and will prepare them for secondary education.

Concluding Comments

I have argued that the learning science is not a process that can be explained by assuming that new knowledge is simply added onto existing knowledge structures, but a process that often requires that basic presuppositions and beliefs about the physical world are revised. It appears that this restructuring process is not trivial but a rather difficult one, because the beliefs and presuppositions about the physical world that are based on everyday experience are robust and resistant to change. The realization that the learning of science is a difficult and time consuming affair is the necessary first step in the direction of preparing the education community to put together the concentrated efforts needed for designing the kinds of curricula and learning environments that have the potential to make students both knowledgeable and enthusiastic about science.

References

Anderson, C.W. and Smith, E.L. (1986) *Children's Conceptions of Light and Color: Understanding the Role of Unseen Rays* Res. Series No. 166. East Lansing, MI: Michigan State University, College of Education, Institute for Research on Teaching.

Bereiter, C. (1984) 'How to keep thinking skills from going the way of all frills.' *Educational Leadership 42*, 75–77.

Bransford, J.D., Franks, J.J., Vye, N.J. and Sherwood, R.D. (1989) 'New approaches to instruction: because wisdom can't be told.' In S. Vosniadou and A. Ortony (eds) *Similarity and Analogical Reasoning*. New York: Cambridge University Press.

Brown, J.S., Collins, A. and Duguid, P. (1989) 'Situated cognition and the culture of learning.' *Educational Researcher 18*, 32–34.

Collins, A. and Stevens, A.L. (1984) *Mental Modes of Complex Systems* (Report No.5788). Cambridge, MA: Bolt, Branck and Newman, Inc.

diSessa, A. (1982) 'Unlearning Aristotelian physics: a study of knowledge-based learning.' *Cognitive Science 6*, 37–75.

Acknowledgement

The work on this chapter was facilitated by a grant from the University of Athens, Greece. I would like to thank my colleagues and students – William F. Brewer, Christos Ioannides and Lianne Kempner – for their contributions to the research projects referred to in this chapter.

diSessa, A. (1993) 'Towards an epistemology of physics.' *Cognition and Instruction 10*, 105–225.

Flavell, J.H., Green, F.L. and Flavell, E.R. (1986) 'Development of knowledge about the appearance-reality distinction.' *Monographs of the Society for Research in Child Development 51*, 1, Serial No. 212.

Ioannides, C. and Vosniadou, S. (1991) *The Development of the Concept of Force in Greek Children*. Paper presented at the biennial meeting of the European Society for Research on Learning and Instruction, Turku, Finland, August.

Kempton, W. (1987) 'Two theories of home heat control.' In D. Holland and N. Quinn (eds) *Cultural Models in Language and Thought*. Cambridge, England: Cambridge University Press.

Lave, J. (1988) *Cognition in Practice: Mind, Mathematics, and Culture in Everyday Life*. Cambridge, England: Cambridge University Press.

Locke, J. (1956) *An Essay Concerning Human Understanding*. Chicago: Henry Regnery.

Piaget, J. (1970) *Genetic Epistemology*. New York: Columbia University Press.

Sadler, P.M. (1987) 'Misconception in astronomy.' In J.D. Novak (ed) *Proceeding of the Second International Seminar: Misconceptions and Educational Strategies in Science and Mathematics* (Vol.3, p.422–425). Ithaca, NY: Cornell University.

Vosniadou, S. (1991) Designing curricula for conceptual restructuring: lessons from the study of knowledge cognition in astronomy. *Journal of Curriculum Studies, 23* (3), 219–237.

Vosniadou, S. (1994b) 'Capturing and modeling the process of conceptual change.' *Learning and Instruction 4*, 45–69.

Vosniadou, S. (1994a) 'Universal and culture specific properties of children's mental models of the earth.' In L.A. Hirschfield and S.A. Gelman (eds) *Mapping the Mind*. New York: Cambridge University Press.

Vosniadou, S. and Brewer, W.F. (1992) 'Mental models of the earth: A study of conceptual change in childhood.' *Cognitive Psychology 24*, 535–585.

Vosniadou, S. and Brewer, W.F. (1994) 'Mental models of the day/night cycle.' *Cognitive Science 18*, 123–183.

Vosniadou, S. and Kempner, L. (1993) *Mental Models of Heat*. Paper presented at the biennial meeting of the Society for Research in Child Development, New Orleans, LA, April.

Further Reading

Baillargeon, R. (1990) *The Development of Young Infants Intuition About Support*. Paper presented at the Seventh International Conference on Infant Studies, Montreal, Canada, March.

Chi, M.T.H., Glaser, R. and Farr, M.J. (eds) (1988) *The Nature of Expertise*. Hillsdale, NJ: Lawrence Erlbaum Associates.

Chi, M.T.H., Glaser, R. and Rees, E. (1982) 'Expertise in problem solving.' In R. Sternberg (ed) *Advances in the Psychology of Human Intelligence, Volume I*. Hillsdale, N.J.: Lawrence Erlbaum Associates.

Cognition and Technology Group at Vanderbilt (1990) 'Anchored instruction and its relationship to situated cognition.' *Educational Researcher 19*, 6, 2–10.

Gentner, D. and Stevens, A.L. (eds) (1983) *Mental Models*. Hillsdale, NJ.: Lawrence Erlbaum Associates.

Johnson-Laird, P.N. (1983) *Mental Models*. Cambridge, MA.: Harvard University Press.

Spelke, S.E. (1991) 'Physical knowledge in infancy: reflections on Piaget's theory.' In S. Carey and R. Gelman (eds) *The Epigenesis of Mind: Essays on Biology and Cognition*. Hillsdale, NJ.: Lawrence Erlbaum Associates.

Tiberghien, A. (1994) 'Analysing teaching–learning situations.' *Learning and Instruction 4*, 71–87.

Tversky, A. and Kahneman, D. (1974) 'Judgement Under Uncertainty: Heuristics and Biases.' *Science 125*, 1124–1131.

Vosniadou, S. (1991) 'Are we ready for a psychology of learning and culture?' *Learning and Instruction 1*, 3, 283–287.

Vygotsky, L.S. (1978) *Mind in Society*. Cambridge, MA: Harvard University Press.

Wason, P.C. and Johnson-Laird, P.N. (1972) *The Psychology of Reasoning: Structure and Content*. Cambridge, MA: Harvard University Press.

Wiser, M. and Carey, S. (1983) 'When heat and temperature were one.' In D. Gentner and A.L. Stevens (eds) *Mental Models*. Hillsdale, NJ.: Lawrence Erlbaum Associates.

CHAPTER 3

Concepts in the Primary Science Curriculum

Paul Black, Jonathan Osborne and Shirley Simon

The first part of this chapter describes methods used in research used as a basis for development of curriculum materials in the Nuffield primary science project in the UK. The approach is a constructivist one based on the need to start from elicitation of children's ideas about natural phenomena. The second part describes a more detailed research with children between ages 7 and 13 about their understanding of forces in equilibrium. The aim of the work was to explore the ways in which children's perceptions, explanations and concepts, as evoked by two experiments, differed between the age groups, in order to establish empirically based hypotheses about progression in learning of the topic. The structure of the questioning and the data analysis lead to a proposal that children's thinking can be described in terms of separate 'dimensions'. For most aspects explored, there was a range of responses within any one age group, which was comparable with the changes across the six years spanned by the four groups. A short trial of a teaching scheme based on the results showed some success.

Introduction

Two pieces of work will be considered. Both are to do with children's learning of science. The first was part of a research and curriculum project called the SPACE project (Science Processes and Concept Exploration). The second is a more recent and detailed research about understanding of forces in equilibrium. It has also produced both research reports and materials for teachers.

The SPACE Project

The SPACE publications consist of nine research reports (with 5 more to come) each on a different topic. In addition there is a set of curriculum materials, teacher's guides, pupils books (see Black *et al.* 1993a, b). The research was designed to be comprehensive - and therefore not as detailed - and to lead to comprehensive curriculum materials for primary school science.

One reason for the project being set up was that there was felt to be a problem as to which science concepts you should teach to young children. Should only process skills (e.g. observation, making investigations) and not concepts, be taught (Black and Harlen 1993)? The SPACE team felt that a 'process-only' curriculum is simply not possible. For example, children cannot develop skills of observation unless they have some idea of what they are looking for. Observation involves selection, from ideas in your head, of what is worth seeing. The criteria used involve conceptual assumptions about the system observed. It is not possible to investigate this without a model - implicit or explicit - of the system you are investigating.

Another concern was that perhaps there are some concepts, for example in electricity, current and potential difference, that are too difficult for primary school children to cope with. The central question is: what aspects of concepts in scientific topics should we analyse and attempt with young children? Are there concepts that pupils can investigate that will change their ideas into scientific ideas and also be opportunities in which to develop process skills?

It should always be remembered that children have their own informal everyday explanations of natural phenomena. We have to work with those explanations, explore, expose and try to change them, to lead into the concepts and ideas we wish to establish.

The SPACE research covered 11 topics as follows:

- Living processes
- Living things in their environment
- The variety of living things
- Rock, soil and weather
- Using energy
- Earth in space
- Materials
- Forces and movement
- Sound
- Light
- Electricity and magnetism

Children's Ideas About Light

This chapter will concentrate only on the topic of light. At secondary school exploring the topic of light involves complex diagrams with lines drawn, lenses, mirrors, the eye and virtual images. Is this too difficult for primary pupils? It is important to realize that some things are assumed to be obvious for secondary pupils that are not at all obvious. Examples are:

(1) What we understand as light can be represented by drawing lines on pieces of paper. That is an unreal step for children.

(2) The assumption that seeing is to do with light entering the eye. Many diagrams in school textbooks on optics are bad because they show the eye at the edge of a ray diagram but do not show what the eye is doing - it is just 'there'. The idea that you only see because of light entering the eye is a very difficult concept and hard even for many adults to accept.

This analysis led to targets being set for the topic of light for primary pupils, as follows:

o Light travels. It is not just 'there' but it comes and goes. It normally travels in straight lines and can be represented by straight lines.

o Light is produced by a range of sources and travels out from the source.

o Many objects (e.g. a wall) reflect or re-emit as well as mirrors.

o Vision occurs because light enters the eye from the object that you see.

o Shadows occur because light is blocked by an object, i.e. a shadow is a lack of light not a reflection.

These are the targets for children aged up to 11 learning about light. When these ideas are clearly understood then children are better able to learn what is taught later at secondary school.

How can these targets be achieved? Researchers from the project worked with teachers who collected the data. There were four phases:

(1) The elicitation and collection of children's ideas; i.e. a start was made by thinking of ways, relevant to the points of interest, which would provoke children's thinking.

(2) Categorization and analysis of the evidence.

(3) Feedback (to the teacher from the analysis) - a feedback of initial results and discussion of intervention strategies to challenge the child and change her ideas.

(4) A further elicitation and collection of children's ideas (post test)

  ○ to look for changes in children's work

  ○ to help analyze the teaching material and evaluate its effectiveness.

For phase (1), pupils were asked: 'where does light come from?' They were asked to draw different sources of light. This was successful with all ages but will not be discussed further here.

Pupils were also set tasks about 'seeing'; e. g. how can you see a book? Can you draw it? Figure 3. 1 shows some examples of their responses. It is noteworthy that in some cases, the light is represented by arrows and lines.

Pupils then worked in pairs. One had a torch; the other had a mirror and sat with her back to the pupil holding the torch. The 'game' was to move the mirror in order to be able to see the torch and say whether and when it was switched on and off. The pupils were then given drawings and told to add to them to show how the mirror was used to see the light from the torch. There were a variety of drawings - as shown in Figure 3. 2 - from different schools and different ages. Some drew lines, others arrows, some arrows went in one direction, others in both directions.

On the basis of the drawings, children's responses could be categorized. This was useful for two purposes:

(1) To explore the effectiveness of any intervention.

(2) In the teacher's books that were produced the diagrams could be used to illustrate typical work of primary school children (which the teachers found both useful and re-assuring).

A final task was: draw where your shadow would be if the sun were behind you (see Figure 3. 3). There was a variety of responses. In general children were unable to predict where a shadow would be. Often there was confusion between shadows and reflections.

In general many methods were used to collect children's ideas as follows:

  ○ drawings (especially good with young children)

  ○ writing

  ○ diaries (written every few days or once a week for slow processes e. g. evaporation)

  ○ discussions (comparing drawings)

  ○ a few individual interviews.

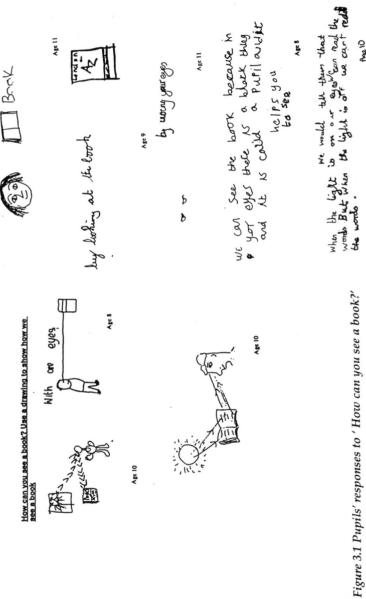

Figure 3.1 Pupils' responses to 'How can you see a book?'

Figure 3.2 Pupils' drawings to represent seeing a reflection of a light in a mirror

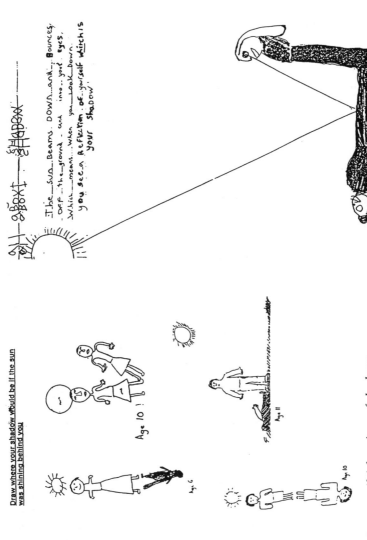

Figure 3.3 Some pupils' drawings of shadows

It should be noted that these difficulties in understanding light are not unusual. Research from Sweden (Andersson and Karrqvist 1983) showed that few 12-year-olds were aware that something needed to enter the eye. After some physics teaching at age 15, one third then got it right, leaving two thirds who failed to understand the phenomena in a basic way (see also Goldberg and McDermott 1986).

Several different intervention activities were employed. For example:

○ Four mirrors were mounted vertically with plasticene on the four edges of a square table-top. The children were given a torch and asked to see if they could bounce the light around the table. The drawings produced could then be used as a basis for discussion with the teacher.

○ The children were given a shoe box with a lid so that it was dark inside. There were small holes in two opposite sides. A narrow light beam was shone through one hole to pass through the other. A pupil looking from a hole in a third side does not see the light and this comes as a surprise (i. e. the fact that the light is there does not mean that you will see it). This experiment can be further developed using a mirror mounted internally on the fourth side to reflect light shone through the first hole at an oblique angle back through the second. Looking directly at (at right angles to) the mirror surface from the third hole, you still see nothing. This surprised many physicists and adults because our instinct tells us that when the mirror is reflecting light it should not look dark. When a piece of white paper is placed over the mirror surface, then we can see an illuminated surface - because the paper reflects diffusely.

These activities lead to the idea that light must come into the eye for you to see. It is not enough for the light simply to be there.

After these activities an attempt was made to categorize pupils' responses (Osborne *et al.* 1990, Osborne *et al.* 1993). Some children drew no links when representing vision. Some drew just one link, for example eye to object or object to eye. A third category would include children who could put in two such links, although the overall picture might not be scientifically correct, whilst a fourth could be for the correct representations. Such analytic schemes were used to see how responses change with increasing age and how they changed before and after the intervention activities. One set of results is shown in Figure 3. 4. The numbers there show, for example, that after intervention with the younger children (5 to 7 years of age) they were beginning to show single links but not dual links. How-

Numbers in boxes in each oval are those whose representations did not change; numbers on arrows represent pre- to post-test changes (e.g. 24 pupils changed from showing no links in the pre-test to showing a single link in the post-test). (a) is for 5- to 7-year-old pupils, (b) for 8 to 10 year-olds.

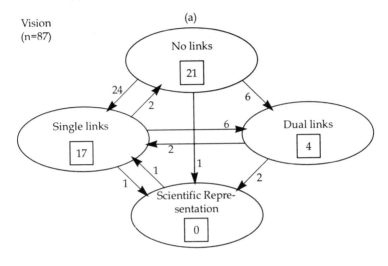

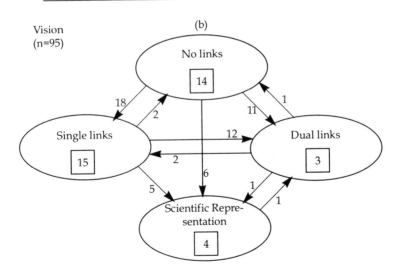

Figure 3.4 Pre to post test changes of pupils' explanations of vision

ever, with older children (8 to 10 years) the numbers showing dual links increased quite significantly. This was fairly typical. Some activities produced a big change for younger children, other activities achieved very little success with them but showed partial success with older children.

On the basis of such results two sets of books have been produced for teachers (Black *et al.* 1993 a, b). For younger primary school children these concentrate on activities about light sources and shadows. For older children the activities are about the representation of light in drawing and about the eye and 'seeing'. These books for teachers are laid out as follows:

o introduction

o guidelines on planning - how to divide into themes/topics (with examples and methods)

o intervention and assessment guide

o a background science chapter; this is important for teachers who are not trained in science and has proved very popular.

Progression in Understanding Equilibrium of Forces

The second piece of work is similar but more detailed and was an attempt to explore children's thinking in more detail. It was designed in two phases; the first was a research phase, the second a teaching trial.

The Research Phase

The research involved pupils at four different ages: 6–7, 8–9, 10–11 and 12–13. Several schools were involved and there were 12 pupils at each age. Each child was interviewed twice, before teaching and after, resulting in 96 interviews. There was no intervention in the teaching by the researchers, i.e. normal school teaching was used. The data were collected by researchers in interviews. The work (i.e. the transcripts of the interviews) produced then needed detailed interpretation (see Black and Simon 1992; Simon *et al.* 1994a, b for a full description).

Two situations were set up to establish the children's understanding of force, as illustrated in Figure 3.5. One involved a box being lifted with a piece of elastic. The other was a model bridge where pieces of card were supported on two blocks. The pupils had a weight which they could put on the bridge to see what would happen.

(a) Hanging box   (b) Bridge

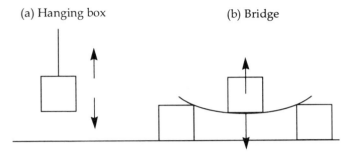

(a) Hanging Box: Children were given a box attached to two elastic bands and a loop of string. The box contained a few stones and could be lifted by pulling up one band, two bands, or the string.

(b) Bridge: Children were shown two bricks, a piece of thick card and a box containing a 400 g. mass. A bridge was built with the bricks and card, and the box placed on the top. Other bridges were built using a thinner piece of card, and an identical box containing a 600 g. mass. The lighter box could bend the thick card slightly and the thin card substantially. The heavier box made the thin card collapse.

Figure 3.5 The tasks presented to pupils

As each situation was presented to the child, questions were asked about:

- what they thought would happen
- what they saw happening
- why things happened
- what pushes, pulls and forces there were in the situation (the word forces was only introduced at the end if the child had not already used it).

From analysis of what was said it is possible to identify 'dimensions' along which a child can progress in the topic. These are:

(1) Progression in processes, notably in prediction and observation and in explanation.

(2) Progression in concepts, in that pupils might identify forces informally, calling them pushes and pulls, or make more formal use of the term force to identify and describe effects and explanations.

A brief summary of the results shows that, in prediction and observation:

○ some pupils could predict regularly, others could not or only occasionally

○ some made predictions about one of the effects involved, e. g. the elastic stretching, elastic breaking

○ some made predictions about two different aspects, e. g. the box is heavy and the elastic will stretch.

The pattern sequence that can be inferred, both in the children's predictions and also in their observations is a progression from observing nothing, to seeing one aspect, to seeing a different aspect, then to simultaneously focusing on two interacting aspects.

There was found to be little significant change pre/post test. Their teaching had not focused on observing and noticing forces. Surprisingly, there was little change in the overall responses for children between 6–7 and 12–13. Previous research has also reported this slow change in understanding with age (Hart 1981, Denvir and Brown 1986).

A similar summary can be proposed for children's explanations. Again there was a range of results. Some pupils could not give an explanation, others gave one single explanation (often 'weight'). A few gave a multiple explanation. The interviewer asked each child about gravity at the end of the interview and they often made no association between weight and gravity. Comparisons can be made using these results of children giving single and multiple explanations, as set out in Figure 3. 6.

It is possible to speculate that perhaps the human action in the first case (elastic) diverted attention away from the problem being investigated. In the second situation with the bridge there was no outside human intervention so perhaps it was easier to see in a more complex, abstract way.

When a child could recognize the concept of force she was asked: 'Do you think the forces are the same? Are some bigger? Which one?' The researcher was careful to ask the question suggesting equality as well as inequality. In fact most children did not think that the forces could be equal even when that had identified two opposing forces. They would argue either that the supporting force must be greater, otherwise the weight would fall, or that the weight force must be greater otherwise the elastic would not have stretched or the 'bridge' would not have bent.

A general conclusion from this work is that in order to teach a child about forces, it is necessary to identify what forces exist all

	Hanging Box	Bridge
Single/Multiple Pre	27 / 14	30 / 8
Single/Multiple Post	29 / 12	21 / 17

Figure 3.6 Comparison of pre/post-test changes in relation to single and multiple explanations

around us. Children need to look at the forces due to distortions of material objects as well as to weight, to magnetism, to friction and so on. Only then can you move on to a more abstract discussion about forces moving and stopping when they are equal. As for other areas in primary science, it seems clear that teaching should always keep close to everyday experience and attempt to make sense of that experience.

A progression can be made through the following main steps:

o recognize forces due to weights and pushing

o broader recognition to include forces due to springs, to elastic bands, then to other everyday materials, when they are distorted

o different forces are often opposing one another

o when there is no movement, the forces must be equal.

It was possible from these results to look at changes with age. There appeared to be two aspects as follows:

Aspect A involves ability to predict, to observe, and to explain. These abilities seem to be context dependent, insensitive to teaching, and slow to change with age.

Aspect B involves formal grasp of concepts, use of scientific language and discourse. For these, pupils' work seems more consistent, sensitive to teaching, and changes with age.

So, language can change but the underlying understanding is slow to change. It is thought that this is because teaching is too focused on B and not enough on A. More attention needs to be given to A. This then gives a different perspective in looking at the early work in the SPACE project.

The two task situations only bear strong similarity in the light of the abstract concepts which they were invented to exemplify. The children's responses have taught the researchers that there are many more differences between the tasks than they had realized, and for the children it is these aspects that are salient. The only exception to these generalizations is the consistency in respect of children's identification of upwards and downwards forces across the two tasks. This should not be surprising, since this is the aspect of the questioning and responses which came closest to the abstract scientific analysis of the two tasks. It is also the one aspect for which there were some significant changes with age.

The teaching observed between the pre and post tests was concerned with some aspects of the concept of force. Between various classes it used a variety of phenomena and exercises in measurement. However, in general, little attention was paid to developing children's explanations, to identifying multiple forces or to the concept of equilibrium. Some work was done with more formal approaches to the concept with the older children, and this could have been expected to improve their ability to identify forces.

The Teaching Trial

A small scale teaching activity was designed and tried out in order to explore whether it is possible to enhance young children's understanding of forces in equilibrium through activities designed in the light of the research results. The trials were carried out with two groups of six children each, in Years 3 and 6 respectively in the same school. The activities were first designed by the research team, and then reviewed by the class teachers who modified the proposed organization and presentation in the light of their knowledge of the children. Each pupil was also interviewed, both a few days before the teaching and about six weeks after it, using the same interview design as for the main research.

The activities for both years were based on the application of a force (by children's bodies or by heavy weights) to cause distortion in different objects. Children were encouraged to predict, observe and explain what happens when the objects are pressed on with their hands or a weight is added. The objects used were a piece of foam, a cushion and a small bridge made of bricks and plywood, all chosen because:

- ° they distort easily when pressed or when a heavy weight is placed upon them

- ° they go back to their original shape when the weight or hand is removed

- ° children can feel the force exerted by the distorted material.

The children subsequently used less easily distorted objects, such as a plank of wood, and were asked to explain the difference in what they then observed.

The approach and detail for the two year groups were not the same. Year 3 children could listen to the teacher for no more than a few minutes, 'talk about' ideas to their peers for a short time, explore practically, then reflect and articulate through writing down what they had done, before meeting new ideas. Year 6 children could listen to the teacher for a more protracted time, follow collective notes on a blackboard, discuss ideas at length with their peers and carry out and remember more lengthy procedures.

For the Year 3 children, the activities had two main aims. One was to provide a range of phenomena involving forces in balance through which children could be encouraged to make predictions and observations and to provide explanations for what they predicted and observed. The other was to help children, through their exploration and discussion of a range of phenomena, to progress in their understanding of the following ideas:

o a downward push is a force downwards

o weight is a force downwards

o objects do not continue to fall when supported because there is a push or force upwards

o when objects are at rest, the downwards and upwards forces are the same.

The whole set of activities took about one hour and comprised three main episodes.

In the first episode, children used their bodies to press down on squashy things. The teacher showed them several objects including a piece of foam, a cushion and a small bridge made of bricks and plywood and explained that they were to see what happened when they pressed down on each object. She told the children to talk in pairs about what would happen before they actually pressed down on the objects, and added that they should also think of reasons for their predictions.

As the children described things the teacher tried to pick up words they were using, explore meanings and extend the children's use of everyday language in describing and explaining the phenomena. As children finished pressing on the objects they were invited to sit on a plank of wood suspended by two bricks. The distortion in the wood was barely noticeable, and so children were encouraged to observe carefully and explain the difference between what happened to the plank and to the other objects.

When the children had all tried pressing on the squashy objects the teacher introduced the second episode with use of some kilogram masses. She asked the children to feel them and think about what would happen if they placed a kilogram on to each of the squashy objects (thus encouraging them to make predictions). She gave each child a small work-sheet to fill in as they tried each object, asking them to write down their 'guess' before actually placing the mass on the object.

While the children did this, the teacher asked them individually if there was a push down when they pressed down with their hands and also when the weight was placed on each object. The aim of this line of questioning was to facilitate a way of talking about force.

The children were very aware that they could make the objects distort more by pushing with their hands rather than placing the kilogram mass on them, however they did say that the weight of the kilogram was pushing 'a little bit'.

When it came to the plank, there was no perceptible movement when a mass was placed on it. Some children said that there was no push down because there was no movement. When asked about other situations they expressed a belief that unless objects moved, they were not being pushed. At this point it was appropriate to ask them to push with their hands various immovable objects like a wall or, by linking hands, the teacher (who stood firm). There was no perceptible movement in each case, but because the children knew they were pushing, they began to extend this idea and to see that the weight of the kilogram mass could be pushing down on the plank.

To introduce the third episode, the children were gathered together as a group to talk about what had happened both with the hand pressing down and the weight. The teacher demonstrated each one as they talked about it. As the teacher talked about pushes down, she introduced the word force. This phase was designed to draw all the children's observations and explanations together in order to talk about force. The word force was applied in the other contexts as well, including the idea that their bodies had lots of force when they sat on the cushion and made it very squashed. The idea of force was then extended to pushing on the wall; the teacher talked about pushing it with a force, although it did not move.

At this point the teacher chose one child to demonstrate and talk about the idea of pushing back (some children had begun to do this when they had finished the work-sheet). The teacher linked hands with the chosen pupil and let herself be pushed backwards; she then held firm so that their hands were still; she then pushed harder so that the pupil moved backwards. As the teacher demonstrated this she talked about force:

Teacher: She's got so much force she nearly pushed me over. Now what happens if neither of us are moving?

Pupil: You are pushing her back.

The idea that things can push back was emphasized as it was the key to the next idea, that of the squashed objects 'pushing back'. The teacher then asked the children to look again at the bridges, bits of foam and the cushion, and to think about whether these were pushing back.

For some children, the idea of pushing back was difficult. One child was encouraged to push down on the bridge with one finger, close her eyes and talk about what was happening. She insisted that it was not pushing back, it moved only so far because her finger was not strong enough. Another child had a similar line of reasoning, but when he did this exercise with his finger, and when he sat on the cushion he expressed a belief that each was pushing back.

The activity was finished by the children drawing one of the objects and if they wanted to, writing about all the pushes and forces they had learned about. The children spent some time drawing and colouring in. All the children drew a straight bridge with a weight on it (not representing the distortion in their drawing).

While they were quietly drawing, some children were asked individually what they had learned that day:

'You can push wood... the cushion... You can make weight with one kg, with those heavy things, and it only goes down a little bit.'

'You can push without things moving'.

In their written work, the children gave reasons for their predictions: these were mostly single explanations focusing on the properties of the materials being squashed.

For the Year 6 activity, the aims here were the same as for the younger group with the addition of a third aim - to build on work previously carried out on force and motion. It will not be described in detail here. The main style was that of teacher-led discussion, interspersed with children exploring phenomena with the use of equipment, followed by written work. There was emphasis on children producing predictions and explanations, and discussing several experiences in terms of forces, directions of forces, and the idea of weight.

Our evaluation of the trial showed that in Year 3 the children appeared to enjoy the activity, became involved in what they were asked to do, and were stimulated by the materials to talk about what was happening. The session did not proceed entirely as predicted because these young children produced unforeseen ideas. It had not occurred to us to make a discussion point of 'pushing even though things do not move'. Also, some of these children had not yet developed a general notion of a push down, that is, something in common between a weight causing distortion and a hand pushing down causing a distortion. This common element has to be perceived by children (even if they don't label it force) before they can perceive the reverse, that is, an upward push.

The Year 6 children also appeared to enjoy the session, and found the ideas stimulatiing - they were talking about them the following week. They were all involved in the activity: they were attentive and appeared to listen, concentrate and assimilate the ideas. The session was successful in that the children showed in their written work that they had learned something (to varying degrees) about forces in balance, but it was felt in retrospect that more time could have been spent on asking children to feed back their ideas at various points, through writing, drawing, or orally.

To look for evidence of progression, the 12 children were interviewed a few days before they experienced the teaching activities and again 6 weeks later. The interview schedule was similar in style to that used in the main study, with some change in the equipment used to show compression. The results were analyzed in a similar way to the results of the research study.

In the dimensions of prediction, observation and explanation the results were similar to those of the research study. Younger children were just as likely to provide single or multiple predictions and explanations as older children. Also, there were no significant differences in these aspects between the two interviews (before and after teaching). It would of course have been surprising if the impact of a single hour of teaching could have been detected six weeks later.

For another dimension, the interviews were analyzed in terms of whether pushes, pulls and forces were identified as downwards, upwards, or in both directions. If in both directions, we looked to see whether children described the bigger push, pull or force as upwards or downwards, or whether they suggested forces were the same in each direction. For each child, there were four opportunities to exhibit progression, on identification of pushes/pulls and forces, and on judging equality for both, in the cases of compression and of stretching. The result showed that both groups progressed for the compression task, but that the stretching task made little impact in Year 3. Perhaps, as suggested before, the personal handling here was a distraction from the analytic thinking required.

This teaching trial can only be a first foray into testing out teaching implications. Its results were sufficiently encouraging to justify further development of the teaching ideas. The work has led to a publication for teachers, which sets out the teaching exercises in some detail and also explains the background science necessary for the understanding of the conceptual targets that are the aim of the proposed work (Simon *et al.* 1994b).

However, the evidence still is that progress between ages is slow, better than in the research phase which showed that in many aspects explored there was little sign of effective learning over a period of six years. This certainly indicates that the topic is a difficult one for children over this entire age range, and that conventional science teaching is not addressing effectively the issues explored here. There is a range of performance within any one age group sample which is comparable with the changes over several years - an outcome which is reminiscent of the 7-year gap given prominence in the Cockcroft report on mathematics (Hart 1981). The significant changes with age were in the identification of forces and in the sophistication of the language they used. This latter aspect has not been discussed in this chapter.

The Reconstruction of Teaching

The work has led, as originally intended, to a quite new formulation of conceptual targets within primary science, incorporating some general assumptions about progression between different ages - this formulation has had some influence on the 1994 revision of the National Curriculum for Science in England and Wales (DfE 1995).

The results have been used to design teaching episodes which have been tried and then presented in a publication for teachers (Simon *et al.* 1994b). These episodes are novel in two respects. One is that they are quite unlike teaching used hitherto in primary science in the UK. The second is that they have worked to explicit conceptual targets, but these targets are new formulations of basic concepts which have not hitherto been spelt out. It is our view that in secondary science, conceptual bases such as these are not taught because they are taken for granted as being too obvious, or because their importance as underlying assumptions to what is taught has not been recognized. Thus, there is an important and achievable role for teaching science concepts at primary school level which is not merely a diluted version of the familiar secondary science curriculum. This approach, albeit based on far less detailed research but covering a wide range of topics, was that developed in the Nuffield SPACE project (Black *et al.* 1992, 1993a, b).

Two problems stand out here. One is that, even given the limitations that arise because this was a cross-sectional study across ages rather than a longitudinal one following one cohort over several years, it has been a quite expensive way of providing a firm research base for one specific topic. If such work is really essential over the whole potential range of topics, then the time and expense would be formidable. Much has been achieved with less detailed exploration in the Nuffield Project referred to above - work at the level of the forces research might be reserved for areas of particular difficulty.

The second problem is that the work has not been guided or illuminated by any explicit model of learning, apart from the adoption of the very general constructivist position that learning has to start from and connect with children's existing perceptions and theories. It is a matter for argument whether this has affected the quality of the analysis and practical conclusions. One possibility would be to analyze the results about explanations in relation to the work of Andersson (1986) and Carey *et al.* (1989). If such analysis were to be productive, it might develop these theoretical approaches. It might also make it possible to generalize the conclusions to other topic areas so that practical advances could be made on the basis of better directed and more economical research.

References

Andersson, B. and Karrqvist, C. (1983), How Swedish pupils, aged 12-15 years, understand light and its properties. *European Journal of Science Education* Vol. 5, No. 4, 387–402.

Andersson, B. (1986) 'The experiential gestalt of causation: a common core to pupils' preconceptions in science.' *European Journal of Science Education*, 8, 155–171.

Black, P. J. and Simon, S. (1992) 'Progression in Learning Science.' *Research in Science Education* Vol. 22, 45–54 Melbourne.

Black, P. J., Harlen, W., Russell, T., Austin, R., Bell, D., Hughes, A., Longden, K., Meadows, J., McGuigan, L., Osborne, J., Wadsworth, P., and Watt, D. (1992) and later *SPACE Research Reports*. Seven separate booklets reporting research on different primary science conceptual areas. Published 1992–1995. Liverpool University Press: Liverpool.

Black, P. J., Harlen, W., Russell, T., Austin, R., Bell, D., Hughes, A., Longden, K., Meadows, J., McGuigan, L., Osborne, J., Wadsworth, P., and Watt, D. (1993a) *Teachers' Handbook: Nuffield Primary Science*. London: Collins.

Black, P. J., Harlen, W., Russell, T., Austin, R., Bell, D., Hughes, A., Longden, K., Meadows, J., McGuigan, L., Osborne, J., Wadsworth, P., and Watt, D. (1993b) *Nuffield Primary Science* (Two sets of teachers' guides and pupils' books, covering respectively the age ranges 5–7 and 8–11, each set treating eleven science topic areas.) London: Collins.

Black, P. J., and Harlen, W. (1993) How Can We Specify Concepts for Primary Science? pps. 208–229 in Black P. J. and Lucas A. eds. *Children's Informal Ideas in Science*. London: Routledge.

Carey, S., Evans, R., Honda, M., Jay, E., and Unger, C. (1989) '"An experiment is when you try it and see if it works": a study of grade 7 students' understanding of the construction of scientific knowledge.' *Internationl Journal of Science Education* 11, 514–529.

Denvir, J. B., and Brown, M. (1986) 'Understanding of number concepts in low attaining 7-9 year olds: Part 2. The teaching studies.' *Educational studies in Mathematics* 17, 143–164.

D. f. E. (1995) *Science in the National Curriculum*. London: Her Majesty's Stationery Office for the Department for Education.

Goldberg, F. and McDermott, L. C. (1986) Student Difficulties in Understanding Image Formation by a Plane Mirror. *The Physics Teacher* Vol 24, 472–480.

Hart K. M. (ed) (1981) *Children's understanding of mathematics: 11–16* London: John Murray.

Osborne, J., Black, P., Smith, M. and Meadows, J. (1990) *Light- Science Process and Concept Exploration Project Report* Liverpool: Liverpool University Press.

Osborne, J. F., Black, P. J., Meadows, J. and Smith, M. (1993) Young children's (7–11) ideas about light and their development. *International Journal for Science Education* 15(1) 83–93.

Simon, S., Black, P. J., Brown, M. and Blondel, E. (1994a) Progression in Understanding the Equilibrium of Forces *Research Papers in Education* 9(2) 249–280.

Simon, S., Black, P. J., Blondel, E. and Brown, M. (1994b) *Forces in Balance* Hatfield: Association for Science Education.

CHAPTER 4

Developmental Pedagogy and Children's Understanding of the World Around Them

Ingrid Pramling

Introduction

People generally think of development and pedagogy as two different and distinct notions. In fact, it does not sound right in English to talk about developmental pedagogy. Pedagogy and development – the very words and concepts fit together much better in Swedish, German, Finnish, etc. The Swedish word *pedagogik* does not stand merely for the act of upbringing, teaching and learning, but also for a discipline that focuses on studying upbringing, teaching and learning in a scientific way. In most languages, however, the word 'pedagogy' refers to teaching – something done to or with children.

The word 'development', on the other hand, leads our thoughts to biology and psychology, the individual, the organism, the entity progressing more or less by itself. In the area of educational psychology, we most often think of development in relation to developmental psychology, that is, the child's mental growth stages, maturity – changes that come about for internal reasons (Piaget and Inhelder, 1969). I think we can all agree that, when we talk about babies and young children, including those attending pre-school, we are focusing on the concept of development rather than on pedagogy. When we talk about the learning that takes place in schools, however, we are referring to pedagogy. But let's leave the words now and deal with the *conceptions* of development and pedagogy and the features that distinguish and unite them.

Some researchers claim that humans are remarkable in the way in which they teach their young (Barnett, 1973). Premack (1984) argues that teaching arises from the need for an older generation to affect a younger one. Human beings are more particular than other species in the way in which they bring up their young. Marton and Booth (unpublished manuscript, p. 169) argue as follows:

First, teaching is seen as an activity which deliberately sets out to bring about some sort of change in another member of the same species. Second, the activity directed to bringing about this change is not a casual occurrence, it has to persist until the change is achieved in some measure. Third, and implied by the second criterion if we take it to its logical limit, the teacher has to have grounds for evaluating the behaviour, in order to judge if it is satisfactory or not.

This means that human beings use pedagogy for the purpose of reaching specific goals and persist in intervention until a change occurs. The institutions of education – schools, nurseries, universities and colleges – have been constructed by society to formalize the human pedagogical project – the effort to transmit one generation's experience, knowledge and values to the next generation – and teaching is the instrument that has been developed to bring this about. In a wide sense *the main purpose of pedagogical activities is to bring about a change in the child.*

But even though we can see that pedagogy and development are both concerned with change, development in the context of pedagogy may still seem strange to some, since development in relation to psychology is traditionally viewed as *internal*, while development in relation to pedagogy is viewed as *external*. In everyday life, also in the context of pre-school or school, people most often take the traditional views described above for granted. If we, on the other hand, turn our interest towards more recent theories of human change, learning and development may not be so clearly distinguished (Marton, 1994; Pramling, 1991; Rogoff, 1990; Valsiner, 1987; Wertsch, 1991). Instead these two aspects seem to be indistinguishable. It may be considered that development does not take place without external influence, or, on the other hand, that external influence which does not lead to development may not be considered as learning.

The manner in which these two distinctly different conceptions have begun to be interwoven can be seen, for example, in practice in New Zealand. The New Zealand government has recently introduced an extended project called 'Parents as the child's first teachers', in which one of the aims is to make parents aware of their role as educators of their offspring. In Sweden we can read, in the visions for the new curriculum for elementary school, that the plans for the different subject matters are formulated from the perspective of the pupils' development, which I think is a quite unique way of talking about learning in the school context (SOU, 1992:94). This means that development today has begun to be viewed as a pedagogical question, *i. e. how to bring about a change in the child.*

Thinking about pedagogy in these terms is far less radical in the context of pre-school than in that of school. As early as 1850 Friedrich Fröbel introduced the idea of development as a principle of pedagogy in pre-school (Johansson, 1995). There are, of course, many kinds of development in the context of pedagogy. The focus of this particular chapter is how the child widens its experience through interaction with the world around it. The basis of the pedagogical act is how the child experiences or understands aspects of the world, as opposed to the developmental approach to learning in which the child's psychological development forms the basis for activities (Clay, 1992). The question asked by a teacher is not, 'what can I teach children at the level each child is at?', but, 'how can I as a teacher, in interaction with the child, contribute to the child's development and learning?'.

The aim of the pedagogical act that we are looking at is to develop the child's awareness (experience, understanding) of specific phenomena. This means that one has to thematize and make certain relationships or features visible to the child. Relationships or features in the present context deal with aspects that could be considered as a basis also for science education.

The approach on which this chapter is built is phenomenographic. From a phenomenographic standpoint learning is considered as development and development as learning, that is, learning is viewed as a change in people's ways of experiencing the world around them.

Phenomenography

A phenomenographic approach to research was developed in relation to university students' conceptions of learning and their way of understanding different texts (Marton, Dahlgren, Svensson and Säljö 1977; Marton and Säljö, 1979). A qualitative analysis was made of the students' answers to different tasks; this showed the different ways in which one and the same text was understood. It became clear that students' reproduction of what the text was about differed in that they interpreted or experienced it in different ways. It was, in other words, not a question of whether or not they had understood the text, but rather of how they had understood the message conveyed by the text.

In interviews with students about their conceptions of learning it also became obvious that learning appeared to students in a number of qualitatively different ways (Marton and Säljö, 1976). Students' conceptions of their own learning have been studied in other cultures and contexts (see, e. g. , Dahlin and Regmi, 1995; Marton, Wen and Nagle, 1995; Trigwell, Prosser and Taylor, 1994). Some conceptions seem to be general and found in all cultures while others are more culturally specific. Children's conceptions of their own learning have also been described by Pramling (1983). Children's awareness about their own learning was described in terms of *what* children experience when they learn and *how* this learning comes about. The 'what' aspect of learning was described in three overriding categories which formed a developmental progression. First came *learning to do* something (a skill, activity or some sort of behaviour), then *learning to know* something (facts or knowledge), followed finally by *learning to understand* something (getting a different meaning, relating things or drawing conclusions). The 'how' aspect was described in terms of *learning as doing, learning as growing older* and, finally, *learning by experiencing*. Experience, again, could be related either to occasional incidents or to practice, a conscious approach towards being able to master something.

The phenomenographic approach to research focuses upon ways in which a phenomenon is experienced by a group of people. The variation of categories of conceptions constitutes the results (Marton, 1981a). Categories of conceptions have been found by using open interviews, drawings, essays, etc. The categories of conceptions are the meaning formulated by the subject about the phenomenon studied as it is understood by the researcher. The categories formulated by Piaget (1976) in his early work could be viewed as phenomenographic categories, although the notion did not exist at that time. Piaget (see, e. g. , Piaget, 1976, 1978) described children's conceptions of specific phenomena and later related his categories to developmental stages, whereas within phenomenography it has been shown over and over again that there is a variation of conceptions which are not related to age. Different ways of experiencing something can be found in a specific age group or among adults who seem to have the same background or partake in the same learning context. Piaget's interest changed from content-specific thinking to general structures in thinking (see, e.g., Piaget, 1970; Marton, 1981b). To describe categories in a phenomenographic study means to take the others' perspectives and try to uncover the subjects' taken for granted way of thinking about something. This means that the categories are formulated on the basis of their thinking and not on the words as such. Examples of children's conceptions of learning can be found in Pramling's dissertation (Pramling, 1983). In answer to a question such as: 'Can you tell me something you have learnt?' children obviously suggest a lot of different things. A child may, for example, suggest that he has learnt to ride his bike, to jump on one foot, to build an aeroplane, etc. For the researcher the question is then: 'In what way do children think about learning when they suggest the things they do?'. This leads to such considerations as in what way do these ideas differ from suggestions made by someone else, such as: 'I have learnt what time the children's programmes start on TV', or 'I have learnt that there is a planet called Saturn'. The first set of the children's suggestions described above were interpreted in the study as learning *to do* something, while the second set of suggestions were interpreted as learning *to know* something. So the categories are descriptions of peoples' taken for granted ways of experiencing a phenomenon, a base on which their ideas are formulated.

Children's conceptions of, for example, learning, expand and give them access to new and different ideas. This does not mean that they totally leave the earlier ideas behind, but that these ideas exist simultaneously with more advanced conceptions. It has also been shown that conceptions of different levels of advancement exist simultaneously in adults too (Brumby, 1979). This means that conceptions are not always stable, but can vary in children as well as in adults depending on the context and the content.

The result of a phenomenographic study is the variation in the ways of experiencing something and is denoted *the outcome space*. The categories of conceptions are superior to the individuals.

An Experience-Oriented Approach to Learning

The phenomenographic research approach was later developed into an approach to learning. Within phenomenography we have developed a non-dualistic way of viewing knowledge. The ontological assumption is that the object and the subject are not separate, but form one whole made up of two parts that have an internal relationship. There is one world only. It is both subjective (experienced by people) and objective (it transcends the experiences of individuals). In other words, knowledge is deeply personal. On the other hand, the non-dualistic perspective assumes that there are not two different worlds, one real and objective, the other subjective and consisting of mental pictures. Only one world exists, which people experience in different ways. This world is subjective and objective simultaneously. When the child makes a certain piece of knowledge his or hers, it is integrated into his or her personal way of understanding the world. The child also goes beyond itself and participates in something superior – collective knowledge. So although knowledge always exists in relationship to people, it transcends the individual. Experiencing something means that there is a relationship between the object and the subject which encompasses both (Marton, 1992). Children cannot gain an understanding of something that they do not have any experience of; they cannot form conceptions without any point of reference or relation to their world. When Fia, 20 months of age, started pre-school she had a very limited command of language, but became interested from the first day in the circle-time – a daily activity in which the class sang and played guitar. By focusing her attention and interest Fia grasped the idea of singing and songs from the very first day. She then spontaneously practised, day after day, the different songs that she heard. She invented her own fantasy words and moved her fingers as she had observed others doing during circle-time. After three months, Fia still does not talk much but knows five or six songs by heart (Lindahl, 1996). From the initial understanding, that it is possible to sing songs (the idea of singing), her awareness about songs was thematized and she learnt to sing songs.

Since each new experience contributes to the child's understanding of the world, he or she grows in awareness and changes. What he or she has learned or experienced modifies his or her way of experiencing, that is, *a development has taken place.*

All the things a child experiences from birth, or even earlier, will remain and form the foundation for new experience, while earlier experience will change as a result of the new. Or, in the words of the Nobel prize-winner Aaron Klug: 'One doesn't see with one's eyes, one sees with the whole fruit of one's previous experience' (Marton, Fensham and Chaiklin, 1994).

This means that we cannot separate our understanding of a situation and our understanding of the phenomena that lend sense to that situation. Moreover, to experience something we must be able to see it as something distinct from something else. The perspective presented here is based on a theory of awareness (Gürwisch, 1964). This means that when we talk about learning, we are focusing on awareness. It also means that, although our experiences are in our awareness or, rather, constitute our awareness, we are not simultaneously aware of everything in the same way. Instead, our awareness is assumed to have a structure, and at any one instant certain things come to the fore (they are figural or thematized) while other things recede into the background (they are tacit or unthematized).

In daily life people talk and make statements about the world, about phenomena or about situations. We always do this from a specific perspective and for certain purposes. This means that the perspective is taken for granted, both by the person making the statements and by the person listening. Although we think we are talking about reality, we are talking about the world as it is experienced by a particular individual.

Phenomenographic research refers to particular points in time and to particular situations. The very object of research is the variations in how something is (and can be) experienced. To transform a research approach into a theory or principles for bringing about learning or development, one must have an idea about what constitutes the change.

The assumption here is that it is: (1) children's thinking, reflecting and expressions (verbal, visual, etc.) at different levels of generality; and (2) the use of a variety of conceptions as a content (e. g. of group discussion, viewing each other's pictures) that lead to a widening of the child's experience, and thereby to change.

By expressing itself verbally or in other ways, the child will remain unaware of his or her idea as an idea, while if the child's ideas are exposed to other ways of thinking than its own, a way of thinking that has been taken for granted will be challenged (Doverborg and Pramling, 1995).

Learning to Learn

Some illustrations will be given here of the approach to learning discussed previously in general terms. The examples are derived from a study named 'Learning to learn. A study of Swedish pre-school children' (Pramling, 1990).

The background to the study was Pramling's dissertation 'The child's conception of learning', published in 1983, in which children's awareness of their own learning was discovered and described.

Since children's ways of experiencing their own learning were shown to have an effect on the way they went about learning, and the consequent outcome of learning, a new project was set up to try to influence children's learning.

Before the intervention in the classroom began, all of the children were interviewed about their own learning. Half of the children did not have any idea about what they might learn during the coming year, and those children who had an idea of what they might learn expressed it in terms of learning to do something.

Four classes of five- and six-year-old pre-school children who had similar class backgrounds were chosen. The teachers were all fairly competent and had a lot of experience of working with this age group. Two of the classes (C and D) continued to work as normal as control groups, while the other two (A and B) incorporated certain principles, designed to promote the children's metacognitive reflections into their activities. To promote metacognitive reflections the teachers worked at three levels: the level of content, the level of structure and the level of learning. This was done mainly by the teacher distinguishing between, and drawing the children's attention towards, certain features at the three levels of generality, as well as making them express their own ideas about the phenomena that were focused upon. This approach served to make the children aware of the variation, the dimension of variation and the fact that their own view was just one of several possible views.

One example from the content level is found in an experimental class in which quite some time was spent studying the theme of water. The teacher wanted the children to develop an understanding of symbols – that different symbols stand for different things – so that she would later be able to draw their attention to the fact that we need a system of similar symbols (e. g. letters) to be able to communicate in written language (Pramling, 1990; Pramling and Mårdsjö, 1994). First the children were asked to make up their own symbols for different kinds of weather, such as high and low pressure, thunder and lightning, storms, sunshine, cold and warm air, etc. When the drawings were ready they were put up on the walls of the classroom and the children were encouraged to talk about each other's ways of depicting weather phenomena in symbolic form. Many of the symbols were similar, while others differed widely. They then compared their symbols with the ones used on television, which they found in a book. They talked about why particular symbols had been chosen and why some were easier to understand than others. This way of learning about symbols differed radically from the more traditional approach in which standard symbols are presented and discussed and given to the children to learn as if they were self-evident. In the experimental class, alternative symbols were drawn from the children's own experience and used to raise their awareness of symbols, to embrace what they mean to others, and to elucidate the variation in symbolic meaning. In this way, from the activities of their own imagination and experience, they reflected upon the variation to be found in others' experience and meaning.

Reflecting at the second level, structure, may be exemplified by different groups' thoughts about getting drinking water into a house (Pramling, 1990) and getting the dirty water out of the house (Pramling and Mårdsjö, 1994). In sessions that lasted for several days, the children discussed various aspects of the problems of getting clean water as well as getting rid of used water. Most of this discussion focused on the structure of the process involved: piping water into and out of homes, the process of purifying water, the cycle of how water is used, and the rain cycle. Cycles of purification were schematized: a map of the town with its underground pipes and drains was drawn; experiments were performed with steam, and so on, all focusing on the structure of the different processes.

Thus when children are learning about water (the content), the variation in how water appears in the structure of different cycles (the structure) can be made the subject of reflection.

Finally, at the third level, about learning itself, we can look at another example (Pramling, 1994). To develop children's understanding of their own learning means making them aware of both what they learn and how this learning comes about (Pramling, 1983). While working on the theme 'Growing new plants', one boy in one group said: 'Which is larger, the Earth or the Sun?'. 'Well, what do you think?' the teacher asked. Marcus replied: 'The Earth, because there is air there!'. Isaura said: 'The Sun, because it can shine so far away'. Zandra continued: 'They are the same size, because the Sun shines all over the Earth'. The teacher pointed out that the Sun can't be both larger, smaller and similar and asked them how they would go about finding out the answer to the question. Isaura said: 'I will call the radio for finding out the weather'. Stig: 'Call TV. People there go up to the sky and examine the weather. They can look...or you could go there yourself'. Marcus: 'I can ask Håkan. He goes up into space sometimes'. Gabi: 'I'll think about it'. Zandra: 'Read it in a book. My mother can read for me'. Nanette: 'I'll read in a book too'.

In the afternoon when the children were picked up by their parents, the teacher talked with each parent and child about what he or she should find out for the next day. The parent whose child wanted to call the radio seemed very embarrassed, so the teacher said to her: 'If you find it difficult, you can look up the telephone number, and we'll call from here tomorrow'. And so they did! When each of the seven children brought their answers the next day, the teacher drew diagrams of (1) the Sun and Earth as equal, (2) the Sun as larger and (3) the Earth as larger. Each child had to give his or her answer, and the teacher put a mark beside the diagram. After a while they realized that everybody now knew that the Sun was larger than the Earth. The teacher then focused on the learning aspect again, and asked each child how he or she had found out. She finished this short session by bringing to the children's attention the many different strategies that they had used to get their answers.

The teacher tried to make the children aware of their own learning by taking a question asked by one of the children and creating a situation in which they had to think and reflect. They had to follow up their ideas practically. And finally, once again they saw the variation in the ways of finding something out. Here the teacher used the children's own ideas about finding out what they wanted to know and helped them to appreciate the various ways of learning. Thus the session took a metacognitive turn, and the children were given the opportunity to reflect on their learning, getting to know the process itself (Pramling, 1994; Pramling and Mårdsjö, 1994).

To sum up, one can say that teachers A and B worked according to Figure 4. 1, which means that they created situations and events in which the children had to reflect on both the content, the structure and their own learning, as well as on how they think at different levels. Sometimes it is a question of moving from the specific to the more general and sometimes the reverse. On certain occasions attention is focused naturally on the three levels and sometimes only on one level, fixing on the next level on another occasion.

---

1. The content --> Metacognition
2. The structure --> Metacognition
3. Learning --> Metacognition

Figure 4. 1.

When we look at the results of the study (Table 4. 1) we see that the children in groups A and B, who had been involved in the approach presented here, were the first to develop metacognitively, that is, their awareness of their own learning was more advanced than that of the children in the comparison groups C and D.

**Table 4. 1. Children's understanding of their own learning
before (1) and after (2) the intervention**

	Pre-school							
	A		*B*		*C*		*D*	
Occasion	*1*	*2*	*1*	*2*	*1*	*2*	*1*	*2*
To do	16	4	18	11	17	16	13	10
To know	2	11	–	9	1	1	1	5
To understand	–	3	–	–	–	–	–	–
Don't know	1	1	2	–	2	3	1	–
Number	**19**	**19**	**20**	**20**	**20**	**20**	**15**	**15**

Not only did the children's metacognitive awareness of their own learning develop, but also their capacity to learn new things, that is, the cognitive aspect of learning was determined. One of the three learning experiments in which all four groups participated took place at the Natural History Museum. The attendant gave the children a short 'interactive lecture' on the ecological cycle. It consisted of first showing a stuffed bird and listening to its song. Then they went on to consider and discuss what happens when a bird dies. Beetles come and feed on the carcass, digest the matter they eat and excrete it. That matter in turn nourishes the soil it falls on, which feeds the trees, which produce leaves, which fall to the ground and feed worms, which birds eat. Thus the cycle is completed.

All through the discussion the attendant illustrated the cycle by displaying the parts on the floor and putting arrows from one link to the next, talking about cycles. At the end, he went in the opposite direction and took away different sections while asking the children questions such as: 'What would happen if there were no worms in the fields and woods?'.

All the children were then interviewed in their ordinary classroom by an outsider who did not know what any of the children in any of the groups had been working on. One of the main questions in the interview focused on finding out how the children had understood the presentation by the museum attendant. It was possible to distinguish four distinctly different ways in which the message had been understood by the children.

The most comprehensive category was experiencing *the cycle as a whole*, seeing how the parts depended on each other for their nutrition. The next category focused on *the food chain*, which meant some children understood that certain parts supply food to others but failed to see the whole cycle. The third category concerned *fragments of the food chain*, meaning that some of the parts of the story were focused upon, or that they were taken up one by one. Finally, the fourth way of dealing with the story was to *name or mention parts* without relating them to one another or to the cycle.

Table 4. 2 shows the distribution of the four different ways in which children understood the ecological cycle as it was described to them at the museum. One could claim that children's different un-

Table 4.2. Distribution of conceptions of the ecological cycle

	Pre-school			
	A	B	C	D
The cycle	10	8	1	2
The food chain	8	6	1	5
Fragments	1	2	6	9
Naming a part	–	3	10	1
Number of children	**19**	**19**	**18**	**17**

derstandings are parts of a whole, in the same way as many university students focused on parts of the same text in the early studies of phenomenography (Marton *et al.* 1977). To understand is to be able to grasp the whole, and relate the different parts to this whole.

It is evident that the children from the experimental groups (A and B) grasped the ecological cycle much better than those in the other groups. The children in Group A expressed the most advanced understanding; they had worked during the year in pre-school with ideas connected to the ecological cycle, although not with the specific content mentioned earlier. Group A might have given even better answers if the attendant at the museum had not actually confused the cycle with the food chain.

The results of the intervention in the study mentioned above were evident with reference to both children's metacognitive development (their ways of reflecting about their own learning) and their cognitive development (their capability of making sense of a message). Some years later a new study was carried out (Pramling, 1994). Study 2 had several similarities to study 1, the main purpose in both cases being to apply and evaluate a phenomenographically oriented approach to learning in pre-school. The main difference between the studies was that while the content of the first study was defined by the teachers, that of the second study was defined by the researcher. The content in study 2 was also much more extensive, as it was supposed to form the basis for future learning in the different content areas in primary school. The procedures, however, were the same, as well as the structure in terms of different levels of generality.

The results of study 2 are similar to those of study 1, i. e. the children, this time taken from a broader range of social backgrounds, developed both metacognitively (their understanding of their own learning) and cognitively compared with children from traditional pre-school programmes. The children's cognitive capabilities were traced both by finding out how well they understood different content areas and how skilled they were at solving arithmetic problems, at expressing themselves in written language, and at making sense of a story told to them (Pramling 1996).

Conclusions

I want to bring to the reader's attention the idea that learning science from early on in the school setting could be a question of making it possible for children to become aware of certain structures and relationships in concrete activities. It is also important to give children an opportunity to reflect upon phenomena that are often taken for granted by teachers, and that are invisible to children without assistance from someone who can see them. This idea differs from merely giving children experience of science and nature. From an adult perspective we can view children's experience in play as experience of science, and be satisfied with that as a base for later learning. But from the perspective presented here, the experience has to appear in children's awareness in particular ways in order to form a base for later learning. If a child does not experience what the teacher thinks he or she experiences, there is no base to build teaching upon. Learning about science means *forming children's awareness of discovering science*. A traditional way to work with changes in nature is to take children to a particular place and observe the changes. But however good these experiences are, children will not become aware of the reason for the changes if that aspect is not thematized and made into a topic for their reflection.

This means that we, as researchers and as teachers of young children, must find out what structures, relationships or meanings are basic to beginning to understand different aspects of science, and which of these can be relevant to work on with children in this age group.

The teacher must first have an idea of what it is he or she wants to make the children aware of. Then he or she must create situations or use events in everyday life to draw the relevant phenomena to the children's attention and to make them reflect and express themselves about the understanding to be developed. The various ideas must also form part of the content of teaching and learning. The relationship between the teacher's role and the children's is that the teacher knows in which direction to focus the children's thinking, but the children's own reflections upon their various levels of understanding constitute the dynamic factor that brings about change in children or expands the world around them.

References

Barnett, S. A. (1973) 'Homo docens.' *Journal of Biosocial Science 5*, 393–403.

Brumby, M. N. (1979) Students' perceptions and learning styles association with the conception of evaluation by natural selection. Unpublished doctoral dissertation, University of Surrey, England.

Clay, M. (1992) 'Developmental learning puzzles me.' *Australian Journal of Reading 14*, 263–276.

Dahlin, B. and Regmi, M. (1995) Conceptions of learning among Nepali students. Paper presented at the 6th European Conference for Research on Learning and Instruction, Nijmegen, The Netherlands, 26–31 August.

Doverborg, E. and Pramling, I. (1995) *Mångfaldens pedagogiska möjligheter.* (Diversity as an educational tool.) Stockholm: Liber Utbildning.

Gürwisch, A. (1964) *The Field of Conciousness.* Pittsburgh: Duquesne University Press.

Johansson, J. -E. (1995) *Friedrich Fröbel: Människans Fostram.* Lund: Studentlitteratur.

Lindahl, M. (1996) *Erfarande och lärande. Ettåringars första tid i förskolan.* (Awareness and learning.) Göteborg: Acta Universitatis Gothoburgensis.

Marton, F. (1981a) 'Phenomenography – describing conceptions of the world around us.' *Instructional Science 10*, 177–200.

Marton, F. (19981b) 'Studying conceptions of reality – a metatheoretical note.' *Scandinavian Journal of Educational Research 25*, 159–169.

Marton, F. (1992) 'På spaning efter medvetandets pedagogik.' (In search of the pedagogics of awareness.) *Forskning om utbildning 4*, 28–40.

Marton, F. (1994) 'Världens bästa kunskapssyn.' (The best way of looking at knowledge in the world.) *Lärarnas tidning 14/1994*, 28.

Marton, F. and Säljö, R. (1976) 'On qualitative differences in learning. 1. – outcome and function of the learner's conception of the task.' *British Journal of Educational Psychology 46*, 115–127.

Marton, F., Dahlgren, L. O., Svensson, L. and Säljö, R. (1977) *Inlärning och omvärldsuppfattning.* (Learning and conception of the world around them.) Stockholm: Almqvist and Wiksell.

Marton, F. and Säljö, R. (1979) 'Learning in the learner's perspective. III. Level of difficulty seen as a relationship between the reader and the text.' Report no. 78 from the Institute of Education, University of Göteborg.

Marton, F., Fensham, P. and Chaiklin, S. (1994) 'A Nobel's eye view of scientific intuition: discussions with the Nobel prize-winners in Physics, Chemistry and Medicine (1970–1986).' *International Journal of Science Education 16*, 457–473.

Marton, F., Wen, Q. and Nagle, A. (1995) 'Are culturally different conceptions of learning conflicting or complemenatory to each other? A comparative study of Chinese and Uruguyan university students.' Paper presented at the 6th European Conference for Research on Learning and Instruction, Nijmegen, The Netherlands, 26–31 August.

Piaget, J. (1970) *Structuralism.* New York: Basic Books.

Piaget, J. (1976) *The Child's Conception on the World.* New Jersey: Litterfield Adams and Company.

Piaget, J. (1976) *The Grasp of Consciousness.* Cambridge, MA: Harvard University Press.

Piaget, J. (1978) *Success and Understanding.* London: Routledge and Kegan Paul.

Piaget, J. and Inhelder, B. (1969) *The Psychology of the Child.* New York: Basic Books.

Pramling, I. (1983) *The Child's Conception of Learning.* Göteborg: Acta Universitatis Gothenburgensis.

Pramling, I. (1990) *Learning to Learn. A Study of Swedish Preschool Children.* New York: Springer Verlag.

Pramling, I. (1991) 'Föreställningar om barnet.' (Perspectives on children and youth.) In M. Tamm (ed) *Perspektiv på barn och ungdom.* Stockholm: Utbildningsradion.

Pramling, I. (1994) *Kunnandets grunder. Prövning av en fenomenografisk ansats till att utveckla barns förståelse för sin omvärld.* (The foundations of skills and knowledge. Testing a phenomenographic approach to developing children's understanding of the world around them.) Göteborg: Acta Universitatis Gothoburgensis.

Pramling, I. (1996) 'Understanding and empowering the child as a learner.' In D. R. Olson and N. Torrance (eds) *The Handbook of Education and Human Development: New Models of Learning, Teaching and Schooling.* Oxford: Blackwell.

Pramling, I. and Mårdsjö, A. -C. (1994) 'Att utveckla kunnandets grunder. Illustration av ett arbetssätt.' (Developing the foundations of knowledge. Illustration of a working method.) Rapport nr. 7 från Institutionen för metodik i lärarutbildningen. Göteborgs universitet.

Premack, D. (1984) 'Pedagogy and aesthetics as sources of culture.' In M. S. Gazzaniga (ed) *Handbook of Cognitive Neuroscience.* New York: Plenum Press.

Rogoff, B. (1990) *Apprenticeship to Thinking.* Oxford: Oxford University Press.

SOU (1992:94) Skola för bildning. (School for education.) *Huvudbetänkande av läroplanskommittén.* Stockholm: Utbildningsdepartementet.

Trigwell, K., Prosser, M. and Taylor, E. (1994) 'A phenomenographic study of academics' conceptions of science learning and teaching.' *Learning and Instruction* 4, 33, 217–232.

Valsiner, J. (1987) *Culture and the Development of Children's Actions.* New York: John Wiley and Sons.

Wertsch, J. (1991) *Voices of the Mind.* Cambridge, MA: Harvard University Press.

CHAPTER 5

Criteria for Identifying Progression in Scientific Ideas for Primary School Pupils

Wynne Harlen

Introduction

What does progression in science ideas mean? Where does it start and where is it appropriate to stop for primary school children? This chapter addresses these questions in discussing what are realistic aims in the development of scientific ideas at the primary level. There is a fair consensus across national boundaries about the aspects of science to be included in science education. Thus the main foci in this chapter are the nature of progression, in the first section, and, in the second and longest section, the criteria to be used in deciding how far along the progression of ideas primary children should be taken. The final section of the chapter touches on how progression can be facilitated in the translation of curriculum statements into classroom practice.

Progression in Scientific Ideas

Looking across some of the various national statements of curriculum requirements, guidelines or standards (AAAS, 1993; DfE, 1995; NAS, 1994; SOED, 1993) we find considerable consistency in the general areas of knowledge and understanding set out, just as we do in the skills and attitudes relating to scientific enquiry. Of course, the various documents present the ideas in different ways, grouping them differently and making different distinctions among them, all of which are to some extent arbitrary. Despite these differences, there is common agreement that science education should, from the start, help children towards an understanding of:

- The characteristics and diversity of living things

○   the processes of life

○   the properties, uses, interactions and structure of materials

○   energy sources and transformations

○   forces and movement

○   the Earth and its place in the Universe.

These do not necessarily comprise the total science curriculum, since this often extends to an understanding of the nature of science and its history. However, here the discussion is limited to scientific ideas about the world around us rather than ideas about science.

Of course, identifying similar broad areas of ideas relating to content does not mean that the more specific ideas within them are necessarily seen in the same way. For even when these very broad headings are broken down into more specific ideas – identifying particular properties of materials, or the cellular structure of living things – each one still represents a continuum of ideas which I find it helpful to represent by wavy, branching lines (Figure 5.1).

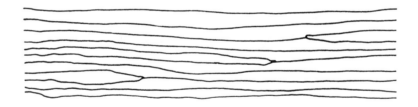

Figure 5.1 Representation of development of ideas from less to more mature

Along the flow of this stream, from less to more mature thinking, the meaning of the ideas changes. Two examples may help to illustrate this progressive change. The first is dissolving. Young children's own ideas of what happens when, for example, salt is put into water is that the salt simply disappears. Thus the first step in developing a scientific view of this phenomenon is to realise that the salt is still there. Note that a whole range of experience is needed to help children develop this idea; it is not a matter of telling them. After all, their idea does not conflict with the evidence: the salt has actually disappeared from view. Children whose ideas about matter have developed so that they reject the idea that it can simply disappear, in the sense of no longer existing, will realise that it makes more sense to regard the salt as no longer being visible, rather than having ceased to exist. When they test this idea, by tasting the water, or even by reclaiming the salt by evaporating the water, they are likely to confirm the idea that dissolving means that the separate substance can no longer be seen in the water but is still there. However, this idea will not serve to satisfy curiosity about what happens to the salt in the water that makes it invisible. It is necessary to call upon ideas about the particulate nature of matter to begin to answer this question, which takes us to a more sophisticated view of dissolving. It is necessary to go further still, in order to begin to understand why some solids dissolve in water while others do not. So there is a range of ideas about dissolving, reaching, as it were, from the kindergarten to the degree course.

A second example is the reflection of light on various surfaces. There is hardly a sighted person who does not look in a mirror every day. Young children, however, do not connect this with the reflection of light; indeed they are likely to consider a mirror as a source of light (Osborne *et al.* 1990). Understanding how an image is formed by reflection depends on bringing together several ideas: that light travels from a source in a straight line, that seeing something involves light from it entering the eye, that mirrors send light back in a particular way, and that the eye interprets light as having travelled in a straight line from the object and does not 'see' any change in direction which may have been caused by something in its path. These are each complex ideas in themselves and so it is no wonder that even many adults do not understand how images are formed in a mirror (Harlen, Holroyd and Byrne 1995). Even when these ideas are brought together it is, of course, not the end of the story. We need ideas about light behaving as waves to explain the change in direction at the surface and that not all is reflected. With these ideas it is possible to explain reflection on any surface and phenomena such as the greenhouse effect.

So, again there is a continuum of ideas which interconnect to explain everyday events. Clearly there are different kinds of knowledge along this continuum, such as 'knowing that' and 'knowing why', for instance, underlining the point that there are many different levels at which scientific ideas can be understood. It is not difficult to see that the idea of interdependence among living things, for instance, could be grasped by quite young children at the level of animals depending ultimately on plants for their food, whilst understanding in terms of ecosystems requires a great deal of experience and other ideas to be brought together. The changes taking place along this continuum are that the ideas become 'bigger' in that they link more experiences together and thus are more widely applicable. They are also more abstract since they concern the general features that quite different objects or events have in common. These changes are of the very nature of progression; if ideas are not changing in these ways then we cannot say there is progression but perhaps only an accumulation of ideas which remain separate instead of forming more powerful ways of linking experiences together.

The 'stream' in Figure 5.1 can be helpful in giving a representation of what anyone specifying appropriate ideas for the primary years is trying to do. If a time scale is laid along this progressive stream of ideas, the question being addressed is what is appropriate as a cross-section of ideas at, say, age 7/8 and age 10/11? To answer this question and try to judge where along the continuum are the ideas at levels appropriate to primary school children, it is necessary to consider the criteria to be applied.

Criteria for Identifying Suitable Ideas for Primary Pupils

The criteria used in identifying curriculum requirements or standards are not always stated explicitly but are likely to be similar to those indicated in the National Science Education Standards (NAS, 1994). The three criteria set out there concern: the accurate representation of science as appropriate to grades K-12; and alignment with the ages and stages of learners from K-12; presentation in a form usable by implementers such as teachers and curriculum developers.

The criteria suggested here (taken from Harlen, 1993) are more specific to the primary years, although there is clear correspondence with the first two of the NAS criteria. According to these criteria, the ideas should:

(1) help children's understanding of everyday events and the world around them and be applicable to their experience
(2) be within the grasp of their understanding, taking into account their limited experience and mental maturity
(3) be accessible and testable through the use by the children of science process skills
(4) provide a sound basis for further science education.

The following discussion attempts to justify these criteria and to set out the implications of each one.

1. Relevance to Children's Everyday Experience

This first criterion is justified by the very purpose of teaching science, that is, to help understanding of the living and artificial world around us. Moreover, it is to ideas about these things that children can relate their previous experience and the ideas they have generated from it. The importance of this is related to the way children learn. It is through being applied and used that ideas develop and become part of children's own ways of understanding. Ideas that do not link in with experience – and so have to be learned by rote – are unlikely to remain long in children's minds. What this means in practice is that it would be unhelpful to include ideas at this stage about the formation of the Earth, for example, or molecular structure or even evolution, since these are not parts of everyday events in life obvious to children.

2. Within the Grasp of Children's Understanding

This second criterion indicates that we should take into account what is known about children's ideas and how they make sense of the world around them. There is now a considerable body of research that has explored these ideas across a wide range of concepts. Other chapters refer to these findings (see Black, Osbourne and Simon in this volume), and so just a few examples will be given here in order to justify some general points about these ideas.

Children's Ideas about Light and Seeing

Children were asked to use drawings and words to explain how it is that they can see a bottle on a table in a dark room after the light is switched on, but not, as they agreed, with no light. Figure 5.2 is

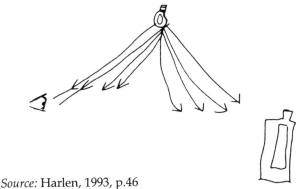

Source: Harlen, 1993, p.46
Figure 5.2 A common example of the response of children aged 7–9 explaining how you see a bottle on a table

typical of the responses of children aged 7 to 9 years. All but four of the 27 in the class showed light spreading to the eye and the bottle, but nothing from the bottle to the eye. It was as if having light was synonymous with seeing; there was nothing to explain: if there was light, then you could see.

Figures 5.3–5.5 show responses from older children of 9 to 11 years of age. Figure 5.3 is typical of the 'active eye' view of seeing which has been found by many researchers (Andersson and Karrqvist, 1983; Guesne, 1978; Osborne *et al.* 1990). Only four children out of 26 had the arrows from the bottle to the eye and two had them going both ways, as in Figure 5.4.

The explanation in Figure 5.5 shows how the child reconciled the 'active eye' idea with the observation that we cannot see in the dark. As many researchers have pointed out (see Osbourne *et al.* 1990), it is understandable that the eye is seen as an active agent rather than a receiver, for this fits the subjective experience of 'looking' by turning one's eyes and the everyday use of expressions such as someone 'cast his eyes around' or 'shot a glance across the room', where the eye as an active agent is implied.

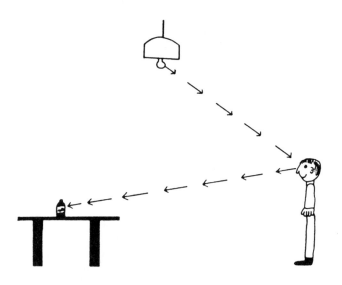

Source: Harlen, 1993, p.45
Figure 5.3 A common example of the response of children aged 9–11 explaining how you see a bottle on a table

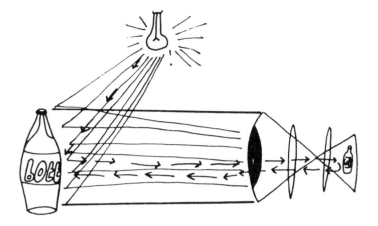

Source: Harlen, 1993, p.45

Figure 5.4 A less common example of the response of children aged 9–11 explaining how you see a bottle on a table, showing light going both ways

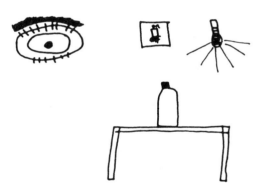

'With no light your eyes cannot see anything as soon as you turn the light on your eyes can see again your eyes sort of work like a light when there's no light you can't see but when there is light you can see'

Source: Harlen, 1993, p.46

Figure 5.5 A 10 year old's explanation of how light 'operates' the eye

Children's Ideas about Sound and Hearing

The drawings in Figures 5.6 and 5.7 were by a younger and an older primary child, repectively in response to being asked to represent how a drum makes a sound and how a person hears it. The younger child suggests no mechanism for the production of sound or for how it reaches the person hearing it; it is as if being 'very loud' and

Source: Watt and Russell, 1990, p.36
Figure 5.6 A 7 year old's representation of how a drum makes a sound and how she hears it

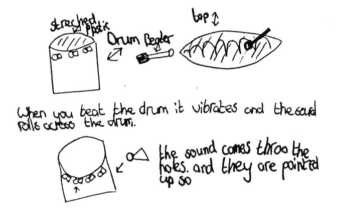

Source: Watt and Russell, 1990, p.23
Figure 5.7 A 10 year old's representation of how a drum makes a sound and how the sound travels

'listening very hard' are enough explanation in themselves. The older child, by contrast, suggests a mechanism in which the impact makes the base vibrate and makes the sound which comes out of the holes. The implication here, confirmed by talking to the child, is that sound only comes out through holes and not through solid material.

Figure 5.8 indicates another idea about sound and vibration commonly found to be held by primary children. This is that sound travels along string as vibrations, but is converted to 'sound' in the air.

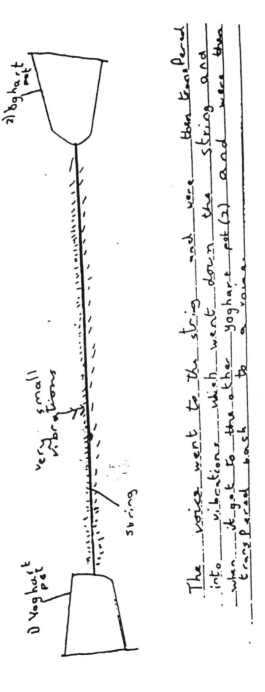

Source: SPACE research, unpublished

Figure 5.8 A 10 year old's representation of sound travelling

These examples illustrate some of the general characteristics of pupils' ideas which can be drawn from a thorough review of the
findings of research:

(1) Up to about the age of 7 or 8 children do not seem to see any
    need to explain why things happen in terms of a causal
    mechanism. They are content to say *that* they happen in
    particular circumstances. As we have seen, the presence of
    light is enough to explain seeing and listening explains how
    you hear. Many other examples could be given: when water
    evaporates it just goes by itself; a clockwork toy moves because
    of the key; plants need to be by the window to grow, and so on
    (Russell and Watt, 1990a,b).

(2) When children do see the need for an explanation, they naturally
    base their ideas on their direct experiences of them, but of course
    their experience is limited and therefore the evidence is partial.
    So, for example, we find the bizarre idea that rust is inside metals
    waiting to be revealed, based on observation of rust being found
    under flaking paint or chrome plate.

(3) Children pay attention to what they perceive through their
    senses rather than the logic which may suggest a different
    interpretation.

(4) Young children in particular tend to pay attention to one
    feature as cause of a particular effect, ignoring the possibility
    of a combination of factors. For example, they may regard light
    or water as the essential for growth of plants, but not both and
    only later will air and appropriate heat be included.

(5) Even though their ideas are the result of using experience – and
    not the result of childish fantasy – their reasoning may not
    match up to scientific reasoning. They do not test their ideas
    rigorously and thus tend to retain what ought to be rejected by
    the evidence available.

(6) Children may use words without a grasp of their meaning, as
    in the case of 'vibration'; thus when they use words such as
    'dissolve', 'evaporate', 'melt' and 'reflect', these words may not
    be bringing with them the range of related phenomena which
    they evoke for a scientist.

(7) Children may hold on to earlier ideas despite the existence of
    contrary evidence if they have no access to alternative ideas
    which make sense to them. For example, the idea that 'the light
    turns the eye on' (Figure 5.5) is a modification of the 'active
    eye' idea that avoids the difficulty that otherwise it should be
    possible to see in the dark.

Each of these characteristics has implications for teaching and for helping children to develop their ideas further. This thread will be picked up in a later section.

3. *Accessible and Testable to Children through using Process Skills*

The third criterion emphasises that the ideas children are expected to learn should be within the grasp of their reasoning skills. This is another way of saying that it must be possible for the children to learn with understanding; to develop ideas that make sense to them because they have worked them out for themselves. (This does not mean that children have to 'discover' ideas or work them out on their own without the help of the teacher; the teacher's role is crucial, but it is the children who have to do the thinking.) How do children's own ideas become transformed and what does this mean for the level of the ideas to which they are exposed? To try to answer these questions let us consider a model (from Harlen, 1996) of how children come to grips with a new object or event.

Children, like everyone else, when faced with a new experience, search around in their minds, perhaps unconsciously, for previous experience which links to it and can be used in the first attempt to make sense of it. The difference with children is that their experience is limited and they therefore have less to call upon. Also, because it is characteristic of their way of thinking that they may consider only one aspect of a situation, they may well make connections which are unhelpful. For example, faced with the evidence that varnished cubes of wood stick to each other when wet, several groups of eleven-year-olds concluded that the blocks became magnetic when wet (Harlen, 1993, p.21). The resemblance of a block sticking to the underside of another, without anything to hold them together, to a magnet picking up another magnet or a piece of iron was clearly very strong. An equally good alternative explanation was not available to them and so they held on to their explanation in terms of magnetism, modifying it to accommodate the observation that the blocks only stuck together when wet by concluding that 'they're magnetic when they're wet'.

This example illustrates several points which are generally found in learning. Figure 5.9 attempts to represent a new experience and various previous experiences which might be linked to the new one in trying to explain it. It is the role of ideas, or more broadly of concepts, to link the new and previous experiences since concepts are the generalised features through which objects or events can be categorised as similar, even though they may differ in many ways.

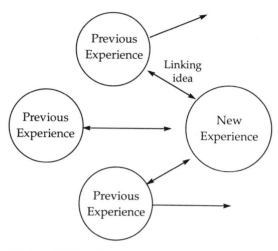

Source: Harlen, 1996, p.11

Figure 5.9 *A model of ideas linking previous to new experience*

For example, the concept of 'living' links many things which are of widely differing form and structure.

The linking concept may not be scientific, nor a property of the objects involved; an association of words may be the basis of the connection of one experience to another. Creativity and imagination have a part. Indeed, in the case of the scientist faced with an unexpected phenomenon, it is the ability to try ideas from outside the immediately obvious that provides the start of a 'breakthrough'.

At this stage the linking idea has not yet been shown to be really useful in explaining the new event; it is still a hypothesis, a possible explanation. To find out how useful it is, the idea has to be tested (Figure 5.10). The testing has to be done scientifically if the result is to be of value in making sense of the experience. In essence, this means that the idea has to be used to make predictions and more evidence has to be sought to see whether it is consistent with these predictions. If the evidence does not support the predictions the process may be repeated for alternative linking ideas, if these exist. The 'testing' can be as simple as tapping an object of unknown origin to see if it makes the kind of sound which would be expected if it were made of a natural material or plastic. In that case the idea of what the object is made of is a hypothesis which leads to a prediction and the tapping is the means of testing this prediction.

More complex tests will require the conducting and interpretation of an investigation, involving skills of planning, collecting evi-

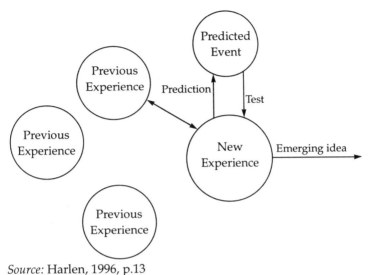

Source: Harlen, 1996, p.13
Figure 5.10 Extension of model to test a linked idea

dence, recording, interpreting and evaluating. For the moment let us assume that the learner is capable of carrying out these processes with scientific rigour and consider what may happen as a result. There are three main possibilities:

- that the linking idea is confirmed, in which case it becomes strengthened by successfully explaining a new phenomenon and having its range extended

- that the linking idea is not confirmed and so an alternative is tried (if there is one)

- that the linking idea will fit the evidence if it is slightly modified.

Which of these is the case will determine the nature of the idea (or one of the ideas) which will link this new experience to future experiences. The first and third possibilities above result in a change in ideas which enables the new experience to be understood in terms of previous experience. Ideas have been extended or changed so that what was not previously understood can now be understood because it fits into a pattern of experiences that are linked by particular ideas or concepts. In other words, ideas have been developed; learning has taken place. Emerging ideas are 'bigger' than previous ones because they now link new and earlier experiences together, an aspect of progression indicated in the first section of this chapter. Thinking is further along the stream of developing ideas.

This model, then, represents learning as a *change* in ideas, rather than as a process in which ideas are taken in from scratch. In practice, ideas which are not related to previous experience and thinking are of very little use to us. They do not arise from past experience and so are not called forth when past experience is used to explain new experience. Such ideas have to be committed to memory by rote and are usually usable only in contexts close to those in which they were learned. *Understanding*, which by definition is applicable learning, is created by development and change in ideas.

But note that when ideas are tested, the outcome in terms of changed or rejected ideas will depend on the way in which the testing is carried out. It was assumed in the argument above that the testing of ideas was rigorous and systematic, in the way associated with scientific investigation. When this is so, then ideas which do not fit the evidence will be rejected and those which do will be accepted and strengthened. But it may not be the case that the testing has this quality. The skills of young children – and those of some adults – have not developed to the appropriate degree. Children may ignore contradictory evidence in interpreting findings and hold on to their initial ideas, even though these do not fit the evidence. Thus the extent to which ideas become more scientific (by fitting the evidence available) depends on the way in which the testing of possible explanatory ideas is carried out, that is, on the use of the process skills. *The development of understanding in science is thus dependent on the ability to carry out process skills in a scientific manner.* This is the reason for attention to development of these skills in science education: because of their role in the development of scientific concepts and not just because they are valuable skills in their own right.

In terms of the ideas which we wish children to develop, according to this model they must be ones which can emerge from this process of testing against evidence by the children themselves. Sometimes this kind of criterion is taken to mean that primary science must concern only that which the children can physically manipulate themselves. This is too restrictive and ignores the fact that a large part of children's everyday experience concerns things far from their physical reach – the Sun and stars, for example, and the remote parts of the Earth brought to them through film and television. These things should not be excluded from study. Process skills are mental skills, and children can develop ideas through their own thinking as long as there is evidence against which they can test ideas (their own and those which may be suggested to them), to see how well they explain the phenomena observed. This evidence can be from secondary sources, from film, video, photographs, on-line databases, etc. and children should be encouraged to use these to extend their experience and to test their emerging ideas.

4. Providing a Sound Basis for Further Science Education

There are two aspects to this fourth criterion, one being to provide a sound basis in terms of good understanding of what is learned and the other to ensure that the early learning provides a foundation for the content of later learning so that there is continuity throughout. I have argued that the first of these, learning with understanding, is likely to follow if the previous two criteria are met. The other, continuity of later with earlier learning, is a matter of effective teaching as well as sound curriculum planning. An effective teacher will help pupils to create conceptual links between new and earlier experience, and will do this at the individual pupil level as well as in planning the overall sequence of lessons. Less effective teachers may neglect links which are there to be made. However, the potential is provided by the ideas set out in the curriculum framework.

Returning to the 'wavy line' representation (Figure 5.1), progression and continuity mean that there should be no sharp changes in direction of the lines, nor, worst of all, gaps or discontinuities. In the past decade a great deal of work has gone into identifying ideas to be developed at different stages and, although we shall perhaps never be able to say that a definitive framework has been achieved, there is evidence of a consensus. In the appendix to this chapter are examples from four different national statements of ideas relating to forces and movement. Although the way of expressing them varies, there is no doubt that they are saying very much the same thing in terms of the progression of ideas, and suggesting much the same stage or age levels for points in this progression. However, unless the statements are elaborated to an extent which is arguably inappropriate for national guidelines, there is room for varying interpretation. It is important, then, for appropriate criteria, such as those discussed above, to be borne in mind by those who work with the statements to translate them into classroom practice.

So, given that all this work of defining the ideas on paper has been done, attention can be turned to how these statements are translated into practice. How is the progress to be brought about, not on the pages of a document, but in the minds of children? What is the role of the teacher, of the pupils and of materials in furthering progression? This is the subject of the next section of this chapter.

Helping Pupils' Progressive Development of Ideas

It is important to begin by reiterating that, as indicated in the model presented earlier, learning with understanding involves development of ideas through the learner's own thinking and action. This means that process skills are used and developed to deal with new situations. There is a close and essential interdependence of ideas, skills and attitudes and it is not the intention to deny this by focusing on ideas only at this time, as required by the remit of this chapter.

It is also apparent from the earlier discussion that the teacher can best help pupils' development by starting from the ideas children bring to the classroom. Ways of gaining access to children's ideas are discussed in Chapter 13 and so will not be taken up here, but the importance of this step must be underlined. The focus here is on the action to take which helps children to move forward from their existing ideas and particularly on the difficult matter of catering for the obvious differences between pupils even if they are in the same class or group. The kinds of action can be considered under four headings: practical activities; exposure to new ideas; discussion of words; and expectations and individual support.

Practical Activities

Activities designed to develop children's ideas are mainly of two kinds: those which are intended to extend children's experience and those which involve children in testing their ideas.

Children's ideas may be limited by their experience as, for example, when they assume that soil is essential for plants to grow since they have only seen plants growing in soil or have little clear idea about how living things are adapted to their environments because they have studied few plants and animals and their environments in detail. In one sense activities designed to extend children's experience will be challenging views based on very restricted evidence, but they do not do this in a way that suggests that the children's ideas are wrong; it is more in the spirit of, 'find out about all of this and see if you still think that...'

To involve children in testing their ideas more explicitly, the ideas may first have to be put in a testable form, as a hypothesis from which a prediction can be made. They often do not start this way. 'Oh, I know, it's...' does not sound like a hypothesis but it will contain some sentiment that a particular effect has a certain cause. 'The ice melts because it is outside' is one such statement from a child which at first caused some surprise to his teacher. The hypothesis was based in this case on the location of the ice (which was, after all, where ice had been seen to form and melt) and not on the temperature of the place. A prediction from this was that if the ice was somewhere else (inside) then it would not melt. The prediction could readily be investigated and thus the idea tested.

The context in this case was a class discussion of what made ice melt, during which several different ideas were put forward and tested. The children whose ideas were not supported by their investigations therefore had immediate access to another idea which worked better in practice than theirs. Thus the whole experience, of discussion and sharing ideas – and not just the activity itself – is important to the development and change in ideas.

No one has made more contribution to the understanding of talk during activity than Douglas Barnes (1976). From observation of children working in groups, he showed how an idea of one child is taken up and elaborated by another, and then perhaps challenged by someone else's idea, leading them back to check with the evidence or to seek further evidence. The challenge and elaboration can only happen if the thinking is made open and public through the use of language. It is not difficult to see that talking is exposing children to the different ideas of others, as well as compelling them to think about how those ideas relate to previous and new experiences. This links to the next point.

Exposure to New Ideas
Children need to be introduced to new ideas which they can consider as alternatives to their own. The same secondary sources suggested above for extending their experience are also sources of new ideas. These alternatives should be introduced, however, in a way which encourages children to test them and not to accept them as necessarily correct, even if they come backed by the authority of a book or a teacher.

As already noted, too, children's peers are sources of new ideas and particularly useful ones since children will feel able to challenge them and not necessarily accept them because of the authority behind them. That such exposure does lead to development has been shown experimentally by the educational psychologist, Christine Howe, who assessed the progress of children working in groups formed in different ways according to their preconceptions relating to activities to be undertaken (on floating and sinking and motion down an inclined plane). One set of groups was formed of children whose ideas about the activity varied widely and the other set was formed of children whose ideas were similar. After activities designed so that the children made predictions and tested them practically, and which they undertook in groups of four, all the children were questioned again about their ideas. The research provided strong and consistent evidence that children in the groups whose initial ideas differed progressed markedly more than those in the groups with similar initial ideas. It was found that this applied as much to those with initially advanced ideas as to those with initially poor ideas (Howe, Rodgers and Tolmie, 1990; Howe, Tolmie and Rodgers, 1992). This is important evidence that creating mixed groups in which children hear and respond to views different from their own helps them to develop their own ideas, far more than working with those of similar ideas.

Discussion of Words and Other Representations

As an accompaniment to practical activity, discussion focused on words and ways of representing things can make all the difference to the thinking which is provoked by experience. In an activity about sound, for instance, children in the early junior years may begin to use the word 'vibration'. It will naturally be used at first for vibration which can be felt or seen and thus related to the use of the word in everyday experience, that is, for the experience of being in contact with things which have motors in them, such as a washing machine, vacuum cleaner, electric mixer or power drill. So it will be easy to use the word in relation to a drum which is beaten or a guitar string which has been plucked, where the thing vibrating can be seen, but not so for wind instruments or a loud speaker. Careful questioning can help to make clear both to the pupils and the teacher just what collection of linked observation is being evoked by the word vibration. What examples of vibrating objects can the children give? Do they think that things which are not vibrating make a sound? Can you have a sound without vibration? What do children think is happening in a vibration?

Discussion of these things, with the children supplying instances of objects explored in their practical work, will help them to think again about what they have done (and perhaps go back to check things they took almost for granted), as well as to reflect on the words they use. At a later stage, and with older children, the questions would be more challenging, aimed at taking their notion of vibration further and towards vibrations which cannot be seen, such as those in air.

Expectations and Individual Support

The teacher's expectations and support can be varied from one child to another so that each is enjoying the challenge of extending ideas but within the range of present capabilities. Adjusting the degree of support and the form of encouragement for each child is a hidden but yet a most powerful means of matching experiences to individual needs. Within a group the amount of help given to children can be different and a teacher can monitor the progress made by individuals in terms of the support they need. Similarly there can be different goals for the children in the teacher's mind. In many cases very different responses to the same activities are accepted and praised because the teacher judges them against the effort made rather than the performance in more objective terms. This is a form of assessment which is appropriate in the context of helping children's learning but not in other contexts (see Chapter 13).

An important judgement for a teacher is how far to press forward in the development of ideas at one time. Being sensitive to this is essential to ensuring that the children stay in control of their learning. Stopping at the appropriate point may mean leaving children with incomplete, even inaccurate, ideas for the time being. This need not matter providing opportunity is made later to return to the subject and take the ideas further.

For each child there is gap between present ideas and those which we aim to help him or her achieve. The question of how to bridge this gap is one to which there is no universal answer. If there were, education would be more an exact science than a form of art; we would be able to build a child's learning rather as building a house, knowing just how one brick should be placed on another. As we know, it is not like that. With children's learning the 'bricks' are not ready formed; they need time to take shape and until that has happened there can be no further building. So it often happens that children's ideas need time before there can be further development. This is the time to stop and it is as important to recognise this as it is to stimulate thinking at other times.

As in other subject areas, children's general reactions will indicate in science when it is time to stop: when they become easily distracted after a period of working with full attention on something; when they lose interest and adopt a mechanical rather than a thinking approach to their work. These can be signs that the child is no longer in charge of the learning and things may have got ahead of him or her. But in science the signs are also to be found in what may seem to be stubborn persistence in ideas despite evidence which conflicts. For example, the teacher who challenged a class's notion that the sound from outside the room must be coming through air round the sides of the door by putting sticky tape all around and over the key hole, found that the children were not convinced that the sound they could still hear was coming through the wood. They claimed that there must be holes which had not been taped over and were letting the sound through. At that time she could not provide convincing evidence of sound passing through solids and was wise enough to leave the children with their idea. At some stage later, with more experience, the idea could be tested more convincingly and further evidence of sound travelling through solids and liquids could be provided. When children hold on to their ideas in this way it is a sure sign that they are not ready to relinquish present ideas for different ones.

So the time to stop trying to help children advance their ideas is when they do not see other ideas as being as useful as their present ones. The time to stop is also *before* falling to the temptation of pressing different ideas with the force of authority, giving the impression that 'this is how things are'. If children feel obliged to accept ideas different from their own because these are clearly 'right' and their own are 'wrong', then they will quite soon lose confidence in their ability to think things out and come to a useful conclusion. It is far better to leave them with an imperfect notion of how sound travels than to turn science into something which they have to accept but don't understand.

References

AAAS (1993) *Benchmarks for Science Literacy, Project 2061.* New York: Oxford University Press.

Andersson, B. and Karrqvist, C. (1983) 'How Swedish pupils aged 12–15 years understand light and its properties.' *European Journal of Science Education* 5, 4, 397–402.

Barnes, D. (1976) *From Communication to Curriculum.* Harmondsworth: Penguin.

DfE (Department for Education) (1995) *Science in the National Curriculum.* London: HMSO.

Guesne, E. (1978) 'Lumière et vision des objets: une exemple de representations des phenomènes physique, preexistant a l'enseignement.' In G. Delacote (ed) *Physics Teaching in Schools,* 265–273. London: Taylor and Francis.

Harlen, W. (1993) *Teaching and Learning Primary Science.* Second Edition. London: Paul Chapman Publishing.

Harlen, W. (1996) *The Teaching of Science.* Second Edition. London: David Fulton.

Harlen, W., Holroyd, C. and Byrne, M. (1995) *Confidence and Understanding in Teaching Science and Technology in Primary Schools.* Edinburgh: Scottish Council for Research in Education.

Howe, C.J., Rodgers, C. and Tolmie, A. (1990) 'Physics in the primary school: peer interaction and the understanding of floating and sinking.' *European Journal of Psychology of Education* 4, 459–475.

Howe, C.J., Tolmie, A. and Rodgers, C. (1992) 'The acquisition of conceptual knowledge in science by primary school children: group interaction and the understanding of motion down an incline.' *British Journal of Developmental Psychology 10,* 113–130.

NAS (National Academy of Sciences) (1994) *National Science Educational Standards. Draft.* Washington: National Academy Press.

Osborne, J., Black, P.J., Smith, M. and Meadows, J. (1990) *SPACE Research Report: Light.* Liverpool: Liverpool University Press.

Russell, T. and Watt, D. (1990a) *Space Research Report: Evaporation and Condensation.* Liverpool: Liverpool University Press.

Russell, T. and Watt, D. (1990b) *Space Research Report: Growth.* Liverpool: Liverpool University Press.

SOED (Scottish Office Education Department) (1993) *National Guidelines. Environmental Studies 5–14.* Edinburgh: SOED.

Watt, D. and Russell, T. (1990) *SPACE Research Report: Sound.* Liverpool: Liverpool University Press.

Appendix

Statements referring to ideas about forces and movement from four national curriculum documents

From Science in the National Curriculum (DfE, 1995)

At Key Stage 1 (5 to 7 years), pupils should be taught:

a) to describe the movement of familiar things, e.g. cars getting faster, slowing down, changing direction;

b) that both pushes and pulls are examples of forces;

c) that forces can make things speed up, slow down or change direction;

d) that forces can change the shapes of objects.

At Key Stage 2 (8 to 11 years), pupils should be taught:

○ that there are forces of attraction and repulsion between magnets, and forces of attraction between magnets and magnetic materials;

○ that objects have weight because of the gravitational attraction between them and the Earth;

○ about friction, including air resistance, as a force which slows moving objects;

○ that when springs and elastic bands are stretched they exert a force on whatever is stretching them;

○ that when springs are compressed they exert a force on whatever is compressing them;

○ that forces act in particular directions;

○ that forces acting on an object can balance *e.g. in a tug of war, on a floating object,* and that when this happens an object at rest stays still;

○ that unbalanced forces can make things speed up *e.g. an apple being dropped,* slow down, *e.g. a shoe sliding across a floor,* or change direction, *e.g. a ball being hit by a bat.*

From Benchmarks for Science Literacy (AAAS, 1993)

By the end of 2nd grade, students should know that:

○ things move in many different ways, such as straight, zigzag, round and round, back and forth, and fast and slow;

○ the way to change how something is moving is to give it a push or a pull;

○ things near the Earth fall to the ground unless something holds them up;

○ magnets can be used to make some things move without being touched.

By the end of 5th grade, students should know that:

○ changes in speed or direction of motion are caused by forces. The greater the forces is, the greater the change in motion will be. The more massive an object is, the less effect a given force will have.

○ how fast things move differs greatly. Some things are so slow that their journey takes a long time; others move too fast for people to even see them.

○ the Earth's gravity pulls any object towards it without touching it.

○ without touching them, a magnet pulls on all things made of iron and either pushes or pulls on other magnets.

From the National Guidelines: Environmental Studies 5–14 (Scotland) (SOED, 1993)

In P1 to P3 (ages 5 to 8), studies should focus on:

○ the effects of pushing, pulling, floating, leading to the ideas of a force;

○ moving and stopping effects, e.g. pulling or pushing a toy;

○ the turning effect of a force, e.g. turning a door handle, twisting an elastic band.

In P4 to P6 (ages 9 to 11), studies should focus on:

○ friction forces on different surfaces, reducing friction's air resistance, streamlining;

○ force of gravity;

○ magnetic materials, forces of attraction and repulsion;

○ motion down a slope under gravity;

○ Earth's magnetic field and compass;

○ magnetic materials in everyday use.

From National Science Education Standards (Draft) (NAS, 1994)

As a result of activities in grades K-4, all students should develop an understanding that:

○ the position of an object can be described by locating it relative to another object or the background;

○ an object's motion can be described by indicating the change in its position over time;

○ the position and motion of objects can be changed by pushing or pulling and the size of the change is related to the strength of the push or pull;

○ magnets attract and repel each other and certain kinds of metals.

As a result of activities in grades 5–8 all students should develop an understanding that:

○ the motion of an object can be described by its position, direction of motion, and speed. This motion can be measured and can be represented on a graph;

○ an object that it not being subjected to a force will continue to move at constant speed and in a straight line;

○ if more than one force acts on an object, then the forces can reinforce or cancel one another, depending on their direction and magnitude. Unbalanced forces will cause changes in the speed and/or direction of an object's motion.

CHAPTER 6

Gender Differences

Messages for Science Education

Patricia Murphy

Introduction

The divergence in girls' and boys' interests and pastimes outside of school has been established by many national and international studies (see Bateson *et al.* 1991; DES 1988a, 1988b, 1989; NAEP 1978; Doran and Tamir 1992; Foxman 1992; Foxman *et al.* 1985, 1990; Gorman *et al.* 1988; Hobbs *et al.* 1979; Keeves 1986, 1992; Tamir *et al.* 1992). What has rarely been examined is how these gender differences emerge and their consequences for children's learning both within and without school. The question considered in this chapter is not what girls and boys can or cannot do, but what is it that girls and boys *choose* to do. What lies behind their choices and how do gendered choices influence achievement?

The chapter in particular examines the consequences of gender differences for learning in science. As part of this examination the sources and nature of gender differences are considered and related to learning outside of school and learning in school. The chapter concludes by looking at the way achievement is defined in subjects, how these definitions shift between the phases of education, and the consequences of this for how 'girls' and 'boys' as groups are perceived both by teachers and pupils.

Background

Research into sex differences in intellectual abilities continues to show a female superiority on certain verbal abilities (Halper 1992). The female advantage is largest for pre-school and adult samples. In relation to quantitative abilities, evidence indicates a male superiority which emerges in adolescence and appears to increase, particularly on tests of mathematical problem-solving. Research continues to show, however, that similarities in male and female performances far outweigh any differences observed (Gipps and Murphy 1994; Halpern 1992). Furthermore, many of the major reviews of studies into cognitive sex differences have revealed empirical trends in the size and extent of differences (Hyde, Fennama and Lamon 1990; Hyde and Linn 1988). Findings such as these have been seen to provide support for psychosocial explanations for gender differences in performance.

The social and psychological factors cited to explain gender differences are derived from the different socialisation processes that research indicates are girls' and boys' experience from birth. Wilder and Powell's (1989) review of the research in this regard is particularly useful. Briefly, their review highlights the different ways parents respond to boys and girls and encourage them to interact with the world and with people. Parents' expectations differ for boys and girls. These different expectations are reflected in the activities and toys they provide for them and in their reactions to the children. Consequently, boys and girls engage in different hobbies and pastimes from an early age, and their interests continue to diverge with age. An outcome of these different socialisation patterns is that children develop different ways of responding to the world and making sense of it, ways which influence how they learn and what they learn. These different treatments also influence children's views of what constitutes appropriate behaviours for them and what others' expectations of them are.

Clearly parents are not a homogeneous group, nor are children passive in this process. Other adults and children are also influential, as are the media and market pressures. How does this general picture relate to what young children do and what might be the consequences for children entering school?

Gender Differences and the Pre-School Child

Browne and Ross (1991) concluded from observations of a large number of pre-school children that from a very young age children develop clear ideas about what girls do and what boys do. The activities girls choose to take part in more than boys were labelled by Browne and Ross as *creative*. Boys, on the other hand, opted for *constructional* activities. Browne and Ross described pre-school children's first choice of activity on entering day care in the following way:

> Many girls chose to play in the 'home corner', to do a drawing, to become involved in a creative activity, to read a book or to talk to an adult. It was extremely rare to observe a girl choose to play with a

construction toy as soon as she entered the class whereas it was very common to observe boys doing so.
(Browne and Ross, 1991, p.42)

In a more recent study (Murphy 1995a), pre-school staff in day care centres were interviewed about their perceptions of gender differences. Some key findings emerged that overlap with Browne and Ross' observations and extend them. For example, staff talked of the importance of role play for children aged two to four years but commented on the differences between girls' and boys' preferred roles:

> You see the maternal instinct in girls from a very early age and this does tend to motivate their play.

> Boys bring their own agendas – they get into some very active, very physically involved games – they do a lot of role play.

> Boys like to be people in authority, policemen, fire-fighters or super heroes.

In playing out different roles children automatically become involved in the activities related to the role. These activities in turn afford children with different learning opportunities. For example, how a mother might interact with the environment will be very different to the way a fire-fighter or super hero interacts. The roles children play also involve them in dressing up. What constitutes an appropriate costume will vary depending on the role. As one member of staff observed, girls like to be the 'grand ladies'. Clearly the needs of a grand lady differ from those of Batman, so children from a very early age are paying attention to different details and developing a different awareness of relevance.

Role play also engages children in talk. Again the kind of talk will vary with the role. If one imagines a mother–child discussion and compares it with an exchange between a policeman and a 'baddie' it is clear that during role play children will practise different types of talk. A recent study of pre-schoolers' communication style found significant gender differences (Thompson 1994). In particular girls' and boys' talk in terms of help-seeking were found to vary dramatically. When children were observed making jigsaw puzzles, it was found that girls more than boys said such things as 'I can't do this', 'will you do this one?', 'where does this piece go?'. However, there were no differences in girls' and boys' ability to solve the puzzles. When adults were shown videos of the children, they were of the opinion that the girls were less confident than the boys and believed boys' performance to be superior to girls'. Girls' equivalent performance was later put down to 'luck'. Thompson suggests that when, 'communicative style does not reflect ability, observer bias seems very likely to occur'. Furthermore, 'adults' beliefs about the ability of girls, particularly at the early developmental ages, may not come in the form of overt disapproval but more often will occur as a subtle shaping of the children's self-concepts' (Thompson, 1994, p.129).

Pre-school children in day care or nurseries spend considerable amounts of time outside. Typical observations from staff included:

Boys are racing all around the garden being somebody else or being the leader.

Girls – you find them sitting in a corner talking, playing their quiet games.

Boys dominate the use of things like the bikes...they think that's their toy.

(Murphy, 1995a)

Again these gendered behaviours result in differences in girls' and boys' opportunities to learn related to the roles with which they associate themselves. It is also possible to see how observers might interpret these behaviours in terms of aggression or timidity. Such interpretations could then, as Thompson suggests, influence children's evolving self-concepts.

Emerging from the interviews was a picture of the boy whose interests had either to be captured or suppressed. In contrast girls' predispositions were considered more congruent with typical nursery activities. One member of staff made the following observation about boys and reading: 'Getting them to settle down to a story was really quite a task. What I resort to is any book that has a tractor, a dumper in it, any sort of machinery. I don't have a problem settling the girls' (Murphy, 1995a).

There was a consensus amongst staff about young boys' interest in mechanical things: 'As soon as you have a sort of machinery, gears or something, the boys are interested straight away'.

It was clear that these interests were exploited to get boys interested in reading and were developed to maintain their interest in other activities. Two potential effects arise from this. First, it can orientate boys towards particular experiences and to observing only certain aspects of their environment and the phenomena within it. Second, because books about vehicles and structures are usually written in a particular style, from an early age boys may be involved with different types of text to girls. It was evident from the study that girls' lack of interest in mechanical things was not considered problematic for them, although one teacher observed about boys' interests, 'I think it inclines them more to the sort of mathematical side of things, science' (Murphy, 1995a).

Girls' interests were characterised by staff in similar ways to Browne and Ross (1991):

Girls are much more interested in drawing and as a result quite often are more forward than boys when it comes to using pencils and scissors.

Girls seem to enjoy the colours and the process of drawing. Boys just aren't interested.

Here girls' interests are also focusing them on different aspects of their environment and engendering the development of particular skills. When asked if boys and girls went to school equally well prepared, staff were not sure but some clearly felt that boys were at a disadvantage.

Starting School

Reception classes in England are dominated by the requirement for children to learn the basics of reading, writing and numeracy (Thornton 1990). If boys go to school having taken longer than girls to settle to listening to stories and with an interest in information-type books already developed, then it is likely that they will find the reading schemes for young children, based largely on stories about people, harder to access. Similarly, boys' less developed skills with using pencils may put them at an initial disadvantage when beginning to write. The implication of this is that boys entering school are potentially more vulnerable than girls to becoming disaffected. As Walkerdine (1989) commented from her study of nursery schools: 'Classroom practices, then, might be for boys a site of struggle where they must work to redefine the situation as one in which the women and girls are powerless subjects of other discourses'. (Walkerdine, 1989, p.71)

Davies and Brember's (1995) longitudinal study of children's attitudes in six primary schools in England found that whilst all infant children were positive about school, girls were more positive than boys. The only topics where boys were more interested than girls in infant school included 'weighing and measuring', 'games' and 'listening to the teacher read'. Browne and Ross (1991) observed that children in infant classes continued to pursue their gendered interests even when participating in the same activity. Girls and boys observed playing with Lego (a construction kit) were found, for example, to make different things. Girls made houses and boys made vehicles or guns using the wheels and rotatable connections in the kits. Browne and Ross commented that boys were using constructional materials in schools in sophisticated ways, incorporating movable parts and focusing on movement and balance. Girls on the other hand were observed to make simple structures as a 'foil for social play'. Thus both boys and girls continue to develop their pre-school interests and learning in school. These observations were consistent across 'cultural and social groups' (Browne and Ross, 1991, p.46). The question considered next is how do these acquired interests and skills influence children's learning as they continue through school? To address it, we turn to national and international surveys of school performance.

National and International Gender Differences in School Performance

The First Science Study of the International Association for the Evaluation of Educational Achievement (IEA, see Keeves, 1986, 1992) was undertaken in 19 countries in 1970–71. The study relied on paper and pencil tests of largely multiple choice items. The study found that boys outperformed girls in all branches of science and the gap between them increased with age. The gender gap was greater in the tests of physical science compared with biological science. Boys also showed more positive attitudes towards science than girls, and reported a higher level of interest in science-related activities. Exceptions to this pattern did occur, however. Girls in England, for example, at ages 10 and 14 outperformed boys in biology. Keeves observed that the gender gap in overall science performance arose because of girls' lower performance on items testing understanding rather than recall of science (Keeves 1986). The USA National Assessment of Educational Progress science results derived using very similar test instruments replicated the IEA pattern of performance for boys and girls (NAEP 1978). The British Columbia Science Survey (BCSS) (Hobbs et al. 1979), however, found boys ahead of girls only on tests of physics and measurement skills.

The second IEA study was conducted in 23 countries in 1983–84 (see Keeves, 1986, 1992). In this survey boys were once again found to outperform girls. The differences between 10-year-old girls and boys was comparatively small but the gender gap increased significantly with age. Differences between boys' and girls' performance were relatively small in biology, intermediary in chemistry and large in physics. It was also found that there were significant reductions in the performance gap for some countries between the first and second surveys. Gender differences in attitudes to science continued in this study and increased with age. Husén (1993) concluded from the findings that the sex of the student had a direct influence on both achievement and attitudes, though he argued that, 'the sex of a student has only a weak, and indirect, influence on science achievement' (p.16).

The reduction in the gender gap in science performance over time was considered to support the view that societal rather than biological factors were influential (Keeves 1992). Humrich's study (1987) provided further evidence for this. She compared the performance of students in Japan and the US, and found that whilst the pattern of performance was the same (i.e. boys outperformed girls) Japanese girls outperformed boys and girls in the USA in physics. Japanese scores were lower than US scores on tests of knowledge but substantially higher on tests of comprehension and application. Humrich linked these differences in levels of performance for girls and boys to the different curricular emphases in the two countries.

In the second science survey, process objectives were identified as important aspects of scientific achievement. The practical skills assessed were divided into three components: performing, reasoning and investigating. Ten-year-olds and 14-year-olds in six countries took part in the practical tests, each student responding to three of six tasks (Tamir *et al.* 1992). At age 10 the results showed very similar performance for boys and girls, with girls performing at a higher level than boys on the 'investigating' component. There were national exceptions with males outperforming females across the tests in Singapore, whilst in Israel girls performed at a higher level than boys in the reasoning and investigating tests, i.e. two out of the three practical test components. For 14-year-olds performance was again very similar for males and females. Boys were slightly ahead of girls in Japan and Singapore and the opposite was the case for Israel (Doran and Tamir 1992).

Two further international studies using NAEP science items (with no practical element) were carried out as part of the International Assessment of Mathematics and Science (IAEP). The first survey in 1988, of 13-year-olds only, found boys outperforming girls in all populations except those of the UK and USA (Lapointe, Mead and Phillips, 1989). The second survey, in 1990, covered fourteen countries for the nine-year-old population sampled. Nineteen countries were involved in the testing at 13 years of age. Boys once more did better than girls in the majority of countries, more so at age 13 than at age 9, and particularly in physical and earth and space sciences. In a number of countries girls were ahead of boys on questions about the 'nature of science' (Foxman 1992). In England girls and boys across the ages performed similarly.

The Assessment of Performance Unit (APU) conducted annual surveys of science for populations of 11-, 13- and 15-year-old students from 1980–1984 in England, Wales and Northern Ireland. The

APU science instruments were quite different in kind to those already discussed and were based on a domain sampling approach. This meant that far more items were used at each age, spanning a broad spectrum of science content and processes including three distinct and extensive practical tests (Murphy and Gott 1984). The results showed girls outperforming boys across the ages on practical tests of making and interpreting observations. Boys continued to demonstrate superior performance in applying physics concepts which increased with age (Johnson and Murphy 1986). The attitude questionnaires showed across the ages girls' interest lying in biological and medical applications, whereas boys' inclined to physics and technological applications.

The latest BCSS found girls outperforming boys across grades 4, 7 and 10 on, '…many of the process skills, and on items involving conceptual planning, abstract and critical thinking and the nature of science and safety' (Bateson *et al*. 1991, p.18).

Boys performed at a higher level on items involving measurement, laboratory techniques, numerical problem-solving, earth/space science and energy topics, particularly electricity (Bateson et al. 1991, p.18). Males performed at a higher level on practical items using scientific equipment but on the practical items to do with the environment females outperformed males. This performance difference in favour of females increased with age. The attitude measures revealed similarities between boys and girls. The exception was that, 'females are more strongly positive than males in the area of environmental issues. These differences tend to become larger as students get older' (Bateson et al. 1991, p.8). The BCSS surveys also showed a decline in the science gender gap over time.

Overall, the research from national and international surveys and the evidence of children's different early experiences suggests that students' attitudes to, and achievement in, physics specifically, and science generally, might be related to the cultural expectations of girls and boys and how these are reflected in the organisation and values underpinning the school curriculum and its assessment. In the next sections this argument is developed and exemplified.

Differences in Experiences – Effects on Performance

Both UK (APU) and USA (NAEP) surveys showed that girls' and boys' experiences of scientific equipment and apparatus out of school differed. Where gender differences in the use of apparatus arose in the surveys they were in favour of boys and on precisely those instruments which boys reported more experience of outside school (DES 1988a, 1988b, 1989). These performance differences increased in range and magnitude as students progressed through school (Johnson and Murphy 1986).

The Davies and Brember study (1995) referred to previously, found that boys' early interest in school in 'weighing and measuring' continued through primary school. The APU maths surveys also found that 15-year-old boys' performance was superior to girls' on tests of measures which included 'units and mensuration' (Foxman *et al.* 1985). However, this performance difference disappeared in later surveys when students were *asked* to use particular instruments rather than being expected to choose the appropriate instrument (Foxman *et al.* 1990). The different experiences students acquire not only affect the skills and knowledge they develop but also their understanding of the situations and problems in which to apply them. For example boys in the APU science surveys were better able than girls at ages 13 and 15 to use ammeters and voltmeters, yet they did not report experience of these instruments outside of school. Boys, however, continue to play more than girls with electrical toys and gadgets outside of school. Such play allows boys to familiarise themselves with the effects of electricity and to develop a tacit understanding of how it can be controlled.

Confidence and Alienation

Browne and Ross (1991) refer to gender domains and discuss the effect on children when placed in situations that were perceived by them as out of their 'territory'. In situations which children perceived to be part of their territories they behaved with confidence whereas being out of territory rendered them diffident. Children's early years' experiences are crucial in forming their perceptions of what constitutes 'girls' and 'boys' domains.

The APU science surveys used 600–800 questions at each age. Spanning the question banks revealed that patterns in gender differences occurred in ways not associated with the tasks set. Questions were labelled by several dimensions, one of which was referred to as the *content*, i.e. what the task was about. For example in Table 6.1 the task is to interpret a table of data but the content is to do with washers and types of materials. This content could easily be altered and the task, i.e. to interpret the figures, kept the same, as such content is not believed to influence performance.

The APU results showed that girls and boys reacted to the same content differently irrespective of the task. Questions which involved content related to health, reproduction, nutrition and domestic situations were generally found to show girls performing at a higher level

Table 6.1 Example of exercise in interpretation of figures

Material	Size						
	$\frac{1}{2}in$	2cm	2.5cm	$1\frac{1}{8}in$	$1\frac{1}{4}in$	$1\frac{1}{2}in$	3.5cm
Rubber	16	18	12	11	3	29	36
Nylon	29	2	4	6	19	1	35
Steel	14	7	3	8	16	52	47
Cord	31	14	9	17	17	37	74
Neoprene	49	10	12	16	16	5	73

Table 6.1 comes from a spare parts catalogue. It shows the number of washers of different types used with nuts and bolts.

In a new catalogue washers are to be shown in the table below. Complete this table by using the information in Table 6.1

Material	Size in cm		
	2	2.5	3.5
Rubber			
Neoprene			
Nylon			
Cord			

than boys across the ages. It was also the case that more girls than boys would attempt such questions. Hence the gender gap in performance arose because of the increased confidence of girls combined with the lower response rate of boys. In questions where the content was more overtly 'masculine', such as in Table 6.1, the converse occurred. Typical 'masculine' contents included cars, building sites, submarines, machinery, etc. Talking to students revealed that they had definite views about content areas where they expected to be competent and content areas where they anticipated failure. Many boys and girls typically avoided those contents which they judged were outside their realm of competence – their territory.

Exactly the same response was found with questions involving electrical content, where girls more than boys anticipated failure. In the APU practical investigation tasks, although girls were found to be equally as competent as boys, more girls than boys lacked confidence in handling the equipment. This effect has been linked to observations of boys' and girls' behaviours in laboratories where boys typically dominate the use of apparatus and equipment (Whyte, 1986).

The content-related performance effects can be traced back to the different learning opportunities that children's gendered play affords them. It is also possible to see links between these content effects and the gender differences in achievement and attitudes established by the national and international surveys discussed. As children engage with activities they develop skills, knowledge and confidence in them. In classroom situations these effects are often undetected by teachers and children. Hence children build on the strengths and interests they bring to school and continue to develop them both within and without of school. The downside of this is that children's alienation from certain content areas and activities related to them similarly goes undetected. It is very difficult to observe the effects of low confidence because children may appear to be pursuing an activity but actually have a low level of engagement with it. Task engagement is an essential prerequisite for learning. Unfortunately lack of confidence is all too often interpreted as a lack of ability. Consequently the effects of alienation go unchecked and lead to underachievement as children miss out on learning opportunities.

Gender Differences in Views of Relevance

Earlier in this chapter it was noted how children's play led them to attend to different features in phenomena. Girls across the ages in the APU surveys were found to consistently outperform boys on the practical tests of making and interpreting observations. It was not the case that girls' performance was higher than boys across all tasks. Indeed, closer review revealed that girls more than boys took note of colours, sounds, smells and texture. Boys on the other hand took note of structural details. Thus when asked to observe phenomena or objects and events in an open way, girls and boys paid attention to different details given the same circumstances. Girls' and boys' observations indicate their differing views of relevance, views that can be traced back to their play and interests in the early years. If boys were directed to observe sounds etc. they were perfectly capable of doing so, but the relevance of these observations had to be pointed out more often for boys than girls. Children's views of relevance influence their learning both in science and in design and technology in very similar ways. A brief review of gender differences at 15 years of age in the APU design and technology survey showed that girls focused on aesthetic variables and empathised with users' needs. Boys more than girls focused on manufacturing issues and were more competent than girls in their application of knowledge of structures and properties and uses of material and energy systems (Kimbell *et al.* 1991).

Just as it is difficult to detect content effects it is very difficult for teachers to be aware of children's differing views of relevance and how they might influence their learning. A simple strategy that has been used (Murphy 1991a) is to set students open tasks to elicit their initial perceptions of what might be relevant. For example, one task asked students to imagine they were designing a boat to go around the world. They were told to give details of things they thought were important. Figure 6.1 shows examples of a typical girl's boat and a typical boy's boat.

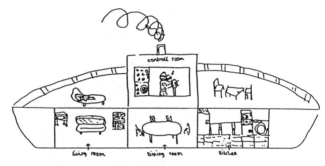

A typical girl's boat

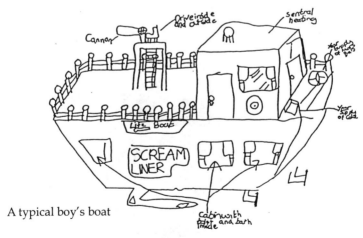

A typical boy's boat

Figure 6.1 Older pupils showed the same kinds of differences although their designs were more sophisticated

A similar task focused on the design of a vehicle. The children chose the vehicle and the purpose they wished to examine. In general, both primary and secondary students' designs varied in gender-related ways. Boys' designs included elaborate weaponry, next to no living facilities but detailed mechanisms for movement and navigation. Girls' designs showed a total absence of weaponry and little mechanical detail. The detail girls included related to living requirements, human needs and safety. It is clear that there is merit in both types of response, as well as limitations. Using such responses as stimuli for discussion can open up to children and teachers how they view the world and others' alternative perceptions.

In another such task primary children were involved in a language lesson looking at different forms of writing for different purposes (Murphy 1991b). The teacher had selected estate agents' use of language when selling houses as a focus of study. However, prior to showing children typical estate agents' literature it was suggested

Girl's house

Boy's house
Figure 6.2

that the children be given the opportunity to be estate agents first. Again, as Figure 6.2 shows, there were striking differences in the detail children considered relevant in their houses which was also found in their descriptions of the selling points of their houses. Girls' descriptions paid much more attention to the broader issues related to family life in a community than boys'.

This finding overlaps a finding established in the APU surveys that girls tend to value the circumstances in which tasks are set and take account of them when constructing meaning in the task. They do not abstract issues from their context. Conversely, as a group, boys tend to consider issues in isolation and judge the content and context to be irrelevant (Murphy 1991a). The consequences are that girls and boys perceive different problems and solutions to them – given the same set of circumstances. Again it is difficult for teachers to recognise when such a gender effect occurs and the consequences of it for children's learning.

The task in Figure 6.3 was given to a class of 9–10-year-olds as part of the normal work in science. The scenario of dissolving sugar in tea was the context for the task in the box.

Molly always teased her dad that he would stir a hole into the bottom of his teacup.

He said that he wanted to make sure the sugar had dissolved properly.

Molly suggested that if he put the sugar into the tea as soon as it was poured (instead of five minutes later), it would dissolve quicker and not need so much stirring.

> Find out how the time taken for sugar to dissolve depends on the temperature of the liquid.

Check that your investigation is sensible – for instance, use reasonable temperatures and use a reasonable amount of sugar for each test.

When you have finished, write a short account of what you did. Did you stir the tea? Explain why you did this (or didn't do it).

Figure 6.3: Dissolving

A mixed group of three children was observed tackling the task. It became clear that the girl in the group took the context and integrated it into her task. She was trying to find out the time taken for sugar to dissolve in tea under 'normal' circumstances. One boy in the group was unaware of the 'tea drinking' context. He did not reject it, it was irrelevant as far as he was concerned. He went straight to the 'science' task in the box and wanted to test a range of temperatures starting with a low temperature. The girl disagreed vehemently. It was not, in her view, what they were supposed to do. As she said, 'nobody drinks cold tea'. Neither the boy nor the teacher could understand the girl's perception of the task. The teacher in interview described her behaviour as 'difficult and quirky'. For the girl who, after the teacher's intervention, had to pursue a task she could not understand the relevance of, the experience was profoundly alienating, as she reported in interview (Murphy *et al.* in press).

In science it is assumed that children will focus down on a single variable effect when they are given opportunities to investigate phenomena. It is further assumed that focusing is something that all children can do equally well. To address this potential source of alienation and underachievement in science, it is essential that teachers and students become aware of the significance of contextual variables for the task perceived. Further, if it is important to observe a single variable effect in a particular way, the reasons for, and relevance of, doing this needs to be made clear to students from a young age. Gender differences in performance in other domains provide further support for this. For example, whilst a 'girls'' typical contextualised response might be devalued and misinterpreted in a science context the converse occurs in design and technology. The APU surveys in design and technology found, for example, that girls were ahead of boys in identifying tasks and investigating and appraising ideas. Girls, in addition, dramatically outperformed boys on evaluating products. All of these tasks in a design and technology context give value to responses that reflect a broad perspective and which recognise a range of relevant variables. Boys were ahead of girls at generalising, an achievement that requires students to abstract from specifics. Again links can be discerned between children's learnt ways of responding to the world and giving value to aspects of it, and their achievements in schools.

Expectations and Achievement

In most of this chapter so far, attention has been drawn to the consequences of children's learning out of school for their subsequent achievements in school. In this final section brief consideration is given to the consequences of gender differences for children's evolving attitudes to school and to achievement in domains. Teachers' role in this will also be touched on.

In recent years in England and Wales, since the introduction of: (1) a national curriculum which reduced students' ability to opt for certain subjects at 14 years of age; and (2) the General Certificate of Secondary Education (GCSE) which broadened both the definition of achievement and the means of assessing it for students at 16 years of age; there has been a trend for girls to outperform boys in that girls achieve more GCSE grades A* – C than their male counterparts (Elwood and Comber 1995). Table 6.2 shows the mean difference between male and female performance for each of the major curriculum subjects (from Elwood and Comber 1995, p.4).

Table 6.2 Percentage of male/female entry and grades A*–C (all GCSE groups): main GCSE subjects, 1994

Subject	%Entry Male	%A*–C Male	%Entry Female	%A*–C Female	Mean Difference %A*–C (M–F)
Art/design	48.3	47.0	51.7	64.8	-17.8
Biology	48.5	68.0	51.5	61.6	7.2
Chemistry	60.9	74.9	39.1	76.3	-2.2
Combined science	49.8	45.3	50.2	45.5	-0.2
Economics	66.5	58.0	33.5	58.7	-0.7
English	50.1	50.3	49.9	66.6	-16.3
English Literature	47.3	55.7	52.7	68.9	-13.2
French	46.1	42.2	53.9	55.6	-13.4
Geography	57.0	48.9	43.0	55.5	-6.6
History	48.0	52.0	52.0	58.4	-6.4
Mathematics	49.2	47.2	50.8	45.4	1.8
Physics	66.9	72.9	33.1	76.3	-3.4
All subjects	49.3	48.8	50.7	56.7	-7.9

Source: 1994 Inter-group Statistics, Associated Examining Board, Surrey

Trends such as this are not restricted to the UK context. Concern about the underachievement of boys has been voiced in many countries of the world, recently in the USA and Australia, for example. Reference was made earlier to the longitudinal study conducted by Davies and Brember (1995). This study found that by the end of primary school girls' and boys' attitudes to school had declined. Girls were less positive about mathematics than when they entered school whereas boys' attitudes remained relatively stable. Boys, on the other hand, were less positive than girls about reading and writing. Importantly, the decline in boys' attitudes to school were related to their views of discipline. By the end of primary schooling, boys were less keen to observe rules and were less concerned about being reprimanded. Girls, on the other hand, were anxious to do as they were told and to please their teachers.

A major study conducted by Keele University in England in 1993–94 surveyed the attitudes of 7000 secondary aged students. The interim results (Barber 1994) of the study show that boys' disaffection with school in comparison to girls' continues, particularly in terms of their motivation to learn. Girls were consistently more positive, better motivated, better at getting on with their teachers and better behaved than boys in their mid teens. Evidence from interviews with students indicates that it is not 'cool' for boys of that age to be seen by their peers as 'achievers'. Boys' greater disaffection with school and lack of motivation has several sources. Research, cited earlier, has highlighted the way boys' behaviours from entering school are suppressed and judged inappropriate compared with girls'. Girls' conformity, on the other hand, is valued. Unfortunately, girls' conformity has been found to influence teachers' perceptions of their ability negatively. The converse has been found for boys. Ebullient, aggressive, risk-taking behaviour is often interpreted as an indicator of high ability. These research findings from classroom studies have parallels with Thompson's (1994) study of adults' responses to pre-school girls' and boys' behaviours discussed earlier.

Girls' conformity has other consequences for their learning. Evidence from classroom interaction studies indicates that girls and boys typically receive different feedback from teachers. Teachers' feedback to girls typically focuses on their work rather than their behaviour, whereas the reverse is the case for boys. Dweck *et al.* (1978) found that this leads girls to have low expectations of their abilities and for boys to overestimate theirs. Many studies have found this to be the case, including the APU surveys (DES 1989). The Keele survey, whilst noting the low motivation of young males compared with females, found that males consistently rated their abilities more highly than females. Randall (1987) looked at pupil–teacher interactions in workshops and laboratories. She found that girls received more attention from teachers than boys. However, the girls' contacts were mainly seeking help and encouragement. Randall found that teachers accepted girls' low confidence and thus reinforced their feelings of helplessness.

Differential Performance at 16 Plus

The gender gap in GCSE was singled out for research. The study into differential performance at 16 plus (Stobart *et al.* 1992) examined reasons for the gap between males and females in the core subjects of mathematics and English. The mathematics examinations were differentiated so that teachers had to select the level of exam that students should sit. At the time of the study the gap between male and female performance had narrowed, with males achieving 3 per cent more A to C grades than females, a small percentage which represented a very large number of students. The research found that more girls than boys were entered for the lower foundation level and intermediate level exams, and more boys than girls (21 per cent versus 12 per cent) were not entered for any exam. The reasons for this differentiated-entry policy were explained in interviews with teachers and students alike in terms of the teachers' beliefs about the affective, not the cognitive, characteristics of students. Boys rated their mathematical ability more highly than girls and teachers believed they would be demotivated and hence disruptive if placed in a low exam tier. Both teachers and girls believed that girls lacked confidence in their mathematical ability and were more fearful of failure than boys. Consequently, teachers tended to place girls in the intermediate rather than higher exam tier to protect them from such anxiety. The research and later evidence suggests that both boys and girls underachieved because of teachers' beliefs (Gorman *et al.*, 1988).

Similar beliefs about male and female abilities exist in the domain of science. A simple but effective study was carried out by Goddard-Spear (1987). She found that when the same piece of science writing was attributed to a girl it received lower marks from both male and female teachers than when it was attributed to a boy.

The research into GCSE examined girls' and boys' achievement in English. At the time of the study girls were achieving 14 per cent more grades A to C than boys. The study found that certain English tasks differentially affected girls and boys. Girls were found to do better when responses involved extended writing, when multiple perspectives were required to achieve good marks, and when the stimulus materials were literary in nature. Boys, on the other hand, did better when questions required short responses or right/wrong answers and overall writing competence was not required to succeed on a question. The study found that exam syllabuses tended to emphasise those aspects girls typically do better than boys. Furthermore there was evidence that boys' style of response prevented teachers 'seeing' the value, in terms of achievements in their responses. Hence there were indications of bias both in the selection of achievements and how they were judged. These performance effects can be linked to children's learnt responses to the world. Girls' disposition to consider multiple perspectives in English is mirrored in their typical responses in science and design and technology.

Styles of Expression and Achievement

There is evidence that students' performance in English is strongly influenced by learning outside of school. The APU surveys of English (Gorman *et al.* 1988) described girls' preferred style of written response as, 'extended, reflective composition'. Boys' style of response was more often episodic, factual and focusing on commentative detail. Examples of the styles of response are included in Figures 6.4 and 6.5 from Murphy (1995b) citing White (1988). The responses were to a task to describe two demoiselle flies emphasising the differences, 'most important for telling them apart'. Both responses include these differences but the form of communicating them is very different.

The Demoiselle Fly

The demoiselle fly in general has a short thorax long abdomen and bulbous compound eyes.

Type A has all the aforementioned qualities but differs from type B in the following ways:

1. It has six long black legs with long hairs on top and lower parts of its legs. Type B only has four legs and has hairs on the bottom of its forelegs and top of its hindlegs only.

2. Type A has opaque wings which are short and wide. Type B has transparent wings which are notably longer and thinner .. than type A's.

3. Type A has it's abdomen segmented into fairly small parts, the end section tapering to a point. Type B has it's abdomen made up of fairly small parts the end part tapering downwards to make it triangular.

Figure 6.4 Demoiselle fly: Typical boys' response

There are two points to note about these differences in styles of expression. The APU language surveys found that the students' preferred style of expression reflected their choice of reading material outside of school. At age 11, more boys than girls enjoyed reading works related to hobbies or which involved finding things out. They were also more likely to choose comic books and annuals at home in preference to stories. At age 15 over half the boys compared

It is one of those lazy hot days in summer when everything is warm and very quiet. The trees surrounding the lake at the bottom of the hill are swaying silently and the ripples on the lake give the impression of peace and tranquillity.

At the end of the lake are reeds and lilies. Flies buzz dozily among the tall grasses, looking for food. Bees laze among the pollen filled lilies, drinking their sweet nectar and the demoiselle flies perch motionless on the tall green fronds of the reeds.

There are two in particular, one male, one female, that catch my eye as I lie against the sturdy trunk of an ancient oak. They are the most beautiful creatures I have ever seen, but they are both different.

One has lacy wings, so clear I can see the water's edge through them. Its colouring is of brilliant pinks and blues, and it stands out amongst the yellow buttercups that surround it. Its abdomen is long, like a finger, and incredibly thin. It looks so fragile, as if any sudden movement may snap it, like a twig. Its lacy wings stretch back, almost to the full length of the abdomen, like delicate fans, cooling its body, Its head is small but bold. It is completely blue with piercing black eyes on either side of its head. The legs of this magnificent creature are long and black, with what look like hairs of the finest thread, placed at even spaces down each side.

The thorax, the part next to its head, is large. It is not as slender as the abdomen, but it is very sleek, with patches of blue and black reflecting the brilliant sunlight.

As I watch, its head rotates and then suddenly it has disappeared, hovering over the lake.

The other demoiselle fly still remains. This is not such a beautiful creature as the first, but it has striking markings. The wings are a dull brown in colour. They are much wider and not as long. They appear to be much more powerful than the lacy delicate wings of the other fly. The abdomen of this creature is much thicker, It is dull brown, like the wings, but has flecks of mauve and grey. It appears, just as with the wings, to be much stronger, more substantial, and more useful.

Figure 6.5 Demoiselle fly: Typical girls' response

with a third of the girls said they preferred reading books which gave accurate facts. Twice as many girls than boys liked to read, 'to help understand their own and other people's personal problems' (Gorman *et al.*, 1988, p173).

The language team suggested that there was a link between the imbalance in girls' and boys' exposure to different types of reading material and their preferences and skills in writing (Gorman 1987). There is in addition a link between the pre-school children's interests and teachers' reactions to them already described and their developing interests in particular reading materials.

The second point to make is that certain styles of expression are expected in particular subject areas and thus influence teachers' judgements of students' ability, often in ways that misrepresent students' real achievements. Whilst girls appear to be advantaged by this in English, research indicates that the reverse is true in science. Furthermore, as students progress beyond compulsory education to GCE A level study post-16 a shift in performance patterns arise. Whilst males continue to outperform females in mathematics, males now outperform females in English (Elwood and Comber 1995). In physics only the most able girls (by GCSE performance) take A level. Hence they are a highly selected group but their performance is not at the level that might be predicted from GCSE performance. Such results have puzzled many teachers. As one head commented in trying to explain what was referred to as the 'A' level score dip: 'One thing we need to look at is the nature of the examinations at GCSE. Ongoing assessment [i.e. continuous coursework] seems to appeal to girls who work very diligently at course work' (*Times Educational Supplement*, 30 September 1994).

It is not untypical for girls' achievement to be explained by diligence rather than ability. As one teacher commented about a successful girl beginning her study in English at 'A' level: 'I hope she doesn't crack up doing A levels... I suppose our expectations are that that particular girl over-performed because she worked too hard. Because she is not brilliant, she's very very good' (Elwood and Comber 1996, p.59).

However, a closer look at the form of response expected in English 'A' level is very revealing, as are teachers' comments about male and female students' style of expression at 'A' level:

> The boys go through it like a Panzer division. Their writing is very clinical and clean, you know, point point point. Girls are much more 'if this then that and I might think this and I might think that...' The girls tend to like to take a lot of time.

> He will write you a side-and-a-half where others are writing four or five pages...it's like a knife through butter – almost notes but not quite, a very sparse style of writing. I've *never* seen a girl do that. Never.

> (Elwood, 1995, p58)

Whilst the roots of boys' underachievement in English at 16 plus occur outside of school and are a cause for concern, their preferred choice of reading provides both a content and a style of writing that appears to be valued in science and increasingly in a range of subjects in the later phases of education. This continues into university. For example, history emerges as a subject where males significantly outperform females. A 'women's' style of response was characterised as showing, 'a preference for cautious, discursive and synthetic approaches, a willingness to consider a range of views and a strong personal investment in 'getting it right'. This was contrasted with good undergraduate history writing which was seen to embody, 'an argumentative and self-assertive approach to questions, risk-taking, the bold affirmation of a particular view and a confident dismissal of others' (Gender Working Party Report 1994, p9). It is worthwhile at this point to recall the characteristics of the communication style of the pre-school girls making their jigsaw puzzles that we discussed earlier. Students' learnt styles of communication and ways of working combined with their preferred choice of reading material exert a powerful influence on the solutions or responses they consider to be appropriate. The evidence cited in this paper has demonstrated the consistency in aspects of males' and females' typical responses and how these are viewed differently in certain subjects at different points in students' educational careers. The consequences for students' learning at 18 plus and beyond cannot be covered in this chapter. It is nevertheless essential to consider how learning in the early years may influence achievement throughout education.

Boys and girls are equally able to appreciate the value of different ways of working and communicating for different purposes. However, to develop this appreciation they need opportunities to: (1) examine their own and others' preferred styles and what lies behind them; and (2) to address a range of purposes whose meaning and value makes sense to them where alternative styles are necessary and appropriate.

Concluding Remarks

This chapter has cited several sources of evidence to show how learning outside of school influences learning in school. Young children's learnt gender preferences lead them to pursue particular interests which provide them with different learning opportunities and importantly align them in different ways to schooling and to subject learning. The combination of girls' and boys' differential learning and interests out of school, and teachers' and students' treatment of these in school, lead to differences in performance between girls and boys, often unrelated to students' ability. They also, as the evidence has shown, lead to underachievement as many children channel themselves away from certain learning experiences. Furthermore, teachers often unwittingly compound this by interpreting aspects of students' behaviour and styles of learning and communication in terms of their ability when they actually reflect differences in opportunities to learn. The strong message that emerges from the research is that teachers, and students from a young age, need to take more account of the interests and learning developed outside of school and how these influence attitudes to, and learning in, school subjects. In addition, if particular styles of response are significant elements of achievement in domains then this should be made clear to students and become a matter for teaching and not just assessment.

It is also clear that more attention needs to be paid to the potential value of different styles and approaches to ways of working. It may be that in areas such as science a too narrow view of what constitutes appropriate behaviour and responses has evolved; a view that is covert and possibly limits the potential of many students, girls and boys alike. Interventions in science that have broadened acceptable styles and ways of working and have concentrated on the social implications of science have been found to increase the levels of achievement for both boys and girls, but particularly for girls. However, the improvement in female achievement has not occurred for all girls, in particular not those from low socio-economic backgrounds (Hildebrand 1996). It is apparent that we understand aspects of the problem of gender and learning, but that much more needs to be understood to make science a subject that is accessible to, and enjoyed by, all our children.

References

Barber, M. (1994) 'Young People and their attitudes to school. An Interim Report.' Centre for Successful Schools, Keele University, Staffordshire.

Bateson, D., Erickson, G., Gaskell, J. and Wideen, M. (1991) *Science in British Columbia*. British Columbia: Ministry of Education.

Browne, N. and Ross, C. (1991) 'Girls' stuff, boys' stuff: young children talking and playing.' In N. Browne (ed) *Science and Technology in the Early Years*. Milton Keynes: Open University Press.

Davies, J. and Brember, I. (1995) 'Attitudes to School and the Curriculum in Year 2, Year 4 and Year 6: Changes over Four Years.' Paper presented at the European Conference on Educational Research, Bath, September.

Department of Education and Science (1988a) *Science at Age 11 – A Review of APU Survey Findings*. London: HMSO.

Department of Education and Science (1988b) *Science at Age 15 – A Review of APU Survey Findings*. London: HMSO.

Department of Education and Science (1989) *Science at Age 13 – A Review of APU Survey Findings*. London: HMSO.

Doran, R.L. and Tamir, P. (1992) 'Results of practical skills testing.' *Studies in Educational Evaluation 18*, 3, 365–392.

Dweck, C.S., Davidson, W., Nelson, S. and Enna, B. (1978) 'Sex differences in learned helplessness: the contingencies of evaluative feedback in the classroom.' *Development Psychology 14*, 268–76.

Elwood, J. and Comber, C. (1995) 'Gender differences in 'A' level examinations: the reinforcement of stereotypes?' Paper presented at the European conference on Educational Research, Bath, September.

Foxman, D. (1992) *Learning Mathematics and Science: The Second IAEP in England*. Windsor: National Foundation for Educational Research.

Foxman, D., Ruddock, G., Joffe, L., Mason, K., Mitchell, P. and Sexton, B. (1985) *A Review of Monitoring in Mathematics 1978–1982 Part 1 and Part 2*. London: Department of Education and Science.

Foxman, D., Ruddock, G. and McCallum, L. (1990) *Assessment Matters: No. 3 APU Mathematics Monitoring 1984–1988 (Phase 2)*. London: SEAC.

Gender Working Party Report (1994) *Men's and Women's Performance in Tripos Examinations, 1980–1993*. Cambridge: Faculty of History, University of Cambridge.

Gipps, C. and Murphy, P. (1994) *A Fair Test? Assessment, Achievement and Equity*. Milton Keynes: Open University Press.

Goddard-Spear, M. (1987) 'The biasing influence of pupil sex in a science marking exercise.' In A. Kelly (ed) *Science for Girls?* Milton Keynes: Open University Press.

Gorman, T. (1987) *Pupils' Attitudes to Reading*. Windsor: NFER-Nelson.

Gorman, T.P., White, J., Brook, G., Maclure, M. and Kispal, A. (1988) *Language Performance in Schools: Review of APU Language Monitoring 1979–1983*. London: HMSO.

Halpern, D.F. (1992) *Sex Differences in Cognitive Abilities*. Hillsdale, NJ: Lawrence Erlbaum.

Hildebrand, G.M. (1996) 'Assessment interacts with gender.' In P. Murphy and C. Gipps (eds) *Equity in Classrooms: Towards Effective Pedagogies for Girls and Boys*. London: The Falmer Press.

Hobbs, E.D., Bolt, W.B., Erickson, G., Quelch, T.P. and Sieban, B.A. (1979) *British Columbia Science Assessment 1978, General Report 1*. British Columbia: Ministry of Education.

Humrich, E. (1987) Girls in science: US and Japan, Contributions to the Fourth GASAT Conference 1, Michigan, USA.

Husén, T. (1993) 'Factors behind choice of advanced studies and careers in science and technology.' *Working Papers in Education ED 93–1*. Stanford University.

Hyde, J.S. and Linn, M.C. (1988) 'Gender differences in verbal ability: a meta analysis.' *Psychological Bulletin 104*, 53–69.

Hyde, J.S., Fennama, E. and Lamon, S.J. (1990) 'Gender differences in mathematics performance: a meta analysis.' *Psychological Bulletin 107*, 139–253.

Johnson, S. and Murphy, P. (1986) *Girls and Physics: Reflections on APU Survey Findings*. APU Occasional Paper No.4. London: Department of Education and Science.

Keeves, J.P. (1986) 'Science education: the contribution of IEA research to a world perspective.' In N.T. Postlethwaite (ed) *International Educational Research, Papers in Honor of Torsten Husén*. Oxford: Pergamon Press.

Keeves, J.P. (ed) (1992) *The IEA study in Science III: Changes in Science Education and Achievement 1970-1984*. Oxford: Pergamon Press.

Kimbell, R., Stables, K., Wheeler, T., Wosniak, A. and Kelly, V. (1991) *The Assessment of Performance in Design and Technology*. London: School Examinations and Assessment Authority.

Lapointe, A., Mead, N. and Phillips, G. (1989) *A World of Differences: An International Assessment of Mathematics and Science*. Princeton, NJ: Educational Testing Service.

Murphy, P. (1991a) 'Gender differences in pupils' reactions to practical work.' In B. Woolnough (ed) *Practical Science*. Milton Keynes: Open University Press.

Murphy, P. (1991b) *Assessment and the Primary Curriculum*. Milton Keynes: Open University Press.

Murphy, P. (1995a) *Gender Differences and the Pre-School Child* (Working Paper). School of Education, The Open University.

Murphy, P. (1995b) 'Gender and assessment in science.' In L. Parker, L. Rennie and B. Fraser (eds) *Gender, Science and Mathematics: Shortening the Shadow*. Dordrecht: Kluwer Academic Press.

Murphy, P., Scanlon, E., Hodgson, B. and Whitelegg, E. (in press) 'Developing investigative learning in science: the role of collaboration.' In J. van den Akker, W. Kuiper and U. Hameyer (eds) *Issues in European Curriculum Research*. Oxford: Pergamon Press.

Murphy, P. and Gott, R. (1984) *Science Assessment Framework Age 13 and 15: Science Report for Teachers: 2*. Hatfield: Association for Science Education.

NAEP (1978) *Science Achievement in Schools: A Summary of Results from the 1976–1977 National Assessment of Science*. Washington DC: National Center for Improving Science Education.

Randall, G.J. (1987) 'Gender differences in pupil–teacher interactions in workshops and laboratories.' In G. Weiner and M. Arnot (eds) *Gender Under Scrutiny*. Milton Keynes: UK, Open University Press.

Stobart, G., White, J., Elwood, J., Hayden, M. and Mason, K. (1992) *Differential Performance at 16+: English and Mathematics*. London: HMSO.

Tamir, P., Doran, R.L., Kojima, S. and Bathory, Z. (1992) 'Procedures used in practical skills testing in science.' *Studies in Educational Evaluation 18*, 3, 277–290.

Thompson, R.B. (1994) 'Gender differences in communicative style: possible consequences for their learning process.' In H. Foot, C. Howe, A. Anderson, A. Tolmie and A. Warden (eds) *Group Tutoring*. Southampton: Computational Mechanics Publications.

Thornton, M. (1990) 'Primary specialism.' *Early Years 11*, 1, 34–38.

Walkerdine, V. (1989) *Counting Girls Out*. London: Virago.

White, J. (1988) *The Assessment of Writing: Pupils Aged 11 and 15.* Windsor: NFER-Nelson.

Whyte, J. (1986) *Girls into Science and Technology: The Story of a Project.* London: Routledge and Kegan Paul.

Wilder, G.Z. and Powell, K. (1989) *Sex Differences in Test Performance: A Survey of the Literature.* College Board Report No. 88–1. New York: College Entrance Examination Board.

CHAPTER 7

Exploring, Sensibility and Wonder

Science with Young Children and Using the Senses

Kees Both

When you understand all about the sun and all about the atmosphere and all about the rotation of the earth, you may still miss the radiance of the sunset. There is no substitution for the direct perception of the concrete achievement of a thing in its actuality. We want concrete fact with a high light thrown on what is relevant to its preciousness.

Alfred North Whitehead

I know the answer, but what's the question?

Lazer Goldberg

What is it in the individual scientist's relation to nature that facilitates the kind of seeing that eventually leads to productive discourse?…one must have the time to look, the patience to 'hear what the material has to say to you', the openness to 'let it come to you'.

Evelyn Fox Keller, about Barbara McClintock

Introduction

Twenty-five years ago I was a firm believer in a process approach to primary science. At that time we were impressed by the rapidly growing amount of information that children were immersed in (especially by the influence of the TV) and by the rapidly expanding and changing sciences. A proverb we used frequently was: 'knowledge is like fish, it soon rots'. We also cited the wisdom of good old Heraklitos, who said: 'teaching is not filling a barrel, but lighting a fire'. It was not important *what* was learned, but *how* it was learnt. One had to learn how to learn and develop an attitude for life-long learning. Indeed many of the new science curricula that were developed in the 1970s in the UK and the USA supported us in these convictions. We, in the Netherlands and especially within the movement of the Jenaplan schools, were speaking about 'world orientation'. By this concept we meant a style of teaching and learning about the environment and the world-at-large in which first-hand experiences, seeing and hearing and touching and smelling, were basic and in which dialogues in the classroom about thoughts and feelings and the experiences of children, had a very central place. Developing independent learners and empowerment of children, especially socially and otherwise disadvantaged children, were important goals. Here, primary science had (and still has) much to offer.

Twenty-five years on, it must be said that there is a good deal of continuity between then and now. Despite changes in the political climate, in our country we (the Jenaplan schools in the Netherlands) still believe in the values of developing independent learners, critical thinking, first-hand experiences with the environment and world orientation, especially with younger children. There are however important discontinuities too, for example, we had to acknowledge that content, the *what* of teaching, really matters. Equally the kind of curriculum framework that is developed, whether it is a constraint or a support for teachers and children in their exploration of the world, is very important, especially if you value the quality instead of the quantity: 'less is more' as Americans say.

Continuity and Change: Towards a Creative Synthesis

In the Netherlands freedom in education – freedom for parents to choose a school for their children, freedom to start a school (under certain conditions) and freedom for schools to develop a specific profile – is part of a long tradition of living together with (mostly religious) minorities on a small piece of Earth. Within a common framework of general guidelines (a kind of core curriculum) a great variety of schools developed. Among these were low-profile state schools and schools based on religion and/or a specific philosophy of education: Montessori schools, Dalton schools, Freinet schools, Steiner schools and (the biggest group among these) Jenaplan schools, all financed on the same basis by the state. All schools with a specific philosophy of education have their roots in the 1910s and 1920s, in the innovative movement of the New Education Fellowship (later the World Education Fellowship) and the European part of it that has been named the 'New European Movement for the Reconstruction of Education' (*'Neu-Europäische Erziehungsbewegung'*;

Petersen, 1927). These movements had branches in many countries. Jenaplan schools originated in Jena, Germany where in 1923 Peter Petersen started an experimental school at the university. They were introduced into the Netherlands around 1960. The two main features of these schools are: grouping children in age-heterogeneous 'family groups' and the central place of 'world orientation' (including 'science') in the curriculum (Both, 1995a). Note that in 'world orientation' children are orienting themselves, and schools help them in *their* orientation!

The Jenaplan schools did pioneering work in the field of primary science in our country. They were influenced by curriculum projects of the 1970s such as Nuffield Junior Science and Science 5/13 from the UK, Elementary Science Study from the USA and the African Primary Science Programme.

In my opinion the Jenaplan movement in the Netherlands has shown that it is possible to look for a 'creative synthesis' between old and proven educational ideas, ideals and practices, and new developments in society, culture and educational research. There can be continuity on the basis of an open philosophy of education, and discontinuity and renewal[1] (Both, 1996): 'We need to build our conception of the school upon a broad and deep foundation that will prove capable of bearing a superstructure of flexible patterns. We shall get nowhere by continually demolishing and starting afresh' (King, 1967).

Ask the Spiders Themselves

In autumn there are phenomena that you can hardly escape if you are working with children aged four to ten: the spiders and their webs that are to be found everywhere, coloured leaves, many fungi, fruits and seeds, the spicy smell of decaying organic material and soil, the days that become shorter and temperature that is falling. You can't escape them, because almost all children have some natural interest in these kinds of things: observing; making some 'cloth' from gathering on a bent twig the loose-knit webs of the young spiders, in the form of a 'tennis racket'; collecting fallen leaves, fruits and seeds and where possible eating them. Very few children (and adults), if any, see or hear something of bird migration, despite the many times they have spoken about it and worked on it in school. Very few children (and adults) who have collected acorns and beech-

---

1   The actual philosophy of education of the Dutch Jenaplan schools is expressed in 20 'basic principles'. These are to be discussed and, if needed, revised every ten years.

nuts and have heard about the development of fruits and seeds from flowers, have ever seen the oaks and beeches flowering.

With a group of eight to nine year old children I started a study on spiders, because of the children's natural interest and because of the anxiety some of them expressed. I had seen many children active on this theme during playtime and asked them to express their feelings on spiders, what they already knew about them and what they wanted to ask about spiders. I showed them how to formulate their questions in such a way that they were directed to the spiders themselves: 'spider, may I ask you...?'. This methodology I had learned from the African Primary Science Programme: 'the ask the things themselves principle' (Duckworth, 1978; Elstgeest, 1971). The children were trained to ask questions in this way and asked among others these questions:

○ Why are there many more webs in autumn than in summer?

○ How do you make your thread and your web?

○ What do you eat?

○ Can you see well?

○ How many eyes do you have? (this child had heard that a spider has many eyes)

○ What kinds of spiders are there in our surroundings?

○ Does a female spider really eat the male after mating? (seen on TV)

○ Are you a female or a male?

○ What size of prey can you catch and eat?

○ Are there 'black widows' here? (a poisonous tropical species; the Netherlands does not have indigeneous spiders that are dangerous for humans)

○ I do see your web, but don't see you, are you still there?

○ Where do the threads of gossamer come from?

○ Why is it that I am afraid of spiders and my friend is not?

Before the investigations began I asked the children to draw, individually, a spider that makes the wheel-webs in the schoolgarden (the diadem or garden spider). Almost all the children drew a rather stereotyped spider, with a simple cross on its back shaped by two lines, I think because the name of this spider in Dutch is 'Cross-spider'. The drawings were displayed. After that the children made plans for investigating spiders, in little groups, on the basis of the questions they had put. How could they be answered? Which questions could be answered by the spiders themselves and which by second-hand resources? Could questions be reformulated to get an answer from the spider herself? What would one need to answer them?

All the children then had to make a new drawing of the garden spider, from observation, catching one and drawing it in the classroom or outside. This task led to discovering a surprising variety in the pattern of the spots of which the cross on the back is made and to discussions about this variety and about the parts of the spider's body and the number of legs. This led to better observation and to looking for new types of spiders, as well as a nice exhibition of spider drawings developed in the classroom.

The observation of prey-rests in the webs led to the idea of simple food chains, introduced by me: making little cards, connected like a chain, drawing and writing on them the two links observed and the hypothetical links before and after it. Many other observations and little experiments followed such as; throwing little things into the web and seeing what would happen; blowing a white powder (flour) into the web to make it more visible, the effect of which was that the spider started to eat her own web and build a new one (discussion: why did she do that?); also interviewing children and adults about their fear of spiders, etc. Equally important was the patience children had to show in observing the spider at work or in trying to discover things without disturbing it. I also introduced stories on spiders (about Arachne and Anansi), by telling and introducing reading materials, and we spoke about the anthropological background.

But how do you value this piece of practice as science education?

That depends of your view of the place of science in the primary school.

Why and What?

Why is science important for young children? The answer to this question depends on the kind of arguments for stimulating science in primary schools. David Hawkins once described three motivations for starting with science at an early age (Hawkins, 1984, p.29–31):

(1) Creating a fertile ground for the development of future scientists, especially in relationship to economic competition, to, 'refill the wells of available talent…by earlier and wider and more effective science education'. I would call this 'education for science'. Hawkins calls this, 'the narrow view'.

(2) A wider view, concerned with preparing youngsters for eventual participation in democratic discussion in a society heavily influenced by science and technology. Here it is important to prevent the development of a cultural proletariat. I would label this 'education in science'.

(3) A still wider view: the contribution of science education to the improvement of all education: *education through science*. Of course, this also has to make contributions to 'enlarging the pools of potential scientific talent and enhancing the qualities of intelligent citizenship', but these goals then have their place in a concern for the education of children as persons.

Lilian Weber, dedicated early childhood educator in the USA, expressed this in a nice way:

what I had to come to from my own experience with children – the enormous significance for children of the real world, emotionally and in making sense of what impacts on them and what changes around them – could only reinforce my already-firm conviction that it is absurd to discuss whether there should or should not be primary science in the curriculum. As long as the child inquires there is no way to eliminate primary science…the child of course continues his making-sense of the world anyway, necessarily and inevitably. (Weber, 1991)

Science is a human activity, a way of searching for meaning, searching for newness and for patterns in the natural world, for its own sake and for solving practical problems.

Putting it bluntly, science for young children must, in my opinion, concentrate on:

- learning (better) to see and to hear and to smell and to taste; in the spider example the improvement of observation by drawing and comparing and discussion; other examples: hearing the voices in the choir of birds in spring or of the geese flying over in winter; seeing the colours in soap-bubbles, etc. Of course I know that observation does not exist without some theoretical framework, but nevertheless it is the beginning and the end of science with children o learning to ask questions and devising simple ways to answer them

o inferring, connecting bits and pieces of knowledge and formulating hypotheses, as contributions to concept formation and learning to think

o communication about observations and interpretations

o reflection (dialogue)

o reporting: the reports of children's investigations can become a part of the reference library of the school, as a part of an ongoing movement, building on each other

o discovering that common things are fascinating if you concentrate on them, dive into the material and act on them in new ways

o feeding curiosity and the sense of wonder about nature

o exploring diversity in phenomena, some simple relationships and change

o developing of independence in learning and contributing to a feeling of control, as far as possible (Rowe, 1983)

o contributing to language development and the learning of mathematics (Weber and Dyasi, 1985)

o developing an attitude of alertness

o developing a sense of objectivity or intersubjectivity: 'how do you know?'

o developing a concern with people, animals, plants, things and places; of respect and reverence for life; here there are important links to environmental education and the arts (Margadant van Arcken, 1990).

These are all basic educational aims for the primary years, to which science can make an important contribution.[2]

---

2   Some books on play in the primary years reflect the same philosophy of education, especially if exploratory play is connected with reflection: see Moyles (1989) and Wassermann (1990).

Between Question and Answer

I am well aware of the expression 'the child as scientist' and the discussion around it (Both, 1995a; Driver, 1983). Much depends here upon the definition of 'scientist'. If you are emphasizing science as a means of the education of children and as a human activity, you can see some analogy between children growing into the world and what scientists are doing (cf.Lilian Weber, 1991). In particular, in the primary years an emphasis on process skills is important and legitimate (Harlen, 1992; Hodson, 1985).

In general you cannot grow up with science without having some idea of the processes of doing science. We must have moderate expectations (Millar and Driver, 1987), but most important here is the question: 'I know the answer, but what's the question?' (Goldberg, 1979). All knowledge is the result of people seeking answers to questions, whether on science, technology, the humanities, religion or another area of knowledge. Questions also play an important role in the development of children: explicit questions and questions implicit in the actions of children, their play and work. You can describe the interaction of children and the world around them as a dialogue, an interplay of question and answer. The things around them are asking questions, inviting the child to see, to hear, to manipulate, or sitting there and waiting for what will happen. The child is questioning the things around him or her by seeing and hearing and manipulating, etc., and science with young children develops between the questions and answers. Science can help children in specific ways to find answers to their questions, especially if there is a community of inquiry: the children in the classroom and the teacher, a community in which they can feel safe enough to reach some objectivity as a standard, being challenged by feedback from others, with the question: 'how do you know?'

Researchers of early childhood development (Hodgkin, 1976) including ethologists such as Niko Tinbergen (Tinbergen, 1975) have written about the curiosity in the environment which children show at a very early age, and they warn us not to underestimate the potential of young children. At the same time there is much 'learned helplessness', where, for example, children do not get adequate reactions to their questions. We can have a thorough belief in the powers of young children to build upon the information they receive.

Learning to See and Hear

I do not believe in an isolated training in seeing and hearing, there must be a meaningful context. In the past, educators such as Herbart and Pestalozzi, and later a curriculum-project like 'Science, a Process Approach', were looking for teaching methods that were independent of content and finding and training in general learning skills. Training the sensory skills of children was an important part of this process. Children must, however, understand as much as possible why they have to see and hear better, and also why they have to measure or classify or experiment. Research in the Netherlands revealed that in schools children often do so-called 'experiments' without knowing what they are doing and without any context (Margadant van Arcken and van Kempen, 1990). Training sessions with young children to improve seeing and hearing can be important (if needed), and often can be playful, but as much as possible should be connected with a meaningful context. In one school, for example, the children each year do exercises in handling binoculars and discriminating birdsong (from audiotapes or a CD) as a preparation for the annual bird census, mapping the territories of singing birds in a nearby park. You can't separate process from content in a rigid way.

Trust in Your Senses

Children must first learn to trust and refine their senses but later on they learn that our senses can betray us and have their restrictions. Alas, science education can also cause a premature and unnecessary mistrust in our own sensory perceptions. Fortunately I never found this in young children (there was not enough time to spoil them, I guess), but in older children in primary schools and in teachers I found it more than once. As a warning I will pay this some attention, because teachers can do much harm in this area (Wagenschein, 1977).

Once I gave a workshop for teachers on questioning and investigation (inspired by Harlen and Elstgeest, 1992). The topic was 'water'. The participants had to fill a medicine beaker to the brim and then to estimate how many drops they could add to it by a medicine-dropper, writing down their estimation. Many discovered that they had underestimated the amount of drops that could be added, by a ratio of 6–10. This activity caused a lot of interest and wonder. Later on they had to write down what had been seen and the questions that had arisen. In the collection of perceptions and questions two teachers declared that they had seen 'cohesion'. I asked them what exactly they had seen, and it was very difficult for them to describe. Other teachers tried to express their experience of the mysterious forces inside the water that are pulling the water together in images like a 'skin' over the surface of the water. Elstgeest (1975) gives this example:

I asked a student of mine (a student-teacher), holding a round flask filled with water at arm's length, to look through it at the building on the other side of the road and to tell me precisely what he saw.

'It is an image', he answered.

'No, tell me what you see.'

'It is refraction.'

'No, tell me what you actually see.'

'It is the angle of incidence,' he persisted.

'No, I want to know what you see,' I insisted.

'It is convex.'

'Oh come on, what does that house look like?'

'I see lateral inversion.'

I gave up.

An Heuristic Scheme

An heuristic scheme can help us in the planning of activities. This scheme has been used by Hawkins (1974) among others:

(1) *Organizing an encounter of the phenomena with the children*, for example by:

  o an observation circle: a teaching method or 'form of encounter' in which the children all are observing the same (kind of) thing – an instrument, an animal, a leaf, etc – and trying to communicate in a dialogue what they are perceiving. The other children try to see, etc. the same kind of thing; often questions are raised and little experiments can grow out of this intensive activity[3]. The teacher can prepare this lesson, but at the same time cannot fully foresee what the children will discover

  o a 'discovery-table' in the classroom

  o free exploration of the materials in groups ('messing about', Hawkins, 1974)

---

3 This way of working was first developed by the Belgian educator, Ovide Décroly and was later rather popular in the Jenaplan Schools in the Netherlands (Vreugdenhil, 1995).

- ○ different forms of fieldwork
- ○ children talking about their experiences or showing something they have found (Paull and Paull, 1973).

(2) Children asking questions about the phenomena.

(3) Discussing which questions can be answered immediately and which have to be researched. How can questions be formulated in a way that will get the information from the phenomena at hand? What questions deserve using second-hand resources?

(4) Planning investigations by and with the children about selected questions.

(5) Investigations undertaken by the children themselves.

(6) Reporting to other children. Discussion, criticism.

(7) Lessons by the teacher to place the discoveries in a broader framework.

It is possible for teachers to 'grow' into this scheme during the primary years and teach the children to become more and more independent learners. The scheme can also serve as an important heuristic method in the in-service education of teachers. It can be dealt with phase by phase, first, in a workshop with connected theory, and then trying it out in the classroom, sharing the experiences, and training in some skills.

Learning to ask questions and searching for answers can also be exercised by working with sealed boxes ('mystery boxes'), with something in them. The children have to find ways of finding out what is inside by manipulation, use of models, etc.

Questions: Going Back and Forth

Questions do have a key position in the heuristic method above. Often the questions of children must be reformulated into 'action-questions' and teachers should be trained to do this with children. Wynne Harlen and Jos Elstgeest (Elstgeest, 1985; Elstgeest and Harlen, 1990) developed a simple scheme of questions, each connected with ways of answering them:

- ○ 'What' questions: What is it? What does it do? Have you seen (heard, etc.) that? etc.;
- ○ 'How much?' questions;
- ○ 'How different?' questions;
- ○ 'What happens if?' questions;

- 'How could you?' questions;

- 'How?' questions: How does it come about? How does it work? How are...related?;

- 'Why?' questions.

It's an art for teachers to go back and forth in this scheme of questions. If, for example, children ask why the colours in soap-films are there (a very difficult question for children and many adults!), they can go back to questions like: what colours do you see? Are they always the same ? Can you draw them? Do they change with time? Is it possible to make soap-bubbles without these colours? etc. Comparisons in time, space and conditions can lay a basis for the 'difficult answer', if it can be given. Teachers often stress 'why' questions and children also want to know why, but even if you can't find an exact answer, you can still discuss the question and discover interesting things.

The Book with the Empty Space

Years ago I bought a book on education; at home I skimmed through it and discovered a page without any text or illustration. I guessed it had to be a printing fault and called the bookshop. When someone at the other end of the line was comparing other copies of the book I read the page before the empty page and saw:

Suppose all the syllabi and curricula and textbooks in the schools disappeared. Suppose all of the standardized tests were lost. In other words, suppose that the most common material impeding innovation in the school simply did not exist. Then suppose that you decided to turn this 'catastrophe' into an opportunity to increase the relevance of the schools. What would you do? We have a possibility for you to consider: suppose that you decide to have the entire 'curriculum' consisting of questions. These questions would have to be worth seeking answers to not only from your point of view but, more importantly, from the point of view of the students. In order to get still closer to reality, add the requirement that the questions must help the students to develop and internalize concepts that will help them to survive in the rapidly changing world of the present and future... What questions would you have on your list? Take a pencil and list your questions on the next page, which we have left blank for you. (Postman and Weingartner, 1972)

I apologized to the bookseller and started thinking about this question about questions. If you take children seriously as investigators, searching for meaning, you are touching a powerful source of motivation in children.

In the approach I described above, the questions of the children are taken seriously and at the same time the children are not left alone with their questions, but encouraged to seek answers.[4]

A Framework for World Orientation

Schemes of questions, and going back and forth within schemes of questions, are important for teachers and staffs to give continuity to the work of children. The problem is that teachers experience a conflict between recognizing the importance of in-depth work with children and time-pressure. Teachers feel that 'less is more', that you have to restrict yourself in content, and, for that reason, they also are looking for overlaps in goals and content of primary science with more or less related areas. To help schools in this work, the Dutch Jenaplan Association asked the National Institute for Curriculum Development to develop with and for the Jenaplan schools a new curriculum for world orientation, in which all aspects have their balanced place (Both, 1995b). In addition, it had to meet the guidelines of the national curriculum which was at the end of its development phase.

Seven areas of experience have been defined, that fulfil several criteria; among them:

° not separating nature and human society, but connecting them where possible

° the possibility of connecting predisciplinary goals, content and activities with the subjects later on; the latter have their roots within the 'areas of experience', as is visualized in Figure 7.1.

In Figure 7.2 below an overview is given of the areas of experience, with the domains within each of them.

For each domain, aims and learning experiences have been described for the youngest, the middle and the oldest children of the primary range (in age-heterogeneous groups or 'family groups') that

---

4   See the chapter on 'Encouraging and handling children's questions', in Harlen and Elstgeest (1992) for a discussion of the interplay between children questioning and teachers helping children to find instruments for finding answers to their questions. Dillon (1988) is also an important source on teaching and questioning.

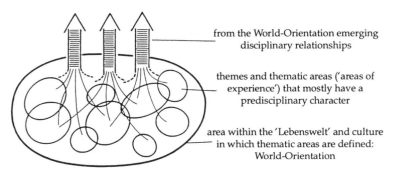

from the World-Orientation emerging
disciplinary relationships

themes and thematic areas ('areas of
experience') that mostly have a
predisciplinary character

area within the 'Lebenswelt' and culture
in which thematic areas are defined:
World-Orientation

Source: adapted from: Köhnlein, 1985
Figure 7.1 World Orientation

A key to the world

Making and Using

Labour/work
Consumption
Sustainability

Technology

Constructions
Machines and tools
Big systems
Matter and energy
Living with technology

Communication

With other people
With and in nature
With the transcendent
(the Other)

Environment and Landscape

Habitat of people
Habitat of plants/animals
The Earth
as a Place to Live
Spatial planning

Living together

Belonging
Conditions
for a good society
One World

All the year round

Seasons
Feasts and celebrations
The schoolyear

My life

Me
Being human
"Great" people

Figure 7.2 Goals and content in World Orientation Science

give (an open) structure to the world orientation in the Jenaplan schools and that enable the schools to make world orientation ever more the centre of their curriculum. I give some examples of the science goals and content in 'Environment and Landscape' below. The basis for this area of experience is the metaphor of the earth as a *home* (*oikos*), an ecological viewpoint. Important key concepts are: life, diversity, adaptation, behaviour (both intra- and interspecific), 'worlds' of a certain organism (auto-ecologically seen), ecotopes (or 'houses', such as a tree, a pond, a plot of grassland, etc., all with different inhabitants that relate to each other and to non-living things and factors; a synecological viewpoint), the food-chain, the progressive cycle of substances and decomposition and the biosphere (the earth as a home in space).

Important skills are: observation, drawing, description of organisms, classifying plants and animals (to self-chosen and given criteria), using and making simple identification keys, mapping and carrying out simple experiments about environmental conditions. Important activities include:

(1) *For the youngest groups (4–6 years old)*: caring for plants and knowing what they need; growing plants from seeds; study of one kind of 'minibeast' in its natural environment and also in some artificial environment within the classroom; visiting the same habitat regularly and looking for plants and animals and at their behaviour; looking at the Sun and following it during the day and seeing where the Sun can throw more and less of its light.

(2) *For the middle-groups (6–9 years old)*: mapping a not too complicated small area and its inhabitants; collecting, observing, describing and classifying invertebrate animals; identifying plants and animals by using simple keys and reference books; soil studies, observing a (species of) animal in its natural environment and trying to learn as much about it as we can, adopting a piece of land and doing conservation work and monitoring the situation from year to year; detailed studies of the sun during the day ('daytime astronomy').

(3) *For the oldest primary groups (9–12 years old)*: designing a simple identification key; mapping/visualizing a structural, more complicated small area and its inhabitants and possible relationships with non-living components, studying the world of one species of plant or animal (including its dispersion), aiming at the idea of adaptation; comparing some closely related habitats (e.g. types of grassland) and their inhabitants; observing the colours, forms and behaviour of some animals

and plants in the environment and trying to find some form–function relationships; comparing these results with species far away; experiencing dimensions in space, by studying the earth in space also by way of pictures from the book *Powers of Ten*. (Morrison, 1982)

In the same way the science content of 'making and using' can be described, with a lot of physics ('kitchen physics') and chemistry (chemical changes in production processes), as well as for 'technology' and the other areas of experience.

Some Concluding Remarks

Some of the insights of twenty-five years ago have now been reinforced in a new way, especially by developments in the cognitive sciences, such as metacognition, while others have been refuted. As a result of working in an open educational tradition, it is possible to find a creative synthesis of the old and the new, without having to make a completely new start and thereby destroying the old before making progress.

I think that in the broad view of science education that I have tried to sketch, it is more important to develop in young children sensibility and sensitivity to the world, alertness and well-rooted knowledge, rather than covering a broad spectrum. Consider the quotation about Barbara McClintock at the beginning of this chapter: taking the time to look...to hear what the material has to say to you, the openness to let it come to you (Fox Keller, 1983). At this level there are still close connections between science and art. The ancient Greeks had a nice concept for the sensual experience that can be the common root of science and art: *aisthesis* (Giel, 1994). It is the sensuous quality of the experience of both that makes sense. Later on in education there is more distance between arts and science, but we can look for connections and interactions. In ecology there are the writings of Annie Dillard (especially *Pilgrim at Tinker Creek* (1975)) and Aldo Leopold (1989) as important examples of such an *aisthesis*. It is possible to work with children in the same spirit. In areas such as pattern, size and scale in nature there is the example of D'Arcy Thompson (On *Growth and Form* (1988)) as a lasting source of inspiration (see also Stevens 1976; Wechsler 1981 and the volumes in the *Science 5/13* series about 'Structure and forces' (James, 1972)). In Germany the 'grand old man' of science education, Martin Wagenschein, developed an approach to science education using (Socratic) dialogues with children. These were connected with hands-on activities, demonstrations (including 'discrepant events'), telling stories and using selected and potentially fruitful examples (*exemplarisches lehren und lernen*; Wagenschein, 1977, 1990, 1992), as a contribution towards teaching for quality, that is, 'less is more',[5] in which there are sensory, bodily and aesthetic experiences and the emergence of objective, 'scientific' ways of thinking (see also Rumpf, 1990, 1993). Questions such as: 'How did people discover how to make fire?', 'How can a ship, made of iron, float?', 'What is a good ball to play with?' are the starting points for an intensive process of searching for answers (Thiel, 1987). In the question about 'the good ball' the teacher starts with a demonstration of dropping two balls and has the children watch and think. After that many activities develop: intense discussions about what happens if a ball bounces, discussions and experiments in small groups (formulating and testing hypotheses), reporting in a circle-discussion, proposals by the teacher for a more precise experiment, all ending with the story about the veterinary surgeon (Dunlop) who invented more or less by accident, but by analogy with the air-filled football, the pneumatic tyre.[6]

In all of this the key word is 'wonder'; developing a sense of wonder (Verhoeven, 1972; Weisskopf, 1979). Rachel Carson (1987) writes in her pedagogical book *The Sense of Wonder* (and I hope you can feel the wisdom behind her somewhat romanticized view of childhood):

> A child's world is fresh and new and beautiful, full of wonder and excitement. It is our misfortune that for most of us that clear-eyed vision, that true instinct for what is beautiful and awe-inspiring, is dimmed and even lost before we reach adulthood. If I had influence with the good fairy who is supposed to preside over the christening of all children, I should ask that her gift to each child in the world would be a sense of wonder so undestructible that it would last throughout life, as an unfailing antedote against the boredom and disenchantment of later years, the sterile preoccupation with things that are artificial, the alienation from the sources of our strength.

I think with young children science has the potential to make an important contribution to cultivating this sense of wonder.

---

5 The approach of Wagenschein and the people that are working in his spirit is to be characterized as: genetic–socratic–exemplary; 'genetic' because of the 'genesis' ('emergence') of the understanding of children and of the use, where possible, of historical examples. There are often some parallels (note: I am not speaking about some way of 'recapitulation theory'!) between the development of scientific ideas in children and the history of science, for example, children sometimes think in 'Aristotelean' ways.

6 I hope that the Wagenschein tradition can be discussed and tried in the English-speaking world too.

References

Both, K. (1985) *De natuur van natuuronderwijs en natuuronderwijs in de basisschool* (The nature of science and science in the primary school). Enschede: SLO, Institute for Curriculum Development.

Both, K. (ed) (1995a) *Jenaplan Schools in The Netherlands: A Reader.* Amersfoort: CPS.

Both, K. (1995b) *Weltorientiering Jenaplan: einige Texte (Worlrd Orientation and Jenaplan).* Amersfoort: CPS.

Carson, R. (1987) *The Sense of Wonder.* New York: Harper and Row.

D'Arcy Thompson (1988) *On Growth and Form.* (Abridged Edition) Cambridge: Cambridge University Press.

Dillard, A. (1975) *Pilgrim at Tinker Creek.* London: Picador.

Dillon, J.T. (1988) *Questioning and Teaching, A Manual of Practice.* London/Sydney: Croom Helm.

Driver, R. (1983) *The Pupil as Scientist?* Milton Keynes: Open University Press.

Duckworth, E. (1978) *The African Primary Science Program: An Evaluation and Extended Thoughts.* Grand Folks (ND): University of North Dakota.

Elstgeest, J. (1971) 'Ask the ant lion: the growth of an African primary science unit.' In P.E. Richmond (ed) *New Trends in Integrated Science Teaching, Vol. 1.* Paris: Unesco.

Elstgeest, J. (1975) New Science and Old Cultures. Paper presented to the International Conference on Physics Education, University of Edinburgh, July 29 – August.

Elstgeest, J. (1985) 'The right answer at the right time.' In W. Harlen (ed) *Primary Science: Taking the Plunge.* London: Heinemann.

Elstgeest, J. and Harlen, W. (1990) *Environmental Science in the Primary School.* London: Paul Chapman.

Fox Keller, E. (1983) *A Feeling for the Organism: The Life and Work of Barbara McClintock.* New York: Freeman.

Giel, K. (1994) 'Versuch über den schulpädagogischen Ort des Sachunterrichts.' In R. Lauterbach (ed) *Curriculum Sachunterricht* (A Search for the Right Place of Primary Science in an Educational Theory). Kiel: Institut für die Pädagogik der Naturwissenschaften/Gesellschaft für Didaktik des Sachunterrichts.

Goldberg, L. (1979) 'I know the answer, but what's the question?' *Science and Children 16*, 5, 8–9.

Harlen, W. (1992) 'Research and the development of science in the primary school.' *International Journal of Science Education 14*, 5, 491–503.

Harlen, W. and Elstgeest, J. (1992) *UNESCO Sourcebook for Science in the Primary School: A Workshop Approach to Teacher Education.* Paris: UNESCO.

Hawkins, D. (1974) 'Messing about in science.' In D. Hawkins *The Informed Vision: Essays on Learning and Human Nature.* New York: Agathon.

Hawkins, D. (1984) 'Nature closely observed.' *Outlook 52*, 27–50. Reprinted from *Daedalus 112* (1983), 2.

Hodgkin, R. (1976) *Born Curious.* London: John Wiley and Sons.

Hodson, D. (1985) 'Philosophy of science, science and science education.' *Studies in Science Education 12*, 25–57.

James, A. (1972) *Science 5/13: Structures and Forces, Stages 1 and 2.* London: Macdonald Educational.

King, R. (1967) 'The bridge of Jena.' *The New Era 48*, 3, March 38–43.

Köhnlein, W. (1985) 'Kindliches Denken und physikbezogener Sachunterricht' (Childrens' Thinking and Physics in Primary Science). *Sachunterricht und Mathematik in der Primarstufe 13*, 2, 73–78.

Leopold, A. (1989) *A Sand County Almanac and Sketches Here and There.* New York/London: Oxford University Press.

Margadant van Arcken, M. (1990) 'Nature experience of 8–12-year-old children.' Phenomenology and Pedagogy 8, 86–94.

Margadant van Arcken, M. and van Kempen, M. (1990) *Groen Verschiet, natuurbeleving en natuuronderwijs bij acht – tot twaalfjarige kinderen* ('Green vista'). The Hague: SDU.

Millar, R. and Driver, R. (1987) 'Beyond processes. *School Science Review 14*, 33–62.

Paull, J. and Paull, D. (1973) *Yesterday I Found...* Boulder: Mountainview Center of Environmental Education .

Petersen, P. (1927) *Die Neu-europäische Erziehungsbewegung* (The New European Educational Movement). Weimar: Böhlaus Nachfolger.

Postman, N. and Wiengartner, C. (1972) *Teaching as a Subversive Activity.* Harmondsworth: Penguin Books.

Rowe, M.B. (1983) 'Science and fate control: implications for the teaching of primary level science.' In W. Harlen (ed) *New Trends in Primary School Science Education Vol.1.* Paris: UNESCO).

Rumpf, H. (1990) 'Von der Stoffbeherrschung zur Weltaufmerksamkeit.' (From Mastery of Content to Sensibility of the World). In H. Mikelskis *Umweltbildung in Schleswig-Holstein*, Flensburg.

Rumpf, H. (1993) 'Erlebnis und Begriff, Verschiedene Weltzugänge imUmkreis von Piaget, Freud and Wagenschein.*Zeitschrift für Pädagogik 37*, 3, 329–346.

Stevens, P. (1976) *Patterns in Nature.* Harmondsworth: Penguin Books.

Thiel, S. (1987) 'Wie springt ein Ball?' ('How does a ball bounce?') *Die Grundschule 19*, 1, 18–21.

Tinbergen, N. (1975) 'The importance of being playful.' *The Times Educational Supplement*, 1st October.

Verhoeven, C. (1972) *The Philosophy of Wonder.* New York: Macmillan.

Vreugdenhil, K. (1995) 'De observatiekring.' (The observation-circle). In A. Boes (ed) *Gesprekken in de kring.* (Dialogue and circle-discussions). Hoevelaken: CPS.

Wagenschein, M. (1977) 'Rettet die Phänomene' (Save the appearances). *Der Mathematische und Naturwissenschaftliche Unterricht 30*, 3, 129–137.

Wagenschein, M. (1990) *Kinder auf dem Wege zu Physik.* (Children on the road to physics). Weinheim/Basel: Beltz.

Wagenschein, M. (1992) *Verstehen lehren.* ('Teaching for Understanding'). Weinheim/Basel: Beltz.

Wassermann, S. (1990) *Serious Players in the Primary Classroom. Empowering Children Through Active Learning Experience.* New York/London: Teachers College Press.

Weber, L. (1991) *Inquiry, Noticing, Joining With and Following After.* New York: Workshop Center City College.

Weber, L. and Dyasi, H. (1985) 'Language development and observation of the local environment: first steps in providing primary-school science education for non-dominant groups.' *Prospect XV*, 4, 565–567.

Wechsler, J. (ed) (1981) *On Aesthetics in Science*. Cambridge, MA: MIT Press.

Weil, S. (1987) *The Need for Roots. Prelude to a Declaration of Duties Towards Mankind*. London: Routledge and Kegan Paul.

Weisskopf, V.F. (1979) *Science and Wonder, the Natural World as Man Knows It*. Cambridge, MA: MIT Press.

Further Reading

Morrison, Ph. and Ph./C. and R. Eames (1982) *Powers of Ten: Dimensions in the Universe*. New York/Oxford: Freeman.

Moyles, J. (1989) *Just Playing? The Role and Status of Play in Early Childhood Education*. Milton Keynes/Philadelphia: Open University Press.

CHAPTER 8

Science and Technology Teacher Education for K-2

Virgin Territory

Naama Sabar

Everything I really have to know about how to live and what to do and how to behave, I learned in kindergarten. Wisdom is not to be found at the peak of the academic hill, but rather in the sandbox of kindergarten.

Robert Fulghum (1989)

Introduction

Education begins at birth, but in the formal process of a child's education, pre-school education is the first and the most notable phase: initial, hesitant steps, leading to more confident strides on the long journey down the highway of information and knowledge. It is universally agreed that early childhood is the critical period for developing the foundations for the mental functions of learning and study habits, for nurturing natural curiosity and for developing observation skills and positive attitudes towards learning.

It is the basic premise of this chapter that the task of pre-school and early childhood education is to set goals which will lead all young children to the fulfilment of their potential, for their own sakes and for the benefit of the society in which they are growing up. Thus major investments in research and in professional development should centre on early child education.

I will first examine the highly developed early childhood educational system in Israel, where the level of science and technology is perceived as an indicator of advancement. Next, I will briefly discuss the situation in other countries, identify some of the universal problems in this area of early science education, state my own beliefs on science for early childhood, mention some generally agreed-upon assumptions on teacher education, and present guidelines recommended for science and technology teacher education for K-2. Finally, I will refer to some of the dilemmas which must still be dealt with.

Science and Technology in Israel's Kindergartens

In the last three years, since the publication of a special report by the Harrari Commission (1992) which studied science and technology needs, a strongly budgeted program called '1998 is Tomorrow' has been underway in Israel's K-2, aimed at advancing science and technology. The formal syllabus for science and technology in early childhood, entitled 'Computers, science and technology in kindergartens' which is part of '1998 is Tomorrow', is reflected in an official report by the Ministry of Education (Levite, 1995), and includes the following aspects:

(1) *Computers in kindergartens.* Today some 3150 of the 4000 kindergartens in the country have computers.

(2) *Fostering science and technology activities for pre-schoolers.* About 50 per cent of the kindergartens have integrated science programs in their curricula, using science kits and aids as part of the basic kindergarten equipment.

(3) *Advancing the study of media and communication technologies.* The aim of this program is to promote understanding of what is seen and heard in the mass media, exposure to the language of communication and the acquisition of critical and effective television viewing habits. During the 1994/95 school year, 600 kindergartens used this media 'consumption' program.

(4) *Preparing educators, inspectors, kindergarten teachers and counsellors.* Training modules were constructed for these educational workers.

(5) *Ongoing counselling and guidance, evaluation and supervision.* A national centre provides counselling for inspectors, teacher trainers, educational counsellors and kindergarten teachers.

The above-mentioned report indicates that this system is currently deployed in seven district centres and that some 70 teacher trainers (all of them active kindergarten teachers) are working with 'Computers, science and technology in kindergarten'. In addition to descriptive data and statistics, the report includes a 25 minute-long video on the many and varied early childhood science activities being carried out in kindergartens and in science museums. The purpose of the film is to demonstrate what can and is being done in practice.

Though in the report and the film these official programs seem very impressive, my visits to K-2 classes, teacher training colleges and science teaching centres, and interviews with teachers, supervisors, curriculum developers, teacher trainers and science educators, indicated that there is a gap between the official reports (the desired curricula) and the outstanding science and technology kits (the written curricula) on the one hand, and in what goes on in the everyday reality (the experiential curricula), on the other.

In the field, I learned that many early childhood teachers do not even open the science kits. They are afraid of teaching science because they lack knowledge and understanding and, even worse, they often hate science and technology, and suffer from 'maths anxiety'. This probably stems from their secondary school science experience, what Janette Griffin (1995, personal communication) characterizes as 'anti-science'.[1] Another possible explanation is the fact that the overwhelming majority of K-2 teachers are female, and it has been found that confidence in females in relation to both information technology and teaching science is significantly lower than in males (Harlen, Holroyd and Byrne, 1995).

The case of computers in Israeli kindergartens is somewhat better since computers are used as a means of communication, but still very different from the image we get from the official report. Here I should like to add a word of caution to those who produce official reports: they too often attempt to paint an extremely rosy picture of their areas of responsibility. In doing so, they may be cutting off the

---

1 Griffin views the current criticism of secondary science in the following way:
    Secondary science is often fact-driven – based on a positivistic view of science, which is not the currently accepted view of the nature of science. The students are set experiments to do using 'science equipment' to 'prove' the theory which they have just 'covered'. Each student does one experiment. If the answer they get is different to what the teacher tells them they should get, they are deemed 'wrong'. They write down the 'right' answer and then write a conclusion based on *one* test. This is hardly what science itself is about! On top of this, all they get is big words, out of context, no clear connections or relationships between ideas, etc.
    Unfortunately, the bulk of today's primary teachers suffered all this! It is no wonder that they do not like or in fact fear science. The thing that we have found we have to do with our student teachers is to tell them to forget all that; that primary science is a different discipline; and that it is possible to learn science without test tubes and Bunsen burners - in fact it is possible to learn, or rather experience science, rather than 'doing' it!
    I think we need to help teachers of young children to recognize that science is about wonder, curiosity, imagination, discovering how *their* world works and why, or in the words of Eleanor Duckworth: 'The having of wonderful ideas' (Griffin 1995).

branch on which they sit: if things are so good, efforts and resources may be diverted to new areas much sooner than intended by those responsible for the reports.

In spite of the criticism I have raised, and though the Israeli case is not as ideal as the official documents would like to pretend, there is a significant awareness of the importance of early childhood science and technology, and steps are being taken to implement changes and make them felt in the schools.

Having observed the gap between the ideal and the experiential science curriculum in Israel (Goodlad, Klein and Tye, 1979; Sabar, 1986), the next step is to examine what is happening in this field in other countries. While some countries, such as England, Scotland, Wales, the United States, Australia and the Philippines, to mention but a few, have highly developed teacher education science programs for primary school, these are mainly geared to grades 3–6. This is the case in spite of the fact that in most countries in the world, kindergarten teachers today are expected to teach health (rules of hygiene) and basic concepts in environmental studies (nature observations), and to do so without the benefit of science education training. In South Korea, a technologically advanced nation, for example, there are only a very small number of computers in K-2. There, it is up to the teacher to take the initiative and enrol in a course in a science centre and to find the means to equip her class with computers if this is what she wants.

We are dealing here with the intersection of three fields of study: early childhood education, science and technology education, and teacher education. When I began to review the literature, I was astonished to discover how few studies had been published. Each separate field has received its share of research; each combination of two fields has received some theoretical and practical attention; but the combination of the three has rarely been studied.

The current situation can be represented through a Venn diagram (Figure 8.1), in which early childhood education, which began receiving formal attention a century ago, represents the largest portion; and the two other fields, which have moved to the forefront only during the last few decades, have less accumulated experience. As a result, the intersecting zone is very small.

Several difficulties have led to the above, widespread, state of affairs. Some of these difficulties are generic to teacher education, to early childhood or to science and technology teaching, and some are specific to the combination of the three fields:

(1) Science education is less attractive than other fields of teacher education. Science and technology are considered difficult

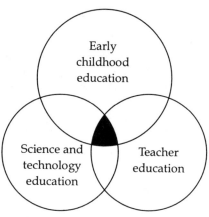

Figure 8.1 Sources of science and technology teacher education for K2

subjects of study, and in Western countries they attract fewer and fewer students (Fraser-Abiter, 1992).

(2) Liking children (the reason for choosing to teach K-2) does not mean liking science. But it should, because liking children should mean letting them do what they like to do (within reason), which is in fact discovering and deciphering their world – which is science (Griffin, 1995, personal communication). However, the formal way in which science teaching is presented to early childhood student teachers, does not define science as such. It is especially difficult to teach science and technology to these student teachers, since they often disliked the subject intensely in their own schooling (Stavy, 1984). Those who enjoyed science and wish to combine it with education, choose, for the most part, to teach in secondary schools.

(3) Science and technology teacher education for early childhood is a newly emerging field. There is no previous experience to draw upon; studies and programs in this area are still in an embryonic state. What we have now, if anything, is rhetoric about the importance of the field rather than a sound basis from which to learn.

(4) Lack of congruency between various teacher educators in teacher training is a hindrance to both the student teacher and the newly qualified teacher. In science teacher education, the university or teacher college lecturers represent one component in the system and the teacher trainers in the classroom, another. Often these teacher educators themselves

have no specific training and rely on their own traditional teacher training. This often leads to clashing approaches. Once the student teacher becomes a practising 'novice' teacher he or she faces additional incongruencies. These may arise from the classroom reality, the principal's expectations, the parents' expectations or even the supervisor's approach, some or all of which may not coincide with the college approach.

(5) Early childhood education prepares generalists who specialize in the cognitive development of this age level. Given that this is the stage where important foundations are laid, many areas of learning compete for time in the teacher education curriculum. Science is not necessarily considered to be as important in early childhood development as other areas such as language, expressive arts or personal development. If a program calls for science and technology training, this will come at the expense of other subjects such as art, drama, language skills, music, etc. It is difficult for a K-2 teacher education curriculum developer to make the decision to replace an existing subject with an alternative one.

These difficulties should be viewed in the framework of what is today accepted as the knowledge base for teaching, as delineated by Shulman (1987):

- Subject matter knowledge – about facts and concepts; the substantive structures by which the discipline is organized; the syntactic structure through which new knowledge is gained; and teachers' attitudes towards the subject matter (Grossman, Wilson and Shulman, 1989).

- General pedagogical knowledge – about classroom management and organization that transcends subject matter.

- Curriculum knowledge – the guidelines, national requirements and materials available.

- Pedagogical content knowledge – about how to teach the subject matter, including useful illustrations, powerful analogies and examples.

- Knowledge of learners and their characteristics.

- Knowledge of educational contexts.

- Knowledge of educational goals, values and purposes, including the history and philosophy of education.

This theoretical model of the knowledge base for teaching, while still being developed, appears to be a relevant conceptual framework for the present discussion. Literature on teacher thinking recognizes the influence that the knowledge base has on the practice of teaching, though research on the links between teachers' knowledge and classroom instruction is still in a primary stage (Shafriri, 1993).

What is clear is that pedagogical content knowledge, no less than subject matter knowledge, is critical for successful teaching. The teacher is expected to be able to delve deeply into the basic concepts of the field, to select suitable examples which clarify the topic, to recognize the difficulties pupils encounter when studying concepts and the processes related to them (Tamir, 1988).

In addition, many researchers contend that there is a connection between teachers' knowledge bases and their instruction, and much research on effective teaching relates to the teacher's content and pedagogical content knowledge, as reflected in the teaching of specific topics in the field (i.e. Baxter, 1990; Grossman *et al.*, 1989). This position is supported by educational psychologists who contend that there can be no content-free instruction (Perkins and Salmon, 1989).

Of the various elements comprising Shulman's knowledge base for teaching, only subject matter knowledge, which continues to develop during a teacher's professional life, can be thoroughly taught during pre-service teacher training. All the other kinds of knowledge develop during the actual instruction and are contextually related to school and teaching. Throughout, it is the subject matter knowledge which is the foundation of the entire knowledge base for teaching.

The difficulty lies in the fact that subject matter knowledge is so often the weakest link in the chain. As practitioners, teachers become professionals who need to know what it means to be scientifically literate. They need theoretical and practical knowledge of both teaching and learning science. All professional development, beginning with undergraduate teacher training and continuing into the professional development of practising teachers, aims at enabling teachers to understand and use the techniques and perspectives of inquiry. Standards for professional development in terms of content, processes and structures, are applicable to all activities and programs that occur throughout a teacher's career.

In order to determine how best to prepare science teachers for K-2, I should first state my own beliefs regarding young children's science education. Then I will present some generally agreed-upon assumptions regarding teacher education. Based on these two foundations I will recommended some guidelines.

Science and Technology Education for Young Children: My Beliefs

These can be outlined as follows:

(1) The integration of the child into his/her environment requires familiarity with natural phenomena, with simple scientific and technological principles and with their daily occurrence.

(2) Introducing the child in an exciting way to subjects in science and technology at an early age is a basis for his or her continuing interest in the subject.

(3) The child's natural curiosity spurs his or her interest in natural phenomena and moves the child towards understanding simple scientific processes and innovative technologies. Science is best understood by young children when presented as part of the world around them, in an integrated form and not in separate fields.

(4) To achieve interesting and pleasurable learning in science the preparation should encompass understanding of both *how* children learn and *what* they learn, and these depend both on the teacher's role and on the organization of the school. Decisions about curricula of primary school science and their implementation should be based on a clear view of the kind of learning that is intended (Harlen, 1993). Many of these decisions need to be taken by the teachers, based on pupils' interests and abilities and the teacher's own inclinations (Sabar, 1994). The teacher should actively provide opportunities for all learners to develop ideas, skills and attitudes.

(5) Familiarity with, and understanding of, processes and phenomena in the physical environment and in nature foster a positive emotional relationship to the environment and contribute to the alleviation of anxieties. Fostering a positive attitude towards the landscape and surroundings, and acquiring involvement and responsibility (Elstgeest and Harlen, 1990), develop in the child a sense of belonging to, and love for, his/her country.

(6) One of the most important scientific skills – observation – really means developing the senses. Children can be taught many aspects of science without calling them science; moving away from teaching separately labelled disciplines could result in teaching science without the fear attached to it.

Complementary to these points are some generally agreed-upon assumptions concerning science teacher education (Fraser-Abiter,

1992; Parker, 1982; Standards for the Professional Development of Teachers of Science, 1995) and the kind of teachers for young children we are looking for:

(1) The aim should be science literacy for all. Science is for everyone and not only for exclusive populations. Science programs should prepare teachers who have appropriate skills and teach multi-cultural populations, including girls and students-at-risk.

(2) Student teachers should be taught in ways that they themselves are expected to teach. Student teachers are as heterogeneous as schoolchildren; therefore training them calls for all the strategies relevant to heterogeneous school populations. Since students of education have usually internalized the practices of their own teachers, they enter the classroom prepared to teach as they were taught (Lortie, 1975). The approach intended for teachers to take – i.e., whether process-oriented science teaching, learning-by-inquiry, integrated science and technology, or constructive learning are advocated – should be reflected in how teachers themselves are taught. Whatever approach is adopted, an effort must be made actively to remove students' negative secondary school views of science lessons (Griffin, 1995, personal communication).

(3) Teachers need to be life-long learners, especially in this age of information; teacher development is a continuous, life-long process (Lieberman and Miller, 1994). Science changes continually, and a teacher's education in the sciences must keep pace. Teachers can not possibly expect to learn at the pre-service stage all they need for their teaching. Therefore teacher education should continue on into the in-service phase when teachers answer their professional needs through continuing education. Life-long learning should also be the message to their pupils.

(4) What kind of a teacher of young children do we seek? The answer to this question is a skilful teacher, since a skilful teacher of young children is well on the way to becoming a good teacher of science. This is the kind of science teacher that teacher training institutions should aim at. In fact, teaching science is easier than teaching many other subjects because most children, given the opportunity, are enthusiastic about learning it. Science provides plenty of opportunity for using materials and for sharing, outdoors as well as within the classroom (Blough and Schwartz, 1979).

Recommended Guidelines for Science and Technology in Early Childhood Teacher Education

Drawing from the above, I would like to recommend the following guidelines which have been designed for science and technology teacher education for K-2.

The professional development of the teacher is analogous to the development of other professionals (Standards for the Professional Development of Teachers of Science, 1995). Opportunities are provided to observe and talk with master practitioners, to study research on learning and teaching practice, and to reflect on and conduct research on one's own practice (Richardson, 1994; Rudduck and Hopkins, 1985).

In presenting specific recommendations regarding science and technology for early childhood teacher education programs, I will first state problems identified earlier and subsequently formulate specific recommendations which aim to alleviate each specific problem.

Problem 1

Science is a subject often disliked by early childhood student teachers, and is associated with lack of confidence resulting in anxiety.

Recommendation 1

Clarify what science is; distinguish the reality of the discipline from what the student teacher did at school; aim at gradually building up a solid science base; teach science in an enthusiastic, joyful way; build up confidence in how to learn about science. All teachers of science should have a strong, broad base of scientific understanding.

Science teacher education should emphasize the 'big ideas' of science, the overarching concepts which pull major components together, and not get bogged down in irrelevant details. Teachers should provide not detailed factual knowledge, but a large range of experiences. Children will then be able to call on this store when needed, to help them develop their own theories about things they meet and questions they have about their environment. These mental and manual experiences will serve as the raw materials for constructing their own understanding.

Science learning experiences should:

○ enable teachers to understand the nature of science itself, of scientific inquiry and its central role in science, and to know how to use the skills and processes of scientific inquiry;

○ involve student teachers in actively investigating scientific phenomena, interpreting results and making personal sense of findings in a way that is consistent with currently accepted scientific understanding, building on their current knowledge of science content;

○ address issues, events or problems significant in science as well as of interest to participants;

○ introduce teachers to scientific literature, media, and technological resources that expand their science knowledge and enhance their ability to access further knowledge;

○ build on the teacher's current science knowledge, skills and attitudes and enable them to make conceptual connections within and across scientific disciplines, including mathematics and technology;

○ incorporate ongoing reflection on processes and outcomes, and on understanding science through inquiry;

○ encourage and support teachers in their efforts to collaborate with others;

○ help teachers use scientific knowledge and disposition of mind as a basis for decision-making when dealing with societal issues.

Early childhood teachers are generalists. They may know the names of birds and flowers, but they may not know that parts of flowers are also concerned with plant reproduction; they may also not perceive science as a tool for children's development. This is why they must be provided with an overall picture of what science really is, and what it encompasses.

Problem 2
Lack of consistency in the messages conveyed by those involved in science teacher education; differences between the ways teachers are taught and teaching expectations.

Recommendation 2
All those involved in science teacher education should aim to continually expect to develop professionally. Professional development of science teachers requires the integration of knowledge of science, theories of learning, pedagogy and the child's cognitive development, and applying all this to science teaching.

Learning experience for teacher educators of science should incorporate the following aspects:

○ The practice of science teaching in actual classrooms to illustrate and model effective science teaching and to allow teachers to struggle with real situations; to practise, to expand their knowledge and skills in an appropriate context and to create and manage the physical, social and intellectual environment that provides the context of the science classroom.

○ Being taught, in both pre-service and in-service courses, to use methods similar to those which teachers are expected to implement in their classrooms. Science should mainly be part of daily learning experiences, observations and inquiry, and only to a small extent a separate course of study. Science teacher educators, both college mentors and classroom tutors, should themselves have professional training and should plan their instruction together in a complementary way. These pre-service trainers should also have ongoing communication with the representatives in the school that absorb the newly qualified teacher, i.e., the school principal and the science inspector, so that they serve as a support system and not a framework in which the teacher drowns.

Learning to teach science – like student learning – is dependent on the ability to articulate questions, pursue answers to those questions, interpret information gathered, propose applications, and to fit the new learning into the larger picture of science teaching. These components of pre-service and in-service professional development do not dictate a certain structure. They should be found in a college course, a sustained in-service workshop, a seminar for new teachers, a teacher study, an action research group or a teacher network. It is the nature of the learning situation that counts, not the structure within which it occurs.

Problem 3
The presence of competing subjects in early childhood teacher education makes it difficult for science teaching to gain sufficient space in the teacher education curriculum.

Recommendation 3
The professional development of science teachers enables them to build the knowledge, skills and attitudes needed to engage in life-long learning. It should therefore be taken for granted that pre-serv-

ice is only the beginning of the process of learning, and whatever is not attained at this phase will receive its share during continuous education. Science and technology are ever-progressing fields, and teachers of science and technology must move ahead with the changes. Therefore the limited time reserved for the K-2 teacher education science curriculum should not be a cause for concern. Professional teachers will uncover further areas later in their education.

Learning to learn science and technology for teachers should include the following elements:

○ Using inquiry, reflection, interpretation of research papers, modelling and guided practice to build understanding and skill in science teaching, and to provide frequent opportunities for individual and collegial examination and reflection on classroom and institutional practice, such as, peer coaching, portfolios and journals.

○ Sharing of teacher expertise, by preparation and utilization of mentors, teacher advisers, coaches, supervisors, and lead and resource teachers to provide professional development opportunities.

○ Opportunities to know and have access to existing research and experiential knowledge.

○ Opportunities to learn and use research skills to generate new knowledge about science and the teaching and learning of science.

○ Aiming at providing the teacher with in-depth experience in at least one subject area of science and technology, including an understanding of inquiry and the structure and generation of new knowledge, both to provide expertise and as a basis for further expansion of knowledge in the framework of continuing education.

Since the primary task of a teacher is to promote learning, teachers themselves should be dedicated learners. Teachers know best what they need to learn and to be able to do, and should have the authority to design their own professional development activities, to guarantee growth and life-long learning. Teachers of science build up their knowledge and abilities as they experience the struggles of their first years in the classroom, work with other teachers, take advantage of professional development offerings, and learn from their own efforts and those of their colleagues. This ongoing development poses several problems: since the responsibility for pre-service education rests primarily with colleges and universities, while that for in-service education rests with the practice community, the transition between the education of prospective to that of practising teachers is usually not smooth. Continuous professional development requires a gradual shift from campus to school accompanied by collaboration among all those engaged in professional development activities.

The recommendations above relate to only a few of the K-2 science and technology teacher education problems. Other problems and dilemmas remain open to further discussion. To mention just a few:

(1) What is more important in training early childhood science teachers – the subject matter, about which they know very little, or the pedagogics and didactics of early childhood? We can introduce specialists in science education to guide them – but then we may lose the dimension of early childhood teaching. A correct balance of different kinds of knowledge is needed with respect to the various knowledge bases identified by Shulman (1987), and listed on page 169.

(2) How should science be taught in early education? Should the teachers present phenomena and topics and describe them – or should they be guided by the children's curiosity and interests, and follow where these lead, answering their questions and helping them to observe what goes on around them? Or should it be a combination of the two, in which the teacher makes the basic decisions using the expression of the children's interests in developing topics?

(3) From the world of science and technology, what should be included in teacher education for early childhood? Who decides what constitutes a core science curriculum for early childhood? How important is accuracy and detail? Is it better to develop intuition among early childhood teachers and their pupils?

(4) While we refer to education of science and technology as one entity, we are actually talking about three different facets: science, technology and teaching. Should science precede technology? We know what science refers to, but what exactly is technology? What contents of each should be taught and in what order? And having agreed on core concepts and skills to be taught, how can the teaching complement the contents?

(5) To what extent should modern information technology be used as a cure for all classroom shortcomings? Should nature films replace field trips and computer simulations replace

laboratory experiments? Technology has been taken to an extreme to cure all ills. Science education is moving further and further from nature. Should we allow this to reach the point where children will become acquainted with chickens on a computer?

We are still at an embryonic stage in the development of science and technology early teacher education; however, today we are also at a potential apex for growth and development. While the issue is complex and multi-dimensional (as we have seen), an encouraging sign of a chance for success in reform in science and technology early teacher education lies in the recent improvement recorded in the Scholastic Aptitude Tests in the USA. This improvement shows that pulling resources together and taking responsibility reflects on results. It seems timely, therefore, to adopt Bybee's suggestion that:

> we must all become leaders and assume responsibility for our portion of the reform which seems to be the only way to take into account the scale, diversity, and power of science education systems while also accomodating both the general demands on the national agenda and the unique needs of state and local systems. Thus distributing leadership among those within the science education holds the greatest potential for improving science education by the year 2000. (Bybee, 1993 p.147)

References

Baxter, J.A. (1990) *The Role of Pedagogical Content Knowledge in Instruction: Contrasts between Experienced Teachers*. Eugene: University of Oregon.

Blough, G.O. and Schwartz, J. (1979) *Elementary School Science and How to Teach It*. New York: Holt, Rinehart and Winston.

Bybee, R.W. (1993) *Reforming Science Education: Social Perspectives and Personal Reflections*. New York: Teachers College Press.

Elstgeest, J. and Harlen, W. (1990) *Environmental Science in the Primary Curriculum*. London: Paul Chapman.

Fraser-Abiter, P. (1992) 'How can teacher education change the downhill trend of science education?' *Journal of Science Education 3*, 1, 21–26.

Fulghum, R. (1989) *All I Really Need to Know I Learned in Kindergarten*, translated by S. Parkol. Tel Aviv: Triwaks (Hebrew).

Goodlad, J.I., Klein, M.F. and Tye, K.A. (1979) 'The domain of curriculum and their study.' In J.I. Goodlad *et al. Curriculum Inquiry: The Study of Curriculum Practice*. New York: McGraw-Hill.

Griffin, J. (1995) Personal communication.

Grossman, P.L., Wilson, S. and Shulman, L. (1989) 'Teachers of substance: subject matter knowledge for teaching.' In M. Reynolds (ed) *Knowledge Base for the Beginning Teacher*. Oxford: Pergamon Press.

Harlen, W. (1993) *Teaching and Learning Primary Science*, 2nd rev. edn. London: Paul Chapman.

Harlen, W., Holroyd, C. and Byrne, M. (1995) *Confidence and Understanding in Teaching Science and Technology in Primary Schools*. Edinburgh: Scottish Council for Research in Education.

Harrari, C. (1992) *Report of the High Commission on Education for Science and Technology* – '*1998 is Tomorrow*'. Jerusalem: Ministry of Education and Culture.

Levite, A. (ed) (1995) *Science and Technology in Kindergartens in Israel*. Jerusalem: Ministry of Education and Culture (Hebrew).

Lieberman, A. and Miller, L. (eds) (1994) *Staff Development: New Demands, New Realities, New Perspectives*. New York: Teachers College Press.

Lortie, D.C. (1975) *School Teacher: A sociological study*. Chicago: The University of Chicago Press.

Parker, S. (1982) 'The preparation of teachers for primary school science.' In W. Harlen (ed) *New Trends in Primary School Science Education*. Paris: UNESCO.

Perkins, D.N. and Salmon, G. (1989) 'Are cognitive skills text bound?' *Educational Researcher 12*, 1, 16–25.

Richardson, V. (1994) 'Conducting research on practice.' *Educational Researcher 23*, 5, 5–10.

Rudduck, J. and Hopkins, D. (eds) (1985) *Research as a Basis for Teaching: Readings from the Work of Lawrence Stenhouse*. London: Heinemann Educational Books.

Sabar, N. (1986) 'Is the disappointment in the implementation of a new science curriculum justified?' *Journal of Research in Science Teaching 23*, 6, 475–491.

Sabar, N. (1994) 'School focused curriculum planning.' In T. Husen and N. Postlethwaite (eds) *The International Encyclopedia of Education*. Oxford: Pergamon Press.

Shafriri, N. (1993) Interrelationships within the practical behavioral system of Logo teachers in elementary school. Unpublished Doctoral Thesis. Tel-Aviv University.

Shulman, L. (1987) 'Knowledge and teaching: foundation of the new reform.' *Harvard Educational Review 57*, 1, 1–22.

Standards for the Professional Development of Teachers of Science (1995) In *National Science Education Standards* (draft). Washington: National Research Council, 1–26.

Stavy, R. (1984) *Contemplations on Science Teacher Education for Primary and Junior High School*. Tel Aviv: Tel Aviv University School of Education (Hebrew).

Tamir, P. (1988) 'Subject matter and related pedagogical knowledge in teacher education.' *Teaching and Teacher Education 4*, 2, 99–110.

CHAPTER 9

The Role of Outside Support Media, Video and Museums

Goéry Delacôte

Introduction

Education, to be successful, and science education is no exception, has to rely on a rich repertoire of experiences on which to build conceptual learning. These experiences pave the way to the construction of meaning, which in turn supports learning. It also helps to entertain, create or re-create a sense of wonder, which becomes the true incentive for learning. It is therefore important to think of education in ecological terms, not limiting the children's experiences to what can possibly take place in the classroom. The role of alternative learning environments therefore becomes critical as a prelude, a complement or a follow-up to the school-based learning process.

Experience comes from interaction with a learning environment. The design of stimulating environments, and the guided process of giving access to them, facilitating exploration and contributing to meaning being built, are therefore critical steps in making the learning easier. This requires that a learning environment should be composed of interactive things (objects, exhibits), of connective tools (computers, multimedia) and of attentive people (explainers, brokers of information, experts, teachers, etc.). Young children, even more than adults, are highly sensitive to experience and media which, if well designed, can be very useful.

At the San Francisco Exploratorium, a sort of learning laboratory open to the public founded in 1969 by Frank Oppenheimer, we have designed together with a publisher, the 'Explorabook', a book which is also a toy (Cassidy and Exploratorium, 1991). The Explorabook incorporates a magnet and other physics flat tools, such as a mirror made out of mylar, a Fresnel lens and a grating, which allow young children to design and carry out their own experiments. In a relatively unique way, the book has moved from a classical story-telling, narrative-based approach to a content that leads to a story-building experience: the young reader uses the book to perform an experimental investigation, to draw a conclusion and to come up with a story of what happened while he was experimenting. The non-linear and non-sequential design of this activity-based book is very similar to that found in the design of some contemporary interactive multimedia. The fact that about one million copies of this book have been sold so far is a result of its well-adapted design and the dire need to find intriguing activities for children aged three to fifteen.

Multimedia programmes can also be conceived with the idea of providing the users with the sort of information, expertise and knowledge which are needed for them to solve a problem or play a role: for instance to become a multimedia designer, to understand the local economy of a little village or to solve a water pollution problem.

Basically this sort of multimedia design tends to blur the boundary between being a narrative reader and becoming a story designer. The author of the multimedia is the one who provides the potential building blocks of the story. The user is the one who makes the story by organizing these building blocks according to a logic of sequencing and of question and answer; the user becomes the author. This important transformation is of a learner who becomes a teacher. Multimedia games such as *Myst*, an adventure game where you build your own strategy, or at least make decisions while the game is going on, are of the same kind.

Phenomenon-based exhibits, little excerpts of the world, if well displayed, can generate a sense of surprise, even of wonder, which can lead the learner into a questioning mode, where formulating a question, trying out an experiment or talking to a companion are all part of an investigatory attitude. The core of this is a mental dynamic of searching for meaning supported by experience and by reasoning.

The problem then is to try to elicit the kind of learning which would be most favoured by these sorts of environment.

What Sort of Knowledge is there to Learn?

One should first pay attention to the kind of knowledge which can be acquired. Here lies the first important dichotomy between knowledge acquired through any sort of media by direct or first-hand experience and by representational or second-hand knowledge. Museums generally accentuate the first sort of knowledge by bringing the child into direct contact with objects. Libraries and networks will provide learning through indirectly represented knowledge, that is through books, films, videos, printed materials, images and sounds. An interesting place where these two sorts of knowledge clearly overlap is the virtual reality environment where you provide an experience about the world and about people experiencing it by proposing user-driven representations of the world; this is still a developing technology (especially for visual experience, sound experience is more advanced).

One can fine-tune the analysis about so-called first-hand knowledge by providing two sorts of access: access to the world or segments of it in keeping with true research like complexity of these segments; or access to a practically reconstructed world based on conceptual representations provided both by designers and users, a sort of post-conceptual didactic practice. In a sense it is the difference between the world as a set of people-mediated concepts and a world with concepts hidden in the background.

It is also possible to categorize knowledge into domains, whether first- or second-hand, for instance one can discriminate between knowledge about nature, technology, the arts, oneself, other people and society, the world of man-made rules and so on. Understanding nature is about understanding natural phenomena, the underlying concepts and theories, and their relationship to the natural world. Understanding technology is about understanding the purposeful design of objects, tools, processes and systems, considering social, economic, cultural and natural constraints. Understanding the arts is about understanding alternative ways of perceiving, representing and even re-creating the world.

One should consider the difference between informal and formal knowledge. Formal knowledge has to do with long chains of inferences connecting sets of principles, sets of concepts and sets of experimental evidence. Most often the use of a formal language has to be mastered and rules of logic applied, and mathematical tools become important. Informal knowledge has to do with qualitative, global and sometimes metaphorical or analogue descriptions of concepts and ideas. This is very often used as *meta* knowledge which helps us to figure out a reasoning pathway, an argument, the planning of a solution to a problem, the raising of a question, or the description of a connection between facts and ideas. It never relies on a long chain of logical inferences and is not a logical demonstration from first principles but rather is connected with intuition.

The Example of the Exploratorium

Let us now apply this categorization of knowledge to understand a little bit better what sort of learning could take place in some of the 'non-compulsory' environments we mentioned earlier. We will consider more extensively the case of the Exploratorium, the leader of hands-on science museums. We can assert that the unguided learning which takes place in this phenomenon-based exhibition environment is mostly of the following type. Visitors are led to do something with the exhibits. The design through specific codes induces a 'natural' doing (building, throwing, feeling, sense-involving) type of personal action. The performance, in its turn, induces a surprise. Again, the design has been such that by interacting with the exhibit, the exhibit itself 'reacts' and something unexpected happens to the visitor. The next, interwoven step is the move from surprise to the question, which very often takes place through a sort of social interaction. The surprise has triggered an interest and a pleasure to share. Friends, family members and other visitors are called on to share in the awakened curiosity. Verbal explanation of the surprise takes place, further investigation may be tried, and a subtle process of progressively building a question is on its way.

Of course, the question will depend on the design of the exhibit and the pre-existing knowledge of the visitor. Nevertheless, what is central is the process by which the visitor discovers that he can raise his own questions and is pleased by so doing. The Exploratorium is a 'question generator' place!

This process clearly implies the existence of a learning environment, in this case centred around knowledge about natural phenomena, providing first-hand experience in a research-like, non-didactic, highly informal mode. It is a Copernical revolution compared with a school learning experience. However, we have found at the Exploratorium that another process of learning seems to operate. The Exploratorium is mostly a place where learning tools are being designed to match the constraint of a museum environment. Teachers working at the Exploratorium have designed learning tools based on the same ideas but which fit a school environment. These have been compiled in a collection nicknamed 'the Science Snackbook,' in four volumes (Doherty, Rathjen and the Exploratorium Teacher Institute, 1995a,b,c, 1996) and pupils in the classrooms are now redesigning these learning tools in order to learn for themselves by doing and investigating at the same time. It is a chain of induced transposition and re-creation, where something is being added to by the different actors along the chain, which facilitates this new process of learning.

There are some 650 exhibits at the San Francisco Exploratorium which allow this questioning behaviour to be triggered among users, including young children. Some examples are the non-linear behaviour of matter, optics, colour and vision, sound and hearing, and mathematics and mechanics. These exhibits are part of larger groups designed like interactive pieces of furniture, which can be grouped in many different ways, therefore allowing the design of an ever-changing, very flexible floor.

Examples of Media-Based Learning Environments

In another spectrum of non-compulsory environments, one may find an institution such as the Museum of the Moving Image (London) which is what I would call a place where 'media is squared' (media^2), a media museum about another media (films and TV). Libraries are also media about other media, but as written material is a less well-perceived medium than photography and film, libraries provide access to second-hand knowledge only. To discover the world (real as well as imaginary) in a medium which offers an experience about a vision of the world that has been created in another medium is apparently a super-distant experience. What really happens is that such a place provides more of an experience about the film medium as a human creative activity and transforms this medium into a sort of reality.

At the San Francisco Exploratorium, in addition to experiential learning we also provide access to the same sort of media-based knowledge but mix first-hand with some second-hand experiences. This was one part of the rationale for the creation of a Center for Media and Communication in addition to the present Center for Public Exhibition, to provide the possibility of 'exporting' the Exploratorium experience. The development of a constantly evolving World Wide Web site is a typical example of a tool which allows home users as well as school users to benefit from these new learning environments. A third component, an innovative Center for Teaching and Learning, allows educators as well as students, by using learning tools, to discover new and hopefully more efficient ways of learning (constructing knowledge, negotiating meaning and assessing performance), either in an individual or a collective mode.

Conclusion

Through books, multimedia, exhibits and field trips (if well designed and carefully introduced), a strong experiential learning can be supported from an early age. This lays the foundation for a deeper and broader learning process which never ends and consists of acquiring experiences as well as skills in handling concepts and at mapping the former with the latter. Based on this evidence, the role of science centres in the transformation of primary education can be quite significant. By design they are open and flexible in content, curriculum, time, and technology. They are also very easy to use by groups, not just peer groups, but especially family groups where social interaction is of primary importance in supporting the learning process. With little change in organization, science centres can become strategic places for helping elementary teachers to feel more supported, educated and connected in their endeavours to help young children grow into active investigators. For instance, visual and spoken dialogues over the electronic networks in a deferred mode, as well as on-line, are recent examples of fruitful interactions between our Exploratorium and San Francisco Bay area fourth grade classes involved in, for instance, investigations on weather. More importantly, teachers, in being supported in their own thinking and understanding, find the conditions that aid and expand their expertise in science teaching. They discover through their own experience what could support their pupils. Thus, science centres can become very active bases of teacher education and support, using the power of an informal approach in discovering about the world and understanding it.

References

John Cassidy and Exploratorium (1991) *Explorabook*. Palo Alto: Klutz Press.

Doherty, P., Rathjen, D. and the Exploratorium Teacher Institute (1995a) *The Magic Wand and Other Bright Experiments on Light and Color*. New York: John Wiley and Sons.

Doherty, P., Rathjen, D. and the Exploratorium Teacher Institute (1995b) *The Cheshire Cat and Other Eye-Popping Experiments on How We See the World*. New York: John Wiley and Sons.

Doherty, P., Rathjen, D. and the Exploratorium Teacher Institute (1995c) *The Cool Hot Rod and Other Electrifying Experiments on Energy and Matter*. New York: John Wiley and Sons.

Doherty, P., Rathjen, D. and the Exploratorium Teacher Institute (1996) *The Spinning Blackboard and Other Dynamic Experiments on Force and Motion*. New York: John Wiley and Sons.

Further Reading

Delacôte, Goéry (1996) *Savoir apprendre*. Paris: Editions Odile Jacob.

John Cassidy and Exploratorium (1997) *The Zap Book*. Palo Alto: Klutz Press.

CHAPTER 10

To Develop an Understanding of the Natural World in the Early Ages

Gustav Helldén

Introduction

During an interview about decomposition a nine-year-old boy explained that the leaves on the ground would become soil. After some seconds he added: 'Well, the more soil there is the bigger the planet will be.' He then described the logical consequence of his own statement that the leaves would be soil. He thought that the biomass was conserved as soil and not as a part of a cycle. The repeated defoliation year after year would result in more soil being formed. He could not see the gaseous state of decomposition where carbon dioxide and water leave the ground. He explained what he could observe and thought that soil was the end point for the decomposition, and drew the conclusion that the planet Earth would grow bigger.

This is an example of how children's thoughts and explanations of natural phenomena start at an early age. Their knowledge exists in their minds as living processes under continuous development. These ideas seem to be very strong and may persist into their life as adults. Even if they are personally coloured, there are certain common features that can be important starting points in the teaching process. Therefore, there is a need for a teaching strategy for the early ages that is keenly alive to children's ideas and has the potential to help them to develop their ideas.

Such a view of knowledge development is also described in a Swedish publication with the title 'A school for education' (*Skola för bildning*) which is a report from the Curriculum Committee (SOU, 1992, p.94). It contains a proposal for a new curriculum for compulsory schools and for upper secondary schools. Such a description of knowledge can be characterised as a constructivist view of learning. It is argued that knowledge develops in an interplay between that which you want to obtain and the knowledge you already have; between problems you experience in that knowledge and the experiences you make. Theoretical knowledge is not a portrayal of reality but a human construction. Knowledge is in that case not true or untrue in a definite meaning, but something that can be argued and proved.

A New Curriculum in Sweden

In the 1994 curriculum for compulsory schools (LPO 94, 1994) it is underlined that the school shall strive to ensure that all pupils develop a sense of curiosity and the desire to learn through which they can develop their own individual way of learning. This is a prerequisite for the development of a deeper understanding of basic concepts, not least in science. The new curriculum concerns ages 7 to 16. Today it is also possible in many municipalities for children to start at school at six years of age. In the curriculum it is emphasised that the school is responsible for ensuring that all pupils completing compulsory school know and understand basic concepts and contexts within the natural sciences, as well as within technical, social and humanistic areas of knowledge.

In the syllabi that define the curriculum, the goals of education are specified in each subject or in a group of subjects. The syllabus for a given subject has two types of goal. First, there are goals to strive for which express the general ambition and direction of teaching where it is a question of developing the pupils' knowledge, insights, understanding, attitudes, skills and so on. These goals are wide and high and concern the subject as a whole. They set no upper limit for the growth of knowledge in the student, but claim that education shall ensure that the pupils shall be able to develop their knowledge, understanding and interests in the different subjects (Andersson, 1995). Second, there are goals expressing a minimum of knowledge in each subject which all pupils are supposed to attain at the end of the fifth and ninth grades, respectively. This means that there are descriptions of minimum knowledge from age 6/7 to 12 (fifth grade) in biology, chemistry and physics.

The stipulated guaranteed study-time for all compulsory school subjects is 6665 hours. Of these, 800 are for biology, chemistry, physics and technology. The distribution of these hours among subjects and grades is decided upon locally in relation to goals and syllabi. All over Sweden groups of teachers from grades 1 to 9 have meetings where they discuss the distribution of time and content of the science to be taught. There is a clear ambition to improve science education in the early years at school.

The syllabi further describe the structure and character of each subject by stating its core: the central concepts, theories and most essential perspectives. Given the fact that subjects are different in character, they are described differently. The following description of goals to strive for, common to all the three subjects, gives a good idea of the general directions and aspirations of compulsory school science in Sweden.

In science education schools shall strive to let the pupil:

o experience the joy of discovery and experimentation and develop his/her inclination and abilities to ask questions about phenomena in nature

o develop knowledge about scientific concepts and models, and an awareness that these are human constructs

o attain an understanding of the scientific way of working and develop his/her ability to present their own observations, conclusions and knowledge in written form

o become aware of how knowledge about nature develops and how it is formed by, and forms, the human image of the world

o develop care and respect for nature and responsibility for both the local and global environment

o develop knowledge about the evolution of the cosmos, the Earth, life and man

o get an insight into how matter is studied at various levels of organisation (e.g. atom–molecule – cell – organism – population and community)

o develop knowledge about the flow of energy from the Sun through the various natural and technical systems on Earth and about natural cycles of matter.

Both the curriculum and the syllabi stress the importance of concept understanding and conceptual development. If we at school are to help children to develop their understanding, knowledge and interests, we must know more about their conceptual development and about their starting points of learning. Only then shall we be able to create teaching situations in which the children's ideas will be challenged.

The 1994 curriculum established that it is important that education provides some general perspectives in all school subjects. Besides an historical, international and ethical perspective, it is emphasised that education shall provide an environmental perspective in the school subjects:

An environmental perspective provides them with opportunities not only to take responsibility for the environment in areas where they themselves can have a direct influence, but also to form a personal position with respect to global environmental issues. Teaching should illuminate how the functions of society and how our ways of living and working can best be adapted to create the conditions for sustainable development.

(LPO 94, 1994, p.9)

It is a tradition in Swedish education to connect teaching on science concepts, particularly in the early ages, to environmental issues often including essential ecological processes. Several important processes in ecology have to do with the transformations of matter between the solid, liquid and gaseous states. Therefore children's understanding of the nature and transformations of matter can be of great importance for their understanding of fundamental processes in ecology and the environment (Helldén, 1995). Teaching about such processes must build upon what the learners already know. In order to know more about the development of pupils' understanding of ecological processes, I am carrying out a longitudinal study of 25–30 pupils' conceptual development concerning ecological processes from 9 to 16 years of age. The first part of the study was reported in 1992 (Helldén, 1992). A description of experiences from this study should help illustrate children's conceptions.

Experiences from a Longitudinal Study

Research Methodology

Let us take three examples from biology and ecology where the understanding of the concept of matter could be problematical:

(1) The organism maintains equilibrium with the environment, i.e. homeostasis, through exchange of energy and matter. This exchange means, among other things, exchange of gases with the environment.

(2) The water cycle plays an important part in several ecological processes. This cycle also involves phase changes between the gaseous, liquid and solid states.

(3) When biomass is decomposed, the products are carbon dioxide and water.

These three examples of gas exchange processes cannot be seen by the ordinary observer. Research in science education has shown that pupils are not initially aware that air and other gases possess material character. They take for granted that everything they cannot observe does not exist (Driver *et al.* 1994).

I wanted to know how children develop their understanding of ecological processes involving such transformations of matter. Therefore, I studied children's understanding of conditions for life and decomposition in nature, and also their ideas of the role of the flower.

The method that has been used most in this project is a revised clinical method. At 16 years of age the pupils answered a questionnaire. They were interviewed about soil and the decomposition of leaves and other things lying on the ground. I used cultivation of plants in sealed, transparent boxes (12 x 12 x 18 cm) with glass lids to challenge the pupils' ideas about conditions for growth and to define the limits for the process we were going to discuss. During the interviews I had materials in front of the interviewee concerning the questions the interview was about. The interviews were recorded.

Conceptions of Matter and its Transformations in Nature

About Conditions for Life

Ten-year-old pupils thought that the living organism was the end station of the flow of matter through the ecosystem. Even if they realised that plants and animals must 'take in' matter of different kinds from the environment, they did not note the passage of matter from the organism to the environment. Initially, many pupils expected the plants to die in the sealed boxes. They constructed a 'used-up model' in their minds to explain how air, oxygen, water and other resources were consumed. When they saw that plants survived over a period of time in the boxes, they constructed ideas about the plants' utilisation of the resources in the sealed box. Their descriptions can be categorised in the following way:

(1) *Life-supporting resources are consumed gradually and are not renewed.* Most pupils thought that there were sufficient resources of water and air in the box when we started the cultivation of plants inside. They thought that the resources would then be consumed or lose their life-supporting quality: 'If they have used the air a couple of times, it is too old and there is no nourishment and no oxygen left'.

(2) *The resources come from a supply.* Some pupils thought that the soil was a supply of one or more of the sources of nourishment

(water, oxygen and carbon dioxide) needed by the organisms. Several of them started to use a 'cycle model' to explain how the resources were renewed: 'The air disappears down into the soil to get more nourishment. Then it moves up again. Then it moves up and down, up and down'.

(3) *The resources are modified, transmuted or disappear.* The condensed water on the inside walls of the sealed box made the water visible and challenged the pupils to develop a 'cycle model' in their minds. This can be called a modification according to Andersson's (1990) descriptions. One of the pupils said: 'Well, because it will be some steam that moves up and then it forms some water and then it falls down'.

Some pupils had the idea that fresh water, air and oxygen were formed by the water cycle. Such ideas can be characterised as transmutations in chemistry or 'forbidden' transformations (Andersson, 1990). One pupil pointed at the plants in the box and described her ideas in the following way: 'Then it will be condensed. If this goes up and it rains down again, then it makes air; so they get air'. Another pupil described how water was transformed into oxygen when it dried.

Other pupils used another way to explain the changes by saying that water, air and oxygen disappeared: 'The air disappeared into the old air', 'Water disappeared by drying up'. The reason why pupils used transmutations and disappearance to explain the transformations of matter can be explained by their lack of a conception of the gaseous state. They did not understand the evaporation and condensation of water but observed the result (Bar, 1989), and used what they saw, the condensed water, to explain the conditions for life in the sealed boxes. Many pupils also applied a 'cycle model' that they had earlier conceived.

(4) *Organisms produce the necessary resources.* It was obvious that some pupils in grades 4 and 5 tried to explain how oxygen was produced by the plants and that there was a gas exchange between the different organisms in the boxes. Such conceptions presuppose that matter can be transported between different parts of the ecosystem. Many described this transportation as a cycle or as parts of a cycle.

At an early stage at school, the pupils constructed in their minds a model describing the water cycle. When the ten-year-olds saw water covering the inside walls of the sealed plastic boxes, their ideas were challenged. Each pupil developed their own idea about the water cycle. Most of the pupils then used their 'cycle models' as prototypes to explain how organisms could survive in the boxes and maintain life-supporting resources such as air, oxygen, water, carbon dioxide and nourishment.

The pupils described two types of 'cycle model'. In one model the cycle was outside the world of organisms and was the first one they developed in their minds. In this model, water evaporated from the soil, was condensed on the inside of the sealed boxes and trickled down into the soil again. Some children described a similar model for the cycle of air and oxygen. Another model described how the organisms were involved. In this model, water evaporates from the plants, is condensed, trickles down to the soil and is sucked up by the plant.

When they saw the plants growing in the boxes, many pupils constructed explanations with the help of a 'cycle model'. Their thinking developed in different ways. For one pupil, both water and oxygen were formed through condensation; for another, air forced its way down into the soil in order to get more nourishment – many pupils thought the condensed water on the walls of the sealed box was 'nourished air'. They could not see the water vapour but could see the result of condensation. They used what they could see and constructed an explanation. In the same way they could not see air and oxygen. They used the condensation of water as a model and some of them constructed an idea that the water film on the inside of the walls of the box contained air or oxygen: 'You can see air here on the walls!'.

Some of the ten-year-olds described an exchange of air, oxygen and carbon dioxide between the organisms in the box. At the beginning, some pupils thought that the plants got their carbon dioxide through the expiration of man. When a couple of pupils saw that the plants survived in the sealed boxes after six months, they constructed the explanation that the plants produced oxygen for each other. One pupil in grade 4 (11 years) said that carbon dioxide could come from the earthworms in the soil. Gradually, the children developed their knowledge about the origin of oxygen, and several pupils thought that the plants themselves could emit the oxygen which they and the animals needed.

About Decomposition in Nature
During the interviews with nine-year-old pupils on decomposition, several pupils answered questions about what happens to leaves on the ground by saying that they disappeared in some way. Oscar said: 'They might have blown away somewhere up in the tree or in the sky. Or they might have been stuck in the snow which has blown away'. According to their conceptions, matter was not conserved.

Some pupils suggested that matter was broken up into smaller and smaller pieces until they could not see anything of the leaves which had then disappeared. Even here, the pupils did not understand the conservation of matter. Soil invertebrates could also be involved in the disappearance: 'Small animals bite and eat small pieces of it. Then it just disappears'. In other cases, the children said that the work of the soil invertebrates was only a fragmentation. Some of them thought that the leaves were moved down into the ground during fragmentation. Only one pupil of twenty-five nine-year-olds described decomposition as a process when organic matter passes through the animal. Seven pupils described a process where organisms were not involved. Instead they described physical factors and age as causing the decomposition.

Hanna can be seen to represent a group of students that developed their understanding towards more developed conceptions of decomposition in nature. Instead of breaking with her earlier ideas she modified them and added new characteristics to the old ideas. You can recognise the same feature through the years. At aged 9 she described the following idea: 'They dry out in some way and shrivel up. Then when they are completely dry, it is enough for it to rain just once more for them to become just small bits'.

As an 11-year-old she had revised her previous ideas by saying that the leaves rot away by being trampled by animals. It was still a mechanical process without any influence from organisms. At 13 she still had an explanation of how the leaves were broken down by the rain and the sun, but she added that the animals ate the fragmented leaves: 'They dry out and then perhaps it rains so that they become soft. Then they dry out again. Then in the end they become...and animals start eating them. Then you get soil of it'.

At the age of 15 Hanna took another step away from mechanical fragmentation when she described how the leaves were eaten and became soil. When she was asked about an alternative process she described something very similar to what she described as a nine-year-old: 'It must be when it dries up. Then when it rains, it is mixed up with some mud. Then it dries and becomes soil. Or also some animals come and eat it. Then their excrements will become soil'. The constructions became more complex. New knowledge was added to the structures Hanna had described six years earlier. There must have been a powerful experience of decomposition during childhood in order for it to exist as a part of her conception in spite of all influences while growing up.

At the end of grade 4 more children began to describe decomposition as a part of a cycle. One of the pupils said: 'First leaves have appeared and then they have grown. Then they move down into the soil and moulder away and then they become nourishment again to plants'. In connection with the next interview, she had the following explanation of why Earth did not increase in size as a result of decomposition: 'There is something like a circulation. It just moves round. Plants and animals die and then...'.

It was difficult for the pupils to associate their 'cycle model' with the circumstances in an aquarium. In a terrestrial environment, they realised that it was possible for the plants to take in decomposed products through their roots. When they saw what happened in an aquarium, they thought that these products were dissolved in water and lost.

Most of the 11-year-olds thought that leaves, grass, wood and paper were converted into soil. This process was seen as taking place with or without organisms. They thought that biomass was conserved as soil. In their conceptions, soil became the 'end point' concerning decomposition in nature and not a stage within the cycle of matter, because they could not observe any exchange of oxygen, carbon dioxide and water with the environment during the decomposition process. It is not so surprising that one-third of the class thought that the Earth would increase in size every year as a result of decomposition of all the leaves. Other pupils imagined Earth to be something like a container. They did not think that the size would change, because all new soil would fill hollows or be compressed. Some pupils in the class thought that the size of the planet would not increase because matter would disappear, for example by blowing away. Others thought that the unchanged size would depend on matter being burned up or eaten by animals. It seemed that many pupils had an intuitive feeling that the Earth could not increase in size and therefore they constructed a number of explanations for this phenomenon.

Other studies have also documented pupils' difficulties in understanding decomposition in nature and the conservation of matter. See, for example Leach *et al.* (1992), Leach (1995), Russell and Watt (1989), Sequeira and Freitas (1986) and Smith and Anderson (1986).

Other Features in Children's Conceptions

The Pupils' Experiences from Everyday Life

Almost all pupils said in the interviews that plants need water to survive. To water plants is an everyday action that they evidently connected with the plants' needs. But they had not seen any water leaving the plants. Therefore they constructed in their minds an 'end-station model' that explained the plants' consumption of water. When I suggested to them that sweet violets might be planted in the plastic box and the glass lid sealed, many of them thought that the plant would die if I did not open the box in order to water the plants. The 'end-station model' was then transformed to illustrate the consumption of air, oxygen and carbon dioxide in the closed boxes. The children thought that the plants in the boxes would die because all the air, oxygen, carbon dioxide and water were used up. The completely fastened lid was a problem to many students. Some pupils tried to prevent me from putting the lid on. Both Linda and Mary interrupted and said: 'Oxygen, it won't work! You must not do it!'.

Because they had the experience that water and nutrients are taken up from the soil, the pupils also thought that other resources were supplied from the soil. For many pupils, nourishment in the soil was the same as food. Food could also be minerals, water, oxygen, carbon dioxide and light taken in from the soil. Several pupils thought that the plants breathed through their roots and others that they took up light with them: 'If it for example shines on the ground, the roots take it in and then it goes the whole way up'. In their minds all life-supporting resources were absorbed from the soil instead of produced in the plant itself by photosynthesis. Several other studies have shown that it is difficult for many pupils to imagine that a plant assimilates a gas as a raw material for building up the plant (Wood-Robinson, 1991).

When the pupils explained what would happen to the leaves on the ground in the autumn, they described early experiences of leaves whirling around in the air, flying up in the sky, being trampled to pieces or being covered by soil. It was usual that children placed a process they could not explain in a place where it could not be observed. It seems that Hanna had seen how raindrops had worked on the ground. She used that experience when she explained what happens to the leaves on the ground in the autumn. This was her way of attacking the problem, even in her explanations as a teenager.

Experiences of picking flowers for decoration were of great importance for some pupils. Anders described it in the following way at the age of 11: 'I think the flowers have...because they have colours to make you think they are nice and want to have them indoors. It gives you something to embroider the table with when you have guests. The food on the table and then you embroider the table with some brightly coloured flowers'. One student used an experience from everyday life when explaining how a plant could develop from a tiny seed. He compared the process with the fermentation of bread under a baking cloth.

Human-Centred Ideas

In the interviews, the children often referred to the human body and to experiences of how their own body functioned. When we were going to seal the vivarium with the plants, many of the ten-year-olds in the class very clearly showed reference to their own breathing.

Some children compared their own eating with the uptake by the plant of resources from the soil. This was used in order to confirm the idea that plants retain and consume what they take up. When I asked the pupils how a seed could develop into a big plant, some of them compared the development to the growth of a human foetus.

Very often children had the idea that a human being was a necessary part of ecological processes. Leaves were decomposed by being trampled to pieces by man. One pupil said: 'In the forest nature waters itself but we must water the garden'. If the pupils had difficulties in explaining what would happen to a plastic cover and an iron nail on the ground, they sometimes said that somebody trampled it down into the soil. Ten-year-old pupils thought that the greenness of the meadow came from seeds sown by somebody or being blown from gardens. They often thought that the purpose of some phenomena was to satisfy the needs of man. Some children said, for example, that the purpose of flowers was to give us a feeling of light and happiness. My study has shown that human-centred ideas can live and develop besides scientifically more correct ones.

Animism, Anthropomorphism and Teleological Reasoning

Many pupils used animistic characteristics to explain what happened to water and air in the sealed vivarium. Eric explained the condensation of water on the lid and walls in the following way: 'Moisture, it will be moisture 'cause nothing gets out. When the air tries to get out, it becomes water; it evaporates'. Another pupil said that the air would die in the boxes. When Oscar explained what would happen to the leaves on the ground he said that the soil ate the leaves.

In order to be able to understand and explain phenomena in nature the pupils often used anthropomorphic reasoning. Morgan gave the following explanation for the decomposition of leaves in the woods: 'They are decomposed by nature. It is nature itself that has constructed them'. Leaves and seeds were given human qualities by the children when they explained defoliation and germination: 'The muscles of the leaves become weaker and the leaves can't stick to the branch'. The anthropomorphic ideas were strongly articulated in the interviews concerning flowers. The pupils thought that the colours made the plants pretty and proud and that the plants could brag to other plants. They used characteristics that they understood rather than biological explanations.

Another characteristic feature of the the pupils' descriptions of phenomena in the environment was teleological reasoning. This refers to ends being used as explanations of how certain structures are built or how certain functions occur. Teleological explanations make us feel that we understand the phenomenon because the explanation is purposeful and fits the way we view our own purposeful behaviour.

It seems that teleological reasoning is of great help, especially for young pupils when trying to understand and explain different phenomena. One pupil said, for example, that cress was growing better in soil than on paper because plants are built to grow in soil. A boy said that defoliation was necessary in order to give space for new leaves.

Some pupils explain the colours of flowers with a purpose from the perspective of man: 'So you can recognise them', 'I suppose it is so we will think they are prettier'. Others said that plants had coloured flowers because they could attract insects: 'They may look more attractive for bees and bumble bees so they will be dispersed more easily'.

Summary

At an early age children develop ideas about phenomena in their environment starting from what they see, hear and feel. Their experiences from everyday life help them to understand and describe the world and assimilate impressions. They use a variety of approaches to understand and describe their conceptions, such as human-centred ideas and anthropomorphic and teleological reasoning. A child's previous experience is the most important single factor influencing meaningful learning (Ausubel, 1968). It is therefore of great importance that we learn more about children's ideas and how they develop over time. We need to take the child's endeavour to describe objects and events in the natural world seriously; it is very important to show children that we appreciate their ideas.

A child does not operate in a conceptual/theoretical vacuum, but has some concepts, principles and theories about phenomena in the natural world. There is a rich diversity of conceptions within different domains; about ecological processes for example. I think there is a capacity in the minds of young children to develop meaningful learning and understand concepts that we wish to introduce later at school (Bloom, 1981; Novak & Mosunda, 1991).

During the early years at school there is a great potential for improving the total result of education at school. Meaningful learning in science may not only focus solely upon the learners' thinking, even feeling and acting are important.

It is important to identify the main concepts with which the pupils ought to be familiar. Children's thinking in relation to such concepts can be starting points to create educational strategies that challenge their ideas. They can then assimilate new ideas into their existing knowledge frameworks and enhance meaningful learning. Perhaps we must leave concepts and experimental settings that have traditionally been the main parts of science education and create new approaches that concentrate on other major concepts and consider young children's thinking.

Another resource that can be used much more is to let children study their own learning in order to help them learn how to learn. This means that we must give children experience of how their ideas can change in the learning process. I have found that children are very interested in their own learning. There is a metacognitive capacity in children's minds that is not fully utilised.

For a successful science education in the early ages we need:

○ to identify a limited number of important concepts

○ to identify children's ideas in connection with those concepts

○ to work out educational strategies to facilitate meaningful learning

○ to help children to learn how to learn

○ to create an atmosphere that gives the children opportunities to recognise, discuss and reflect on their ideas

○ to show children that we find their ideas interesting and valuable.

It is important that such ideas influence both the pre-service and in-service education of teachers. Even teachers for the early ages need a good understanding of basic scientific concepts in order to be able to identify and challenge children's conceptions and help them in their struggle to understand the natural world.

Acknowledgements

I wish to thank Richard Iuli, Cornell University for valuable comments on an early version of this chapter. The research presented in this chapter has been financially supported by the Swedish Council for Research in Humanities and Social Sciences.

References

Andersson, B. (1990) 'Pupil's conceptions of matter and its transformations (age 12–16).' *Studies in Science Education 18*, 53–85.

Andersson, B. (1995) *School Science Education in Sweden. A Description of the System and Dynamics of Change.* Mölndal: University of Göteborg, Department of Subject Matter Education, Science Division.

Ausubel, D. (1968) *Educational Psychology: A Cognitive View.* New York: Holy, Rinehart and Winston.

Bar, V. (1989) 'Children's views about the water cycle.' *Science Education 73*, 481–500.

Bloom, B.S. (1981) *All Our Children Learning: A Primer for Parents, Teachers and other Educators.* New York: McGraw-Hill.

Driver, R., Squires, A., Rushworth P. and Wood-Robinson, V. (1994) *Making Sense of Secondary Science – Research into Children's Ideas.* London: Routledge.

Helldén, G. (1992) *Grundskoleelevers förståelse av ekologiska processer* (Pupils' understanding of ecological processes). (Studia Psychologica et Pedagogica. Series Altera C.) Stockholm: Almqvist & Wiksell International.

Helldén, G. (1995) 'Environmental education and pupils' conceptions of matter.' *Environmental Education Research 3*, 267–277.

Leach, J.T. (1995) Progression in understanding of some ecological concepts in children age 5 to 16. Doctoral thesis, University of Leeds, School of Education.

Leach, J., Driver, R., Scott, P. and Wood-Robinson, C. (1992) *Progression in Understanding Ecological Concepts by Pupils Aged 5 to 16.* Leeds: The University of Leeds. Children's Learning in Science Research Group, Centre for Studies in Science and Mathematics Education.

LPO 94 (1994) *Curriculum for Compulsory Schools.* Stockholm: Swedish Ministry of Education and Science.

Novak, J.D. and Mosunda, D. (1991) 'A twelve-year longitudinal study of science concept learning.' *American Educational Research Journal 1*, 117–153.

Russell, T. and Watt, D. (1989) *Growth. A Research Report.* Liverpool: Liverpool University Press.

Sequeira, M. and Freitas, M. (1986) 'Death and decomposition of living organisms: children's alternative frameworks.' Paper presented at the 11th Conference of the Association for Teacher Education in Europe, Tolouse, France.

Smith, E.L. and Anderson, C.W. (1986) 'Alternative student conceptions of matter cycling in ecosystems.' Paper presented at the annual meeting of the National Association for Research in Science Teaching, San Francisco, California, April.

SOU (1992:94) *Skola för bildning.* (A School for Education) Stockholm: Utbildningsdepartementet (Swedish Ministry of Education and Science).

Wood-Robinson, C. (1991) 'Young people's ideas about plants.' *Studies in Science Education 19*, 119–135.

CHAPTER 11

Primary Science Through a Teacher's Eyes

Rena Barker

Introduction

I teach in a primary school in Warwick in the United Kingdom. It is now a compulsory requirement in England that all children from the age of five should learn some science in addition to other basic subjects such as English and mathematics. I have responsibility in my school for the science taught over the whole age range 5–11.

The style of teaching for the age range 5–11 differs substantially from that which is appropriate for older children. As primary science has developed in the United Kingdom over the last 20 years, one of the first difficulties to overcome was any suggestion that it should be a watered-down version of what is appropriate at the secondary level. The emphasis has to be on the *doing* of science; it is essential that the children should experience things for themselves. In this, we are very much concerned with the *skills* of science, namely:

- predicting;

- observing;

- fair testing;

- collecting data;

- communicating;

- recording;

- evaluating.

Of course information matters, as it certainly does at the secondary stage, but at the primary stage it is the above skills which are amongst the most important things to be acquired.

Criteria for Planning Lessons

When I have chosen a topic which is appropriate to the children concerned, I have certain criteria which guide me in my detailed planning.

First, it must be largely practical. It is the *doing* that helps towards understanding. It is certainly this which results in things being remembered. It promotes interest and concentration. Furthermore, depending on the topics chosen, it involves children with their environment and the materials within it.

Second, it must ensure progression. This will take place within the topic, throughout the year and between different age groups.

Third, it must cater for the weaker child while offering stimulation and challenge for more able children.

Fourth, it must allow and encourage the children to be independent and creative. A docile following of precise instructions would be very much against the spirit of what is expected.

Lastly, in England, it must satisfy the requirements of our National Curriculum, which I see simply as a framework on which to hang my teaching rather than a prescription from which I must not stray.

The National Curriculum

Our National Curriculum has been evolving over the last ten years. The flavour of it is given by the following quotations from its latest edition:

Systematic enquiry

Pupils should be given opportunities to:

a) ask questions, e.g. 'How?', 'Why?', 'What will happen if...';

b) use focused exploration and investigation to acquire scientific knowledge, understanding and skills;

c) use both first-hand experience and simple secondary sources to obtain information.

Science in everyday life

Pupils should be given opportunities to:

a) relate their understanding of science to domestic and environmental contexts;

b) consider ways in which science is relevant to personal health;

c) consider how to treat living things and the environment with care and sensitivity.

Planning experimental work

Pupils should be taught:

a) to turn ideas suggested to them, and their own ideas, into a form that can be investigated;

b) that thinking about what is expected to happen can be useful when planning what to do;

c) to recognise when a test or comparison is unfair.

Obtaining evidence

Pupils should be taught:

a) to explore using the appropriate senses;

b) to make observations and measurements;

c) to make a record of observations and measurements.

Considering evidence

Pupils should be taught:

a) to communicate what happened during their work;

b) to use drawings, tables and bar charts to present results;

c) to make simple comparisons;

d) to use results to draw conclusions.

(Department of Education, 1995, pp.7–8)

Fun

The mere listing of the requirements of our National Curriculum and my own criteria in planning a topic omits the most important ingredient which must be woven into any teaching lesson with young children. This very special thread is *fun*, by which I mean enjoyment, interest and excitement. A teacher who has experienced the thrill of teaching some scientific topic to a group of youngsters knows precisely what this fun means. We are exceptionally fortunate in that we have an infinite range of resources to call upon in our teaching of science – from our lives, our homes and our environment – and when this is combined with the natural enquiring nature of young children, it is not difficult to arouse excitement so that the science lessons become fun. All the above is summarised in Figure 11.1.

Content

I have stressed already the criteria which influence the planning of my teaching and the atmosphere of fun which I like to generate in the classroom in order that the children enjoy their science lessons

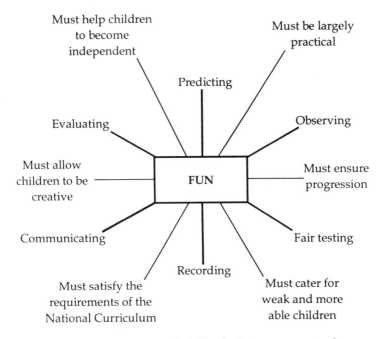

Figure 11.1 Planning criteria and skills of science woven together

and acquire the skills that I want them to have. But, of course, the content matters too. Table 11.1 lists the subject-specific topics which I usually adopt with different age groups.

Inevitably such a scheme must be flexible, but certain topics lend themselves to the summer term and open air while others must take place indoors.

A Glimpse at one of the Topics: Ourselves

I describe this here in order to show something of how I teach seven-year-olds. It is a topic which I use at the beginning of the year and it is divided into two parts: 'outside us' and 'inside us'.

'Outside us' involves a whole series of investigations including the colour of hair and eyes; the strength of hair; the effects of exercise and the differences between left- and right-handedness. It is the opportunity to teach about such things as dental hygiene.

Table 11.1 Plan of topics covered

Age Group	Autumn term	Spring term	Summer term
7+	Ourselves	Colour and light	The soil
8+	Water Substances	Substances Food	Leaves, trees and flowers
9+	Fruits and seeds Electricity and magnetism	Sound and light	The air The human machine
10+	Forces, machines and structures	Planet Earth	Revision Field studies

We measure all sorts of things. How fast can we run? We try to make predictions: will the fastest runner have the biggest feet? How can we measure the area of a foot? How can we measure the volume of a fist? (How very easy it is to tell them how to do it, how much better for them to think out how it might be done.) How heavy are we? How can we measure that? We measure heights and widths and lengths. We produce graphs and charts of, for example, eye and hair colour, and then try to draw conclusions: the children decided that 'most people with fair hair have blue eyes; most people with dark hair have brown eyes'. Sometimes we try to see if the same conclusion also applies to another class. We get practice in graphic presentation by such exercises as plotting the heights of the children in the class (Figure 11.2).

'Care of teeth' is a little project that the children do entirely at home. It is their first attempt at doing some work largely unsupported by the teacher. Over a period of six weeks they carry out their own research, for example, how to brush teeth correctly, what food to avoid, how dentists can help, collect bits and pieces they may wish to use and present their work as they like. It is handed to me by some very proud children!

Then we try to find out about 'inside us', and for this we use Charlie. Charlie was brought to life by seven-year-olds. His body is made from a cardboard box and opens at the front to reveal his internal organs. The bones in his limbs are made from pipe lagging, held together by wire and attached to his body by dowel pushed through the box. For the project, I simply made posters and charts

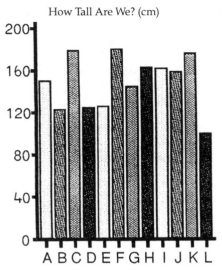

How Tall Are We? (cm)

Name	Number
A Josephine	150
B Sara	123
C Jessica	179
D Polly	125
E Megan	126
F Susan	180
G Charlotte	145
H Jemma	163
I Hannah	162
J Lydia	159
K Michelle	176
L Nicola	100

Figure 11.2 Measuring our heights

available and provided books and models. The children found out for themselves what was needed. They worked in groups and planned how to make the particular part they had researched. They collected the parts needed and then made it. They were not satisfied until Charlie could breathe, hence the tube through his mouth which enables the lungs to be inflated. The children put briefly onto paper what they had found out and I made a book of some of their descriptions of the lungs, the brain, the ribs, the stomach, the heart and so on. Charlie now hangs in the science room and forms the starting point for many activities from food to forces, from electricity to Planet Earth – and of course a basis for the seven-year-olds' work on 'inside us'.

Other Typical Activities

Children love to be imaginative and creative and there are many activities to develop these talents. Nine-year-olds made a range of musical instruments out of recycled materials whilst studying sound. The same children astonished me with their home-made electrical switches – and a 'squeeze me' switch placed under a mat outside the door so that a buzzer sounded in the room whenever the headmistress came along.

I gave each child aged 5 a variety of objects made from different materials to find out which floated and which sank. Very soon they

were predicting what they thought would happen, and some children sorted objects into 'floating' and 'sinking' piles as they took
them out of the water. Then I challenged them to see if they could
make a 'sinker' boat float.
Some children quickly realised that what they had to do was to
make a boat shape. When all the children had made some kind of
boat we talked about how we could test them to see whose boat was
'best'. We decided to use marbles as people and to see how many
people the boats would hold before they sank. The best one held
seven marbles. We then made foil boats and again tested them. We
were all amazed (myself included) to find that the best boat held 63
marbles.
   At age 7, as part of the topic 'Colour and light', someone spilt
drinks on white tablecloths. The drinks were blackcurrant juice and
coffee. We then discussed how we could carry out a fair test to see
which soap powder best removes stains. What a wet, soapy morning
that was! The children recorded their own work as shown in Figure
11.3.

REMOVING COLOURED STAINS
First we stained white fabric

1. What did we use as stains?
    1st stain..............................
    2nd stain..............................

2. We washed the stained fabric
    with different kinds of washing
    powder. How were you fair?
    ....
    ....
    ....

3   Which washing powder was best
    at removing the coffee stain?
    ....

4. Which washing powder was best
    at removing the balckcurrant stain?
    ....

5. What other stains could we have
    tested?
    ....
    ....

Figure 11.3 Testing soap powders

The walls of the room were covered with individual charts, each
with displays of pieces of washed fabric as a record of the evidence.
The children's comments on how to make a fair test were important:
we used the same amount of water; we used the same amount of
washing powder; we put them all in the water for the same amount
of time; the water was at the same temperature; and we 'swished'
them the same.
   I find a worksheet an invaluable tool. I prepare these for every
practical lesson so that I know they will suit the level required. They

concentrate the children on the points I wish to stress. For example, an exercise for eight-year-olds:

Find the coldest place in your house.

(1) Make some ice cubes.

(2) Put each one on a plate.

(3) Put them in different places around your home.

(4) Look at the time.

(5) Watch the ice cubes and see how long it takes for each one to melt.

(6) Record your results.

The worksheet would conclude with the following questions:

(1) Which is the coldest place in your house?

(2) Why do you think it is the coldest?

(3) What could you do to make it warmer?

(4) Do you think it would still be the coldest place if you tried again in summer? Why?

As part of a topic on forces with ten-year-olds, we began an investigation to see which toy car was best. The children carried out their test using the idea of ramps and produced a variety of ways of showing their results. We then wondered why car X was best. A variety of explanations was put forward. We built buggies such as the one shown in Figure 11.4 to enable us to control the variables and test the children's hypotheses.

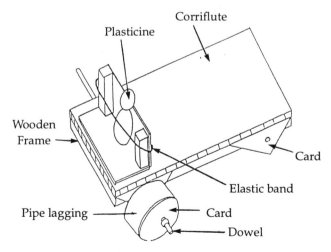

Figure 11.4 A buggy built by the children

We tested the buggies to find which wheel size was best. Did the tyre tread matter? We also added various plasticine loads to the buggy and then varied their position to see if that made a difference. When we had finished our investigation we wrote a letter to an imaginary toy manufacturer giving him our recipe for making a good toy car. All this led to work on seat belts. We crashed our buggies into bricks to see what happened to the plasticine people on board.

Conclusion

I hope that in this chapter I have managed to convey something of my experience of teaching science to young children from five years up over the past 20 years. The teaching is very different from what is appropriate for older children. It can be very exciting. It is almost all practically based. It is just as appropriate to girls as it is to boys – in fact my school almost entirely comprises girls. Science here is fun!

References

Department of Education (1995) *Science in the National Curriculum*. London: HMSO.

CHAPTER 12

Primary School Science in Norway

Anne Lea

Introduction

When talking about school science in Norway, we are talking about science that begins at grade 1 in the primary school when children are seven years old. There is currently no obligatory schooling for children under the age of seven, though many children attend pre-schools. Since one of the themes for the conference 'Growing Up with Science' was 'to suggest changes needed in European pre-school and primary school education', I have chosen to include pre-school science in this chapter. Today, many Norwegian pre-schools work successfully on different science topics. From 1997 onwards Norway will have a new curriculum, with primary school starting at the age of six. This curriculum states that tuition during the first years should be based on the best elements of both the pre- and primary school tradition.

What stands out, then, as the most significant values from the pre-school science tradition that should be forwarded into the new primary school? I will argue that pre-school experiences with learning and playing in nature should be given the highest priority.

Learning and Playing in Nature

All pre-schools in Norway have an 'outside time' during the day, though the amount of time spent outside and the quality of that time varies. In some pre-schools children are only 'watched', while in others there are planned pedagogical goals for the time. It is the valuable experiences from pre-schools that systematically use nature and work on science topics with a clear pedagogical understanding and planning that I will present in the following.

Two or three days every week – rain or shine – the children in these pre-schools pack their backpacks for a day in the forest. This does not mean a 'big' forest. It is more like the 100 metre forest described in A.A. Milne's *Winnie-the-Pooh*. It is more important that the outdoor area is easy to reach and that it contains the necessary variation and challenges that only nature can provide regarding physical and social training for children. These experiences can be summarized as follows.

Language and Concepts

Playing with science while being out in nature gives children a multitude of experiences. The environment is varied, giving children a broad spectrum of sensual impressions as well as movement. Playing and learning can be individualized for different children. Anyone can jump from stones, climb suitable trees, build huts or shelters, collect plants, observe animal traces and experience that they master the situation. Different stones, different trees and related physical tasks represent a variety of challenges, some of which all children can conquer. Nature represents a dynamic learning environment where children can have direct experience of the concrete things that make up the world around them.

Science experiences can lead to language and concept development – an important skill for the total development of the child as well as for science understanding. Conversations about the surroundings and experiences children have in nature serve as the basis for language and concept development, as they use language as a tool for expressing their thoughts.

Social Training

Children will have a different form of social training when being outdoors. Social connections seem to take place between age groups, gender or ethnicities. There seem to be fewer conflicts among children when they are outdoors and those that do occur are solved in a different manner. Children seem to switch between groups according to the activity and social structures. Playing and learning in nature allow children to have shared and common experiences. This is important as children come to the learning environment with different expectations. Common experiences are important when children communicate and when they begin to build bridges between cultures. Social training can, and does, take place through shared experiences when children work with science in nature.

Even children who need special care will profit from a structured pedagogical training outdoors. In 1993 a Norwegian group of specially trained teachers finished a project they called '*Jeg vil mestre. Skoggruppemetoden*', i.e., 'I can do it. Forest Group Method' (Nordahl and Misund, 1996). In this particular project children between five and ten years of age participated, all with specific problems, including difficulties with language, concentration, physical ability and social behaviour. The teachers wanted to try out something new when working with these children, and developed their own model. In brief, this was based on the tuition of children while walking in the forest and staying outdoors. After one year in the 'Forest group' they observed that the children used their language better and more actively, and that their social behaviour improved as well as their ability to concentrate and attend.

The positive results could be due to the structured and well-planned pedagogical work, but the teachers claimed that a very important element was their use of nature and science, both as a basis and as a frame around their work. The interest, curiosity and involvement of the children were easier to evolve and stimulate outdoors (Nordahl and Misund, 1996).

Another Norwegian project with good results due to outdoor work with science is the *'Groblad prosjektet'* i.e. 'Plantago major Project'. *Plantago major* is the latin name for a small plant that in Norwegian traditional medicine has been used for wound treatment. The project included children between five and ten years of age from a rather vulnerable housing area. It was based on playing and learning in nature with the goal of supporting the development of the children and building bridges between different ethnic cultures and between adults and children. Working with science in nature was valuable on its own, but was also a means of reaching other and more special achievements (Halvorsen, 1995).

Health

Many pre-schools and schools have problems with the air quality and noise inside the classroom. A child's resistance to respiratory infections is lower than that of adults. Pre-school teachers that go outside in their work with children report that children are less sick and that they use their bodies in a more all-around way. Many schools even use climbing equipment as the children progress in their activities.

Children's motor development and conditioning improve if they are outside on a routine basis. It is not at all unusual for children of four years of age to walk 4–5 km during a day's hike, even though the walking distance is not a goal in itself. Everything that happens along the way creates a basis for playing, learning, health and communication.

Both children and teachers can be exhausted after a day in the forest, but the exhaustion is different to that felt after a day inside the pre-school. The teachers never complained of tiredness after these tours but they occasionally did on the days when they stayed inside.

Ecological Schools

Some pre-schools in Norway are called 'ecological schools' and emphasise activities that demonstrate connections in nature. They plant and grow food, work with compost and take care of animals. These activities are important not only for children and their experiences in nature, but also for their future life situations as well. Children who are allowed to have positive experiences in nature may also feel a responsibility for preserving natural resources in their adult lives. Outside activities foster attitudes through experience and action which can serve as the basis for good habits.

Through their initiation of new activities these pre-schools have been examples for others and have had an influence on a whole local community. These activities could well be part of the earth science concept.

Could it be Science?

I have presented some of the benefits that outdoor training and science may have for the development of children. A major advantage of Norwegian pre-schools is their freedom to organize their own activities and to adapt them to the children's needs.

Building huts, making dams, streams and waterwheels introduce a variety of science experiences. So does making willow-pipes, colouring wool with birch leaves, picking berries, and collecting different materials and objects from nature. These activities offer many possibilities for, and experiences with, the process skills of science.

Free play is a part of Norwegian pre-school tradition and has a central role in the school day for children. Thinking, memory, following rules and developing relationships with others are all important ingredients in children's play. When playing is connected to nature and science, it can serve as the basis for later interest in the sciences.

Because pre-schools have the freedom to plan the day according to the child's needs, there are differences in the offerings of schools. There is a large variation regarding the use of the environment, and the fact that each school is allowed to make its own plans according to its interests can also lead to the exclusion of science.

I have talked about the sides of science which relate most to children's play and learning in nature. This is mainly because I believe that our traditions in Norway are worth maintaining and building on. There is still a need for research in this area to confirm and develop hypotheses.

New Plans in Pre-school

A weakness of this freedom is that science could 'drop out'. The experimental side of science is almost absent from pre-school practice. To ensure that the plans in pre-schools are balanced and equal, Norway will have its first national plan or national curriculum for pre-school and kindergartens from 1996. The curriculum states that children should experiment with light and dark, sound, natural phenomena and technique. Chapter 5 of the pre-school curriculum plan is called 'Culture and subject' and it provides guidelines for the subject content one should work with at this level. The chapter is divided into six topics:

○ culture and knowledge in the pre-school;

○ society, religion and ethics;

○ aesthetics;

○ language, text and communication;

○ nature, technique and environment;

○ physical activity and health.

Under 'Nature, technique and environment' the following is stated:

The pre-school, which is a female dominated environment, has shown little interest in the areas of Physics and Chemistry in the sciences. Work which will increase children's interest in these areas should begin early. Personnel have a responsibility to provide activities in the sciences for both boys and girls. Girls should be especially encouraged to work in an investigative manner.

Curiosity, fantasy, creativity and concept development all improve when children are allowed to work with the sciences. Nature is also an important environment for inspiring aesthetic development. (Ministry of Children and Family Affairs, 1995)

The curriculum framework states that children should have experiences with science at the pre-school level, even though the content is not specifically defined. The plan goes on to state that: 'Pre-schools shall work to provide children with rich experiences in nature so that they may learn to observe, experiment, order and make conclusions'. Perhaps there is something in this statement that is typical of the Norwegian attitude for raising children. Experiencing nature has always been of central importance. It is almost impossible to talk about one's childhood without talking about experiences in nature. Is this still the case? In general there seems to be a tendency to move outside activities indoors, such as skating, cycling, running, hopping, etc. Even pre-school teachers often have the attitude that it is difficult to take children outside, especially when the weather is bad.

The National Curriculum

With the exception of pre-schools Norway has a national curriculum, and has 'always' had one. Since the first laws for school were formulated in 1739, the political plan has been to provide free and equal education for all children in Norway. Education is seen as one of the most important factors in providing equality in our country. The principles of equality apply to social differences, geographical differences and, not least, to gender differences.

In the general principles for education in our reform document for 1994 it is stated that: 'Education must be based on the view that all persons are created equal and that human dignity is inviolable. It should confirm the belief that everyone is unique; that each can nourish his own growth and that individual distinctions enrich and enliven our world' (KUF, 1994, p.7).

Science has always been a part of the national curriculum documents in Norway. In the first schools, 250 years ago, the goal of schooling was to learn how to read and write well enough to be confirmed in church. Until confirmation one was not a proper member of the community. One could not get married without first being confirmed. Soon after, schools were seen as places where the public could obtain important information for living in a society. It became important for children to learn about their own health and how to obtain food. The first readers made for schools were full of texts which we would classify today as science or knowledge about nature, agriculture and the technology of those days.

Throughout current history we find science as a part of the curriculum in schools. Should we be happy with the situation? If one stops at the level of curriculum plans, the answer would be yes. If one actually looks at classroom practice, the answer is no. The road is long between curriculum ideals and actual classroom practice.

In 1974 Norway went through a curriculum reform that emphasized integration. A new subject, orienteering, was introduced into the curriculum to include the social and natural sciences. The plan's intentions were to integrate topics whenever possible, reflecting the real world. Science and social science each shared about 50 per cent of the time allocated to orienteering as it was written in the national curriculum. However, if we look at the textbooks for orienteering (which are heavily used by teachers) we see that science covers only 25 per cent of the total subject. The situation is even worse, dropping down to 10 per cent science, when we look at actual classroom practice.

Another national curriculum plan launched in 1987 (M87, 1987), continued to integrate science and social science into one subject at grades 1–6. One extension of this plan was adding a section which described how science should be taught with regards to activities and experimentation. For the first time girls were specifically mentioned because of their special needs in science. As we know, girls and boys come to the science classroom with very different experiences and this often tends to favour the boys. Classroom practice should take this into consideration, creating more equal opportunities for all pupils: 'In the science and technical areas, many girls and boys have different experiences and interests. Teaching must take considerations of both sexes and examples should be taken from the experiences of both girls and boys... It is important that girls are allowed to use equipment needed to carry out experiments' (M87, 1987, p.214).

Teachers

Even though curriculum plans may be adequate for science, without teachers who are willing to teach science, we will not go far. Many primary teachers in Norway have little or no science background. These are, for the most part, female teachers who have been able to choose other subjects than science during their education. Until 1992 it was possible to go through a teacher's degree programme without ever taking science. For many primary teachers, the last science course they had was when they were 17 in high school. If teachers refused to choose science in teacher education, they could get by with a 30 hour course which then actually qualified them to teach science up to grade 9. Something was seriously wrong here!

In 1992, teacher education was extended from three to four years. Because the problems with primary science teaching were beginning to surface, a mandatory half year science course was added to teacher education. We are not at all sure of the effect of this change at this time. A new committee will be looking at reform in teacher education in the very near future. Perhaps the new curriculum plan for schools will force teacher education to provide a better science education for our new teachers.

New School-Reform from 1997

From 1997 onwards, for the first time, six-year-olds will become first graders. The new school-reform provides for ten years of obligatory schooling and science is a part of that education from grade 1.

The new curriculum states that the work started in pre-school should be continued by going out and defining a reference area in the school environment. This is almost the same as the 100 metre woods. This place will be their own, where they will practice systematic observation, where they will work and where they will play. Children shall be active in this reference area and, hopefully, will learn about more than science there.

In the new curriculum reform, science is back in the curriculum at the primary level as a separate subject. The new curriculum plan for 1997 stresses an activity-based science programme beginning in the first grade. The plan states the following:

> Teaching shall be organized around the use of a wide range of activities. The experimental and experiential component of the subject shall be central in the teaching of science. Pupils at all levels shall conduct experiments out in nature and inside the classroom... Teaching shall stimulate pupils to ask questions and search for answers. They shall be introduced to and practice with scientific ways of thinking and working. (L97,1997, p.207)

Science topics are organized into five areas:

○ the human body and health;

○ the environment;

○ materials, characteristics and uses;

○ the Earth and the Universe.

Remembering that the starting age for first graders has been lowered from seven to six years, we have a plan that is trying to combine the best of both worlds in the lower two grades. Six-year-olds used to be in pre-schools and those traditions should follow them into the primary schools. The question is whether or not the outdoor traditions from the pre-schools which I have described here will be continued into primary school.

The new plan for primary school states that children in grades 1 and 2 shall:

○ be a part of choosing a reference area which will serve as the basis for their first activities and observations;

o experience both the living and non-living part of nature through free and steered activities and be able to save their experiences through drawing and writing in their own nature book;

o observe some of the plants and animals in the reference area and sort them according to easily observable similarities and differences;

o work with a compost pile at school as an example of a simple cycle. (L97, 1997, p.206)

If these points are put into practice, then the good traditions of playing and learning in the 100 metre woods will be continued. The key words for working with science at the lower grades are: playing, wondering, experiencing, observing, sorting and concept development. If these ideas are implemented then we can also say that the best of pre-school science will be a part of the new primary science program.

One can argue that the best part of the primary tradition would be the concentration on specific topics within a subject area. The new plan states that: 'Through play, experience and observation shall children describe the physical and technological phemomena in our daily lives'. For children in grades 1 and 2 the topics of sound and light are specifically mentioned.

The year 1997 marks the implementation of a new curriculum plan for grades 1–10 as well as the assimilation of six-year-olds into the school system. One of the goals for science education is that pupils should be allowed to experience nature and have the possibility of developing fantasies their abilities and interests for finding out about their environment. As we follow science up into middle school, it will be allocated two hours per week. At grades 8–10 there will be three hours per week.

This new plan once again puts science on the school map in Norway. It remains to be seen if the innovation in curriculum plans and school laws will lead to change.

References

Halvorsen, K.V. (1995) 'Steps in the plantain project.' *Childrens Environments* 12, 4, 434–443.

KUF (1994) *Core Curriculum for Primary, Secondary and Adult Education in Norway.* (full English translation). Oslo: The Royal Ministry for Church, Education and Research. (May be ordered from Akademika A/S, Box 8134 Dep, 0033 Oslo, Norway.)

L97 (1997) *The New Curriculum.* The Royal Ministry of Church, Education and Reasearch. Oslo: Aschehoug.

M87 (1987) *Curriculum Guidelines for Compulsory Education in Norway* (1990) The Royal Ministry of Church, Education and Research. (Full English translation). Oslo: Aschehoug.

Ministry of Children and Family Affairs (1995) *Framework Plan for Daycare Institutions Q-0903B* (In Norwegian). Oslo: Ministry of Children and Family Affairs, p.83.

Nordahl, A and Misund, S.S. (1996) *Jeg vil mestre. Skoggruppemetoden* (I can do it. Forest Group Method). Oslo: SEBU Forlag.

Further Reading

Jorde, D. and Lea, A. (1995) 'Sharing science: primary science for both teachers and pupils.' In Parker, L.H. *et al.* (eds) *Gender, Science and Mathematics: Shortening the Shadow.* Dordrecht, The Netherlands: Kluwer.

Sjoeberg, S. (1995) *Science in School and the Future of Scientific Culture in Europe. National Report – Norway.* Oslo: University of Oslo.

CHAPTER 13

Evaluation of Results

Learning Opportunities and Pupil Achievement

Wynne Harlen

Introduction

There are two different senses in which evaluation of results can be considered: the evaluation of the learning opportunities provided by the curriculum and by the way it is translated into practice, and the assessment of pupils' progress and achievement. Although this chapter focuses mainly on the second of these points it is important not to ignore the first, for as the draft *National Science Education Standards* puts it: 'Students cannot be held accountable for achievement unless they are given adequate opportunity to learn science' (NAS 1994, pp.IV–11). This chapter, therefore, begins with a brief section on the indicators of opportunities for learning science in primary classrooms and an example of how indicators may be used in evaluating opportunities. The longer section on assessing pupils' achievement begins with some general points about the meaning and purposes of assessment before dealing in more detail with two purposes: for helping decisions that have to be made in teaching (formative), and for reporting on achievements at certain times (summative). Methods of assessment appropriate to primary science are then considered and illustrated by examples using data gathered both formally and informally.

Indicators of Opportunities to Learn

Evidence from various sources provided by research (Alexander, Rose and Woodhead, 1992; Harlen, 1977; Russell *et al.*, 1994), inspectors' reports (OFSTED, 1993) and the views of experts (AAAS, 1990; NAS, 1994) suggests that the key indicators of opportunity to learn science at the primary level are:

○ the teacher's understanding of the subject matter to be taught;

○ the teacher's knowledge of the pupils' current levels of achievement and of the next steps to be taken;

○ the balance in the use of whole-class teaching and discussion, group discussion and practical work;

○ the use of questioning to encourage pupils to think and use their knowledge;

○ the use of continuous assessment and feedback to pupils;

○ the availability of suitable equipment for pupils to use.

Each of these deserves discussion and, indeed, they are themes running through the papers in this volume. Some are general pedagogic skills (balancing teaching methods, and the use of questioning, for example) but most are subject-specific and this perhaps raises the point that, whilst sound pedagogic skills will take primary teachers a good way along the road, they are not sufficient for effective science teaching. Recent research (Harlen, Holroyd and Byrne, 1995) showed what happens when teachers 'cope' when they lack confidence in teaching science and lack good understanding and knowledge of the subject matter and of progression in scientific ideas. From individual interviews with teachers about their understanding in science and technology and about their practice in these subjects, there was clear evidence that the effects of low confidence and understanding are associated with:

○ teaching as little of the subjects as one can get away with

○ compensating for doing less of a low-confidence aspect by doing more of a higher-confidence aspect

  — stressing the process aims in science rather than the conceptual development aims

  — doing more biology/nature study and less physical science

  — doing more construction work in technology and less on design, or more on social aspects and less on control technology

○ placing heavy reliance on kits, prescriptive texts and pupil work cards – where pupils have to follow clear instructions step-by-step

○ emphasising expository teaching and underplaying questioning and discussion: 'keeping the progress of the lesson under control'

○ avoiding practical work and any apparatus that could go wrong

○ seeking the assistance of colleagues and outside experts wherever possible.
(Harlen *et al*. 1995)

The same research found that the assessment of pupils was the aspect of teaching science that primary teachers thought most difficult.

Although the above indicators derive from systematic classroom observations or the extensive experience of science educators, they are nonetheless based on value judgements about the kinds of achievement that are desired and hence the opportunities that pupils are intended to have. Turning these indicators into performance criteria which can be used in evaluating opportunities in particular classrooms, involves further value judgements about the kind of learning which is considered desirable. Various lists have been suggested (e.g. Harlen and Elstgeest, 1993; Nuffield Primary Science, 1993) and the one which follows clearly reflects a constructivist approach to teaching and learning. It also implies a role for the teacher which is quite different from the traditional one as a source of information. In this example the criteria are expressed as questions to be used either by an observer or by the teacher for self-monitoring. Used in the latter way it is suggested that the teacher reflects on science activities which have taken place over a period of about two weeks and asks him/herself whether he/she has:

○ provided opportunities for children to explore/play/interact informally with materials?

○ encouraged children to ask questions?

○ asked the children open questions which invited them to talk about their ideas?

○ provided sources of information suitable for helping children to find out more about a topic?

○ provided structured group tasks so that the children knew what they were to do?

° asked for writing, drawings or other products in which the children expressed their ideas about why something happened or behaved in a certain way?

° provided opportunity for children to present ideas or to describe their investigations to others?

° kept silent and listened to the children talking?

° kept records of the children's experiences?

° assessed and kept records of the ideas and skills shown by the children?

° used the records of children's experiences and progress in planning further activities?

° talked to the children about the progress they are making in their learning?

° considered and guarded against bias in activities which may disadvantage children on account of their gender, ethnic origin, religion, language or physical disability?
(Harlen and Elstgeest 1992, pp.148–9)

Assessing Pupils' Achievement in Science

General Considerations

The word 'assessment' is being used here in its broadest sense, meaning the process of gathering information for making judgements about children's achievements. This includes testing and informal methods of gathering information. It even includes the smile or frown with which a teacher reacts to a particular child's action or product, since this is the result of the teacher mentally setting what has been done against expectations and making a judgement which is given expression in the smile or frown.

Assessment involves making judgements since the actual pupil behaviour or artefact is replaced by some kind of record – a mark, remark, score, level, grade. It contrasts with keeping a full record of events such as through video-recording and retaining each piece of the child's work. In making the judgement in assessment there has to be a reference point or standard, and there are three in general use:

° comparing with the norm or average performance of children of the same age/stage, so that the assessment indicates how a child compares with others – this is *norm-referenced assessment*;

- comparing with certain criteria of performance, so that the assessment indicates what the children can do, irrespective of whether others can or cannot do it – this is *criterion-referenced assessment*;

- comparing the piece of work with what the child could do on previous occasions and taking into account such things as the amount of effort put in – this is *child-referenced* or *ipsative assessment*.

The most obvious distinction in methods of assessing pupils is between tests (and examinations) and other forms of assessment. Indeed, some use of the term 'assessment' excludes tests and means only various forms of informal assessment usually devised by, and always conducted by, the teacher.

Tests are specially devised activities designed to assess knowledge and/or skills by giving precisely the same task to pupils who have to respond to it under similar conditions. However, the distinction between tests and non-test assessment is not always all that clear. Tests are not necessarily externally devised; teachers prepare tests (of spelling and arithmetic, for example) and so the feature which separates tests from other forms of assessment is not who devises them but the form they take. Again, however, some 'tests' can be absorbed into regular activities and look very much like normal classroom work as far as the children are concerned, and so they cannot always be regarded as 'formal'.

However, this is not at all the most important and useful distinction to be made in assessment. What is important is, first and foremost, the *purpose* of the assessment. This determines, or should determine, the way the assessment is carried out and the use made of the results. Thus it is important briefly to discuss purpose in general terms before turning to methods appropriate for assessing achievement in primary science and the important matter of using and interpreting the results.

Purposes

Pupils are assessed for many different reasons in their school careers, some of which are directed at helping their learning while others are concerned with performance of pupils as representatives of a particular group. The purposes can be described as follows:

- to help pupils' learning by establishing in what aspects they are and are not making progress, what particular difficulties they are having and what should be their next steps in learning

- to summarise achievement at certain times for keeping records and reporting to parents, other teachers and the pupils themselves, or for the grouping or selection of pupils and, at later stages, for certification and progress to higher levels of education

- to evaluate the effectiveness of teaching (where the individual is of less interest than the performance of the whole class or year group)

- to monitor the performance of pupils across the region or nation, as in national and international surveys of pupil performance, where only a sample of pupils is assessed

- to assist in research or evaluation of new classroom materials or educational reforms.

In the last three of these, pupil assessment, generally by testing, is being used as an indicator of the performance of some other person, innovation or conditions. The interest is not in the individual and the results will not affect the individual, who is generally anonymous in such assessment. This being the case, for these purposes it is not necessary for all children to be given the same test items, providing that equivalent samples are given the different items. In this way a large number of questions can be used and so a fair sample of the full range of curriculum objectives can be included. This is the procedure in national and international surveys, thus overcoming one of the severe limitations of using tests. If testing is restricted to the items that can reasonably be given to each pupil, then the extent of what is tested cannot validly reflect the full breadth of the curriculum. This is the greatest inherent weakness of testing; it is a dangerous one since, 'the relationship of assessment to learning is such that if all the outcomes are not assessed, teachers and students will redefine their expectations to only the ones assessed' (NAS 1994, pp.IV–10). The higher the 'stakes' of the assessment, the greater the tendency of the curriculum to shadow the assessment.

The first two purposes are generally known as 'formative' and 'summative' assessment and are the focus of discussion here. The nature of each of these will be discussed a little more before turning to the question of methods of assessment.

Formative Assessment

Formative assessment is very much a part of teaching, carried out whilst the teaching is in progress and used in teaching decisions. Whatever opportunities teaching provides for developing ideas, skills and attitudes, then the same opportunities are there for formative assessment. Thus it can extend across the full range of objectives, providing these are covered by the teaching. (This is an important proviso reflecting the point made at the start in the NAS quotation on page 219).

Formative assessment is essentially feedback to the teacher and to the pupil about present understanding and skill development in order to determine the way forward. To use information about present achievements in this way means that the progression in ideas and skills must be in the teacher's mind – and as far as possible in the pupil's – so that the next appropriate steps can be identified. (Progression is discussed in Chapter 5.) The assessment is made in relation to where pupils are along this progression and so to this extent it is criterion-referenced. But since this assessment is to help learning and to encourage the learner, it should take effort and the particular circumstances of the pupil into account and therefore will be in part child-referenced. This hybrid does not matter as long as this information is used diagnostically in relation to each pupil and that no comparison is made with other pupils. This is consistent with it being essentially part of teaching and not used for labelling or pigeon-holing the pupil.

The pupil's role in this assessment will be more important as he or she becomes more able to understand the longer-term objectives of the teaching. The use of children's self-assessment in helping their progress is not well developed in primary schools, apart from the areas of language and mathematics where some pupils' materials have built-in means of testing children and recording their achievement of certain skills. Involving children in their own assessment means that they must know what are the aims of their learning. Communicating these aims for science is not easy but the rewards of successfully attempting it are quite considerable, not only for help in assessment but because of the obvious potential for self-direction in learning. Direct communication of complex learning objectives and criteria of achievement is unlikely to be successful. Such things can only be understood by children through experience and examples.

Self-assessment skill has to be developed slowly and in an accepting and supportive atmosphere. The following is an example of one approach:

> The process can begin usefully if children from about the age of eight are encouraged to select their 'best' work and to put this in a folder or bag. Part of the time for 'bagging' should be set aside for the teacher to talk to each child about why certain pieces of work were selected. The criteria which the children are using will become clear. These should be accepted and they may have messages for the

teacher. For example if work seems to be selected only on the basis of being 'tidy' and not in terms of content, then perhaps this aspect is being over-emphasised by the teacher.

At first the discussion should only be to clarify the criteria the children use. 'Tell me what you particularly liked about this piece of work?' Gradually it will be possible to suggest criteria without dictating what the children should be selecting. This can be done through comments on the work. 'That was a very good way of showing your results, I could see at a glance which of the materials you tested was best' 'I'm glad you think that was your best investigation because, although you didn't get the result you expected, you did it very carefully and made sure that the result was fair.'

Through such an approach as this children may begin to share the understanding of the objectives of their work and will be able to comment usefully on what they have achieved. It then becomes easier to be explicit about further targets and for the children to recognise when they have achieved them (Harlen, 1996, pp.156).

Teachers of older pupils can more explicitly share with the pupils the criteria they use both in assessing practical skills and marking written work. One secondary science teacher, for example, did this by writing his own account of a class investigation and distributing copies for the pupils to mark looking for particular features. It led to lively discussion and a keener understanding of what was expected in their own accounts (Fairbrother, 1995).

It is not necessary to be over-concerned with *reliability* in formative assessment since the information is used to inform teaching in the situations in which it is gathered. Thus there is always quick feedback for the teacher and any misjudged intervention can be corrected. This is not to say that teachers do not need any help with this important part of their work, but the help required is to be found in how to identify significant aspects of children's work and to recognise what they mean for promoting progress, not in examples of work judged to be at different levels. The latter are needed for summative teacher assessment, but formative assessment is concerned with the future not with judgements about the past.

In summary, the characteristics of formative assessment are:

- it takes place as an integral part of teaching;

- it relates to progression in learning but depends on judgements which are child-referenced as well as criterion-referenced;

- it leads to action supporting further learning;

o it uses methods which protect validity rather than reliability;

o it uses information from pupils' performance in a variety of contexts;

o it involves pupils in assessing their own performance and helping to decide their next steps.

Summative Assessment

Summative assessment has an equally important role as formative assessment, but the two are essentially different. The purpose of summative assessment, as its name implies, is to give a summary of achievement at various times, as required. It can be achieved either by summing up evidence already gathered for formative purposes, or by checking-up, giving a special test or task.

Summarising information which has been gathered and used for formative assessment means that the summary has the breadth and detail of the record created over time and the advantage of not requiring the teacher to gather any more information. However, it must be carried out by reviewing the records against the same criteria used for every child with the help of a record sheet so that there is uniformity in what is included in the summative report and in the way it is judged. The disadvantage of this approach is that some of the information may be out of date, for example, if parts of work visited earlier in the year have not been revisited to give the teacher opportunity to see if there have been any changes.

The alternative approach, providing summative assessment information by giving a test to check up on the current performance of children near to the time of reporting, has the advantage of being up to date, but the disadvantage is that the range of information is necessarily restricted to what can be included in a test of reasonable length. The notion of providing summative information through a mixture, partly based on rich formative records and partly on a final check-up test, is attractive and is used in national assessment throughout the UK, though with differences among the constituent countries of the UK (see p.239).

Unlike formative assessment, summative assessment is intended to go beyond the teacher and pupil. Its purpose is for reporting to parents, other teachers, pupils, school governors, etc. and to that extent it becomes public. This means that its reliability is important and that criteria have to be used consistently. In brief, the characteristics of summative assessment are:

○ it takes place at certain intervals when achievement has to be reported;

○ it relates to progression in learning against public criteria;

○ the results for different pupils may be combined for various purposes because they are based on the same criteria;

○ it requires methods which are as reliable as possible without endangering validity;

○ it involves some quality assurance procedures;

○ it should be based on evidence from the full range of performance relevant to the criteria being used.

Methods of Gathering Information for Assessment

The options available to teachers for gathering information, for formative or summative assessment as appropriate, are the following:

○ Observing children carrying out their regular work (observing includes listening, questioning and discussing).

○ Studying the products of their regular work (including drawings, artefacts and writing).

○ Introducing special activities into their work (such as concept-mapping and diagnostic tasks).

○ Giving tests.

Observing, Questioning and Discussing Normal Work

Observing is a particularly important means of gathering information about children's development of process skills and for capturing ephemeral learning outcomes. However, observing is not just a matter of seeing if children are, for example, creating hypotheses, making predictions, planning, interpreting, and so on. It requires careful preparation, of two kinds. One is to have in mind what to look for as indictors of these skills being used. General indicators need to be translated into the subject matter of the activities being observed. The second is to focus observation on one group of children who will be the 'targets' of observation for a particular session. Planning which group is to be the target is part of the overall lesson planning, which will ensure that all groups in turn become the target. The children in the target group will not be aware of particular attention being paid to them; the teacher will be interacting normally with them and with other groups. The main difference is that (s)he will taking particular note of their actions and words in terms of a mental checklist of indicators.

Observation includes listening to the way children use words, which will indicate their ideas about certain phenomena. Questioning, using open questions and ones which are phrased to enquire into the children's thinking (person-centred questions, which begin 'what do *you* think…'), can reveal more about their ideas and lead to discussion.

To give some reality to these points, consider an example of a classroom event in which they were used to assess children's ideas and process skills.

Activities with ice balloons (Ovens, 1987; Figure 13.1) provide a spectacular way of enabling children to explore water in its solid form. An ice balloon (created by filling a balloon with water, freezing it and then peeling off the rubber when it is solid) is so much more likely to rivet children's attention than the more accessible ice cubes, that it is worth the effort to make. Working with children aged eight and nine, a teacher prepared ice balloons and gave one to each group of children with a

Source: Ovens (1987)
Figure 13.1 Children investigating 'ice ballons'

tank of water in which it could be floated. The children were fascinated and made many observations and raised questions, some of which were followed up on later occasions. The objectives of the activities were to encourage children to explore, to question and then to set about answering the questions through more systematic investigations, and also to develop ideas about the meaning of 'hot' and 'cold', the notion of temperature, the idea that heat is needed to melt ice and that cooling causes water to solidify.

The experiences of the children in exploring the ice are indicated in the observations they made, which included the following:

(1) There are three types of ice: clear, lined and white, or 'frosted'.

(2) The lines are like spiky objects within the ice; they usually radiate out from a point near the centre; they are fairly straight.

(3) The ice has air bubbles in it, as the ice melts, they are released and, if the ice is in water, the air bubbles rise and pop at the surface.

(4) The ice feels cold, and sometimes dry and sticky, when very cold; the surface is sometimes smooth and slippery, particularly on the clear part, but can feel rough on the frosted part.

(5) When the ice is just out of the freezer it feels very cold; a mist can be seen near it, a white frost grows on its surface, and if it is put into water straight away, cracking noises are heard and cracks appear inside it.

(6) It feels heavy. It floats in water, but only just.

(7) In a tank of water the ice seems to prefer to float the same way up or sometimes in one of two alternative ways.

(8) If you leave the ice floating in a tank of water undisturbed, a ridge shape appears at the level of the water; it melts faster below than above the water, and eventually becomes unstable and capsizes. The water level in the tank rises. The water gets colder.

(9) The ice is very hard, and difficult to break. When it is broken it makes splinter-shaped pieces.

(10) If you put ink on top of the ice, it doesn't soak in, but runs down the side.

(11) If you put salt on the top, the ice melts, the salt mixes with the melted ice, and if it runs down the side of the ice it makes cuts in the surface.

(12) There is usually a pale yellow spot near the middle of the ice balloon.

(13) Larger pieces of ice slide down a slope more easily than smaller pieces.

(14) If you poke the ice with a metal object, a mark is easily made in its surface.
(Ovens, 1987, p.5)

During the children's initial exploration and the follow-up investigations, the teacher observed the children in the target group using the following mental checklist for process skills and attitudes (taken from Harlen, 1996):

Observing:

o made detailed observations (e.g. of 'lines' or air bubbles in the ice);

- ○ used their senses (e.g. to feel the ice, its coldness, its 'stickiness' when just out of the freezer);

- ○ noticed the sequence of events (e.g. which parts started melting first);

- ○ used a simple instrument to aid observation (e.g. looked at the ice through a hand lens).

Hypothesising:

- ○ suggested why something happens or reasons for observations (e.g. why the ice seems to be cracked, why ink runs off and doesn't soak in);

- ○ used previous knowledge (e.g. to explain what happens when salt is put on the ice balloon);

- ○ realised that there were several possible explanations of some things (e.g. several reasons why there were air bubbles in the ice).

Planning:

- ○ used past experience in saying that something might happen that could be tested (e.g. that the ice would melt more quickly in warm water, or in other conditions);

- ○ planned to change the independent variable (e.g. placing some ice in air and some in water to test the idea that this makes a difference);

- ○ controlled variables for a fair test (e.g. keeping the initial mass of ice and the temperature the same in the above investigation);

- ○ measured an appropriate dependent variable (e.g. the change in mass of the pieces of ice over the same time in this investigation).

Interpreting:

- ○ linked pieces of information (e.g. 'the larger pieces of ice slide down a slope more easily than the smaller ones');

- ○ found patterns in observations (e.g. 'the more pieces an ice cube is broken into the more quickly the whole thing melts');

- ○ showed caution in drawing conclusions (e.g. 'it isn't everything that melts more quickly in water than in air').

Communicating:

○ talked and listened in order to sort out ideas (e.g. sharing ideas about why a metal object will make a mark in the ice but a wooden one doesn't);

○ made notes during an investigation (e.g. noting the initial mass of the ice cubes put to melt in different conditions; drawing and labelling the places where they are put);

○ chose an appropriate means of communicating to others (e.g. drawing cubes of diminishing size to show how much melted at various times).

Curiosity:

○ showed interest (by making observations of the kinds reported above);

○ asked questions (e.g. 'why does ice float in water?', 'does it float in every liquid?' 'why does salt make the ice melt?');

○ spontaneously used information sources (e.g. to find out how much of icebergs are below the water).

Respect for evidence:

○ reported what actually happened despite contrary preconceptions (e.g. 'moisture still forms on the outside of the tank when there is a cover on the tank, but I thought it wouldn't');

○ queried a conclusion when there was insufficient evidence (e.g. 'we don't *know* the bubbles are air, we just think they are').

Willingness to change ideas:

○ was prepared to change ideas in the light of evidence ('I thought the moisture on the tank came from the ice, but it can't be that if it happens when the tank is covered').

Critical reflection:

○ was willing to consider how procedures could be improved (e.g. 'it would have been better to have had larger pieces of ice to start with, because the difference would have been more obvious');

○ considered alternative procedures (e.g. 'the cube in air ought to have been supported above the table – it was sitting in water half the time').

The teacher also probed the children's ideas about hot and cold, temperature, melting and freezing, with questions of the following kind:

○ How does the water feel compared with the ice?

○ Touch your arm and then the ice – how does the ice feel in comparison?

○ (If the word temperature has been used): which is at the highest temperature, your arm, the ice or the water?

○ What do you think it means when the temperature of something goes up?

○ What do you think is causing the ice to melt?

○ What would you need to do to stop it melting?

○ What do you think is happening when you put water in a freezer and it goes solid?

Studying the Products of Children's Work
Children's drawings, writing and models provide a permanent record of their ideas and have the advantage over actions and talk of being able to be studied by the teacher after the event. It isn't easy for anyone to represent abstract ideas about such things as melting, but if children are encouraged to put labels on their drawings and to annotate them, they convey meaning more easily. For young children not able to write easily the teacher can talk over the drawings and add annotations provided by the child during discussion, clarifying things which are not easy to interpret in the drawing. Figures 13.2, 13.3 and 13.4 give examples of ideas made clear in children's drawings.

Figure 13.2 is a ten-year-old's drawing of what is inside an incubating egg and shows that the child's idea is that the chick is fully formed and able to feed through its beak on the food inside the egg. Figure 13.3, by a seven-year-old shows that the child considers that the observed disappearance (by evaporation) of water from a tank is due to the direct action of the Sun in sucking it up. Figure 13.4 shows the development of ideas in a nine-year-old of how an echo is formed.

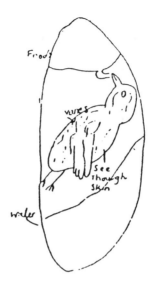

Source: Russell and Watt, 1990a, p.31

Figure 13.2 *A ten-year-old's drawing of what is inside an incubating hen's egg*

' The sun is hot and the water is cold and the water sticks to the sun and then it goes down'

Source: Russell and Watt, 1990b, p.29

Figure 13.3 *A seven-year-old's representation of loss of water from an open tank*

You can here an echo here

caves

tunnel

rooms

showers

The echo are made like this

because when you shout it echoes because

there are roofed and the sound bounces rond

and produes an echo.

Source: SPACE Research, unpublished

Figure 13.4 A nine-year-old's ideas about echos

The greatest benefit for assessment will be gained from drawing and writing if the task is designed and presented to the children in such a form that their ideas and thinking will be revealed. Figure 13.2 would not have given evidence of the child's ideas about the development inside an egg had the teacher simply asked for a drawing of the egg. Similarly, in the following pieces of writing, the children are responding to an invitation to make a prediction (Figure 13.5) and to suggest how a completed investigation could be improved (Figure 13.6).

Using Special Activities as Part of Regular Work

Special tasks used to ensure that children reveal their ideas and skills include general procedures such as concept-mapping and tasks designed to require skills and ideas to be used.

Concept maps are diagrammatic ways of representing conceptual links between words. There are certain rules to apply which are very simple and readily grasped by children of five or six. Asking children to draw their ideas about how things are linked up provides insight into the way they envisage how one thing is related to another. The starting point is to list words about the topic the children are working on and then to ask them to draw arrows and to write 'joining' words on them. Figure 13.7 shows the list and the map which a six-year-old, Lennie, drew after some activities about heat and its

> Our prediction is that people will be able to complete the test when they are much closer to the chart and the chart will be not so clear as the first test when they are further away from the chart. We also think that people with glasses will see better than other people because they have more focus in their glass lenses.

Source: Paterson, 1989, p.18
Figure 13.5 Predicting before an investigation

> If I did this again I would try to think of a way to test the sound and not just guess and try to think of more surfaces and try with different coins at different heights. On the sound I have got two ideas, one, see how far away you can here it drop, and two, get a tape recorder with a sound level indicator.

Source: Paterson, 1989, p.18
Figure 13.6 Reflecting on how to improve an investigation

effect on various things. It is possible to spot from this that Lennie has not yet distinguished heat from temperature, but that he has some useful ideas about what heat can do. As with all diagrams, it is advisable to discuss them with the child to be sure of the meaning intended; the connection between 'liquid' and 'melt' is a case in point in Figure 13.7.

Special activities designed to assess progress are sometimes incorporated into textbooks, more often in mathematics and English language than in science. However, an example of an approach in science of questions designed to assess process skills and the application of ideas is found in Schilling *et al.* (1990). Written questions assessing process skills were devised on the theme of the 'Walled Garden', which the teacher could introduce as a topic or as a story. Questions were grouped into seven sections about different things found in the garden: water, walls, 'minibeasts', leaves, sun-dial, bark and wood. For each section there was a large poster giving addi-

energy
temperature
degrees Celsius
melt
boil
liquid
solid
friction
evaporate
heat
steam
insulate
food
water

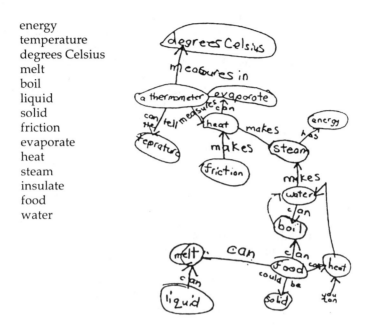

Source: Harlen, 1996, p.164
Figure 13.7 *A concept map drawn by a six-year-old*

tional information and activities and a booklet for children to write their answers. Children worked on the tasks over an extended period, with no time limit; they enjoyed the work, which they saw as novel and interesting, in no way feeling that they were being tested. The examples in Appendix 1 to this chapter are of the questions on 'minibeasts'. They can be used as guides to setting process-based tasks in other contexts to suit the class activities.

Using Tests

Tests are useful for summative assessment through 'checking up' as an alternative or supplementary to summarising existing formative assessment. They are also needed for national surveys and research purposes. The examples in Appendix 2 were devised and used in the Assessment of Performance Unit science surveys between 1980 and 1984 (DES/WO, 1982, 1983, 1984, 1985). They show that written test questions can go beyond testing factual knowledge only and can be designed to assess process skills.

Interpreting and Using Assessment Results

In the preceding discussion it was clear that certain kinds of information were suitable for particular purposes but not for other purposes. An example is the use of information gathered as part of teaching, which can be appropriate for formative assessment but could be misleading or even confusing if used directly for summative assessment. The reality of formative assessment is that it is bound to be incomplete, since even the best plans for observing activities can be torpedoed by unanticipated events, and often the information will seem contradictory. Children are always changing and often appear to be able to do something in one situation but not in another. Such evidence is a problem where the purpose is to make a judgement about whether a child fits one category or level, or another. However, where the purpose is to inform teaching and help learning, the fact that a child can do something in one context but apparently not in another is a positive advantage, since it gives clues to the conditions which seem to favour better performance and thus can be a basis for taking action.

However, these uneven peaks and troughs have to be smoothed out in reporting performance for summative purposes. Thus although the same evidence can be used for formative and summative purposes, for the latter it has to be reviewed and aligned with criteria applied uniformly across all pupils. This means looking across the range of work of a child and judging the extent to which the profile as a whole matches the criteria in a holistic way. Whilst taking this broader view it must not be forgotten that what emerges from this or any other form of summative assessment is still rather uncertain knowledge. It has to be accepted that there is an inevitable uncertainty about just what a pupil has achieved at a particular time; because a child can do something in one context doesn't necessarily mean he or she can do it in another. So the result of assessing pupils is best regarded as an estimate, perhaps no better than the estimate of their height that we can make whilst they are running across the playground.

Using a test taken by all pupils to provide summative assessment is widely thought to be more fair, but what is gained in reliability is lost in validity, for the single test cannot reflect the full range of pupils' work and so it is, perhaps, equally *unfair* to everyone. A combination of the broadly based information derived from teachers' assessment and a formal test is, as mentioned above, used in arriving at summative assessment in the national assessments in the UK. The relationship between the two is, however, significantly different in Scotland from the rest of the UK. In Scotland pupils are not all tested at the same time, as they are in England and Wales, but are given a test at a particular level when their teacher's own assessment indicates that they are likely to succeed at that level. The tests are described as serving to, 'provide teachers with the means to check their own assessments and ensure more consistent interpretation by teachers of what particular levels of attainment mean' (SOED, 1992). Thus they have a moderating or quality assurance role in relation to teachers' assessment, which remains the important assessment.

Where more attention is paid to the test result than to the teachers' assessment, the advantage of this combined approach is lost. This happens when the stakes are raised by using the pupils' results for other purposes than for reporting on their progress as individuals. This happens in England (but not in Scotland) when summative results for pupils are aggregated to give statistics for classes and for schools which are then used for the purpose of evaluating teaching and comparing school with school. There is something to learn here from secondary school experience in the UK, where external summative assessment is carried out by the examination boards and where the results are not only important to the pupils (affecting entry to higher level courses) but they are important also to the school, since examination results are published and are used as a basis for judging the school's effectiveness. Thus the assessment acquires what is popularly called 'high stakes' for those involved. It has for some time been recognised that this situation has largely destroyed the formative purpose of teachers' assessment. As Black and Dockrell pointed out: 'Continuous assessment in action means continual examination for reporting, and to make matters worse, many teachers are doing it rather well because of the skills they have picked up from the examination boards' (Black and Dockrell, 1980).

In the primary context the 'stakes' are raised where pupil assessments are being used to evaluate the performance of a school and to form 'league tables' of schools based on this performance. This has thrown attention on to summative assessment and on to tests, which are regarded as more reliable than teachers' assessment. Thus some teachers are setting a series of special tasks, resembling national test items, as their own continuous assessment. Research has shown that in the assessment of these tasks, 'there was no evidence of any diagnostic or formative element in any of the samples of teachers' assessments' (James, 1994).

It is clearly important to recognise and maintain the distinction between formative and summative assessment. Whilst formative assessment can provide information to be used for summative assessment, the reverse is not true. Formative assessment is essential to support learning, but if teachers' assessment becomes devoted to summative purposes it will have a restricting rather than a supporting impact on learning.

References

AAAS (American Association for the Advancement of Science) (1990) *Science for All Americans: Project 2061*. New York: Oxford University Press.

Alexander, R., Rose, J. and Woodhead, C. (1992) Curriculum Organisation and Classroom Practice in Primary Schools. A Discussion Paper. London: DES.

Black, H. and Dockrell, B (1980) *Diagnostic Assessment in Secondary Schools.* Edinburgh: SCRE.

DES/WO (Department of Education and Science and the Welsh Office) (1982) *Science in Schools: Age 11, Report No 2.* London: DES.

DES/WO (1983) *Science at Age 11. APU Science Report for Teachers No 1.* London: DES.

DES/WO (1984) *Science in Schools: Age 11, Report No 3.* London: DES.

DES/WO (1985) *Science in Schools: Age 11, Report No 4.* London: DES.

Fairbrother, R. (1995) 'Pupils as learners.' In R. Fairbrother, P. Black and P. Gill (eds) *Teachers Assessing Pupils.* Hatfield: ASE.

Harlen, W. (1977) *Science 5/13: A Formative Evaluation.* London: Macmillan Educational.

Harlen, W. (1996) *The Teaching of Science in Primary Schools.* Second Edition. London: David Fulton Publishers.

Harlen, W. and Elstgeest, J. (1992) *UNESCO Sourcebook for Teaching Science in the Primary School.* Paris: UNESCO.

Harlen, W., Holroyd, C. and Byrne, M. (1995) *Confidence and Understanding in Teaching Primary Science and Technology.* Edinburgh: SCRE.

James, M. (1994) 'Teachers' assessment and national testing in England: roles and relationships.' Paper presented at the British Educational Research Association Annual Conference, Oxford, September.

NAS (National Academy of Sciences) (1994) *National Science Educational Standards. Draft.* Washington: National Academy Press.

Nuffield Primary Science (1993) *Teachers' Handbook.* London: Collins Educational.

OFSTED (Office for Standards in Education) (1993) *Curriculum Organisation and Classroom Practice in Primary Schools.* London: OFSTED.

Ovens, P. (1987) 'Ice balloons.' *Primary Science Review 3,* 5–6.

Paterson, V. (1987) 'What might be learnt from children's writing in primary science?' *Primary Science Review 4,* 17–20.

Russell, T. and Watt, D (1990a) *Space Research Report: Growth.* Liverpool: Liverpool University Press.

Russell, T. and Watt, D (1990b) *Space Research Report: Evaporation and Condensation.* Liverpool: Liverpool University Press.

Russell, T., Qualter, A., Mcguigan, L. and Hughes, A. (1994) *Evaluation and Implementation of Science in the National Curriculum at Key Stages 1, 2, and 3.* London: School Curriculum and Assessment Authority.

Schilling, M., Hargreaves, L., Harlen, W., with Russell, T. (1990) *Assessing Science in the Primary Classroom: Written Tasks.* London: Paul Chapman Publishing.

SOED (Scottish Office Education Department) (1992) *Arrangements for National Testing.* Edinburgh: SOED.

Appendix 1

Name.................................... Date of birth...................

Minibeasts

Dan and Tammy kept a note of all the 'minibeasts' they found in the Walled Garden. They drew the minibeasts as well as they could.

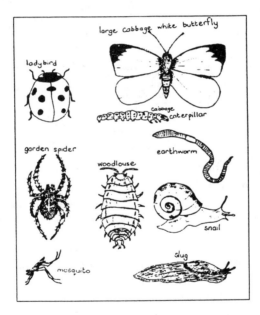

Read about the 'minibeasts' in the project folder before you try to answer the questions.

Later, back at school, they used some books to get information about the minibeasts. They made a special chart, called a table, which showed the information and put it in the Walled Garden project folder. Here is a copy of it.

Minibeast	legs	where eggs laid	eggs hatch into	sheds skin	adult feeds on
woodlouse	yes	under stones, logs	young woodlice	yes	dead animals and plants
snail	no	soil	young snails	no	dead and living plants
ladybird	yes	plants		yes	live greenfly
slug	no	soil	young slugs	no	dead and living plants
earthworm	no	soil	young worms	no	dead things in the soil
cabbage butterfly	yes	leaves	larva caterpillar	yes	plants
spider	yes	in cocoon on leaves	young spiders	yes	flies
mosquito	yes	on water		yes	

1.   Use the information in the table to answer these questions:
      a) What do ladybirds feed on? ....
      b) In the table all the minibeasts with legs have something else
         that is the same about them. Can you see what it is?
         ....
         ....

2.   When they made the table they could not find all the informa-
      tion about the ladybird and the mosquito.
      Please fill in this information for them on their table.
      a) A ladybird's egg hatches into a LARVA.
      b) Adult mosquitos feed on ANIMALS AND PLANTS.

3.   Dan and Tammy's table shows that snails eat dead and living plants, but it doesn't say whether they like to eat some plants more than others.

Suppose you have these foods that snails will eat:

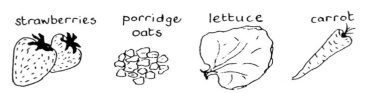

strawberries   porridge oats   lettuce   carrot

and as many snails as you want. Think about what you would do to find out which of these foods the snails liked best.

a) Say what you would do to start with? (Draw a picture if it will help).

b) Say how you will make sure that each food has a fair chance of being chosen:

....

....

....

c) What will you look for to decide which food was liked best?

....

....

....

4.   What other things could you find out about snails by doing investigations with them?

Write down as many things as you can think of to investigate.

....

....

....

....

5.   Dan and Tammy went to visit their Aunt and looked for minibeasts in her garden. They found them all except for snails although they looked carefully for a long time.

a) Write down any reasons you can think of to explain why there were no snails in their Aunt's garden.

....

....

....

b) Their Aunt thought it could be because of the kind of soil where she lived; there was no chalk or limestone in it.

What is the main difference between snails and other minibeasts which Dan and Tammy found?

....

....

....

c) Why do you think snails only live where there is chalk or limestone in the soil?

....

....

....

Appendix 2

1. Tom cut an orange into pieces.

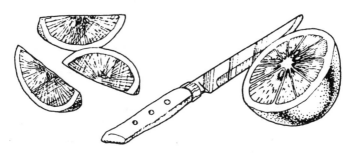

He ate some of the pieces and was going to keep the rest for later.

His mother said: 'Cover them with some cling film so they don't dry up'.

Tom decided to see if covering them really did make any difference.

He decided to cover some of pieces of orange and to leave others uncovered. He would see which ones dried up most by weighing them.

To make this a fair test he should make some things the same in case they make a difference to the result.

Write down three things that should be the same.

1. ....
   ....

2. ....
   ....

3. ....
   ....

2.   When we cut across the trunk of a tree we see growth rings.

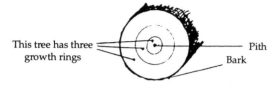

This tree has three
growth rings

Pith
Bark

The trees below were planted at different times in the same wood. The drawings show the trees before they were cut down and, underneath, the growth rings seen after they were cut down.

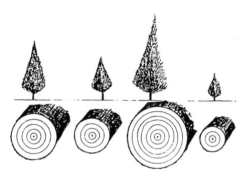

What do you notice about the heights of the trees and the rings in the trunks?

....

....

....

3.   Two blocks of ice the same size as each other were taken out of the freezer at the same time. One was left in a block and the other was crushed up.

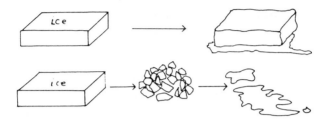

It was noticed that the crushed ice melted more quickly than the block.

Why do you think this was?

I think it was because...

....

....

....

....

4. David and John put equal amounts of dry sand, soil, grit and salt in four funnels.

They wanted to find out how much water each one would soak up. So they poured 100 ml of water into each one.

This worked all right until they came to the salt. When they poured the water in almost all the salt disappeared.

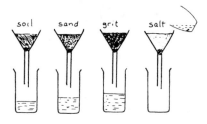

Why do you think the salt disappeared but the other solids did not?

I think this might be because...

....

....

....

....

5. Some woodlice were put in the middle of a tray containing some wet soil and some dry soil. Half of the tray was then covered with a dark cloth.

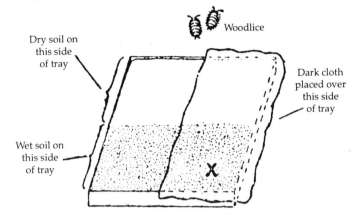

After 30 minutes all the woodlice were under the dark cloth around the area marked X.

a) Use this information to decide where woodlice are most likely to be.

Tick one of these:

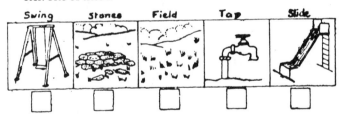

b) Say why you think this is the most likely place to find woodlice.

Because ....

....

....

CHAPTER 14

Consolidating Science in Primary Education

A Review of Policy Issues

Peter Kelly

Introduction

The last 30 years or so has seen an unprecedented output of ideas about the curriculum and, almost as extensive, of innovations in curriculum development. It has been a world-wide phenomenon and from it has come a painful truth. The essential problem we have been left with is not so much to do with having new ideas or initiating new curricula but how can they be implemented effectively.

Science in the primary school has not been omitted from this activity. There have been innovations in many countries (Harlen, 1983). As described throughout this volume there is no lack of ideas about children's learning and teaching methods. Yet we are still concerned about the position and quality of science in primary education.

Given this past experience it is important that we consider what broader educational policies are appropriate for effectively introducing and enhancing science education for the young child, being concerned both with the context in which this is likely to take place and with the factors that are likely to limit and facilitate the changes involved. In this the focus will be not so much on the kind of science education required as the processes of educational social change involved, although let us accept that these two perspectives cannot be completely separated.

I will start by being somewhat of a devil's advocate. Consider the case of primary school teachers with an interest in social studies and a strong conviction of its worth. They are conscious of the pressure of time on the curriculum. They accept that it is essential that young children get a firm grasp of language and numbers and are able to develop their physical and artistic skills. But equally, they would argue, children need to understand the society in which they live and will develop, and to become competent in social skills. In as much as aspects of science – to do with health and the environment, and the role of scientists in society, for example – are part of social studies then there is a place for science, but surely anything else – the technical aspects – really should be left to the secondary stage. And, besides, science educators these days are keen to cover the social implications of science and technology as well as straightforward scientific ideas. Surely pupils need a sound base in social studies before they do this? It would not be unrealistic to suggest that such teachers would argue against a special place for science in the primary curriculum.

Comparable arguments might be put forward by those pressing the case – particularly in a European context – for starting second-language teaching in the early years; those wishing to see a more prominent place for technology; those stressing the importance of health education for young children, and there are many more.

These surmises, in fact, are not so far away from reality. It is a reflection of what in higher education has been portrayed as the battle between the academic tribes. It is seen in secondary education in the contentions of the subject curriculum and the academic versus vocational debate; and, particularly in recent years, there has been a tendency to move the arena of dispute into primary education, fuelled by evidence that early education – primary and nursery – can have a significant effect on future achievement (National Commission on Education, 1993). No doubt of influence, also, is what one might call 'the buck stops with the midwife' tendency in educational debate in which the solutions to problems at one level are perceived inevitably to rest in earlier ones.

However, whatever the merits of subjects and specialisation in secondary and higher education, they surely have minor relevance in primary education. There a comprehensive development of the child is of paramount importance. In the balance, and certainly in the early years, it is better to carefully assimilate the child into the educational process, to encourage confidence, curiosity and both the ability and desire to learn, and to develop a range of skills, interests and conceptual knowledge sufficient to cope with whatever their educational future holds, rather than to introduce subject specialisation. To put this in the specific context of science, the issue is not, for example, to teach Boyle's Law but to provide the experience and foundation concepts pupils can draw on when they study it later. It is, to give other examples, providing studies of the environment which can form the basis for both science and geography when they become separate subjects; encouraging science-based hobbies linking a range of interests; utilising the benefits of children's interest in drama by creating science plays which will support both drama and science as subjects later; and developing a facility in basic concepts of language which will enable students to compete with the variety of types of language found in later subject study.

A Whole-Curriculum Approach

My first suggestion, then, is that 'growing up with science' is only part of a much greater concern. There is a broader educational need for primary schools to develop comprehensive programmes for their pupils aided, in part, by subject specialists but without the obligation of subject demarcation. Unfortunately, however, there have been few initiatives in integrative curriculum development for primary schools which incorporate experiences that provide a basic framework of concepts, attitudes and skills linked to the range of subjects met in secondary schools.

There is a case for subject specialists to come together with non-specialist primary teachers to help develop integrated whole-curriculum programmes coupled, of course, with appropriate assessment procedures. This will need to be done in a cooperative spirit and based on research findings and practical realities rather than rhetoric. It should recognise the considerable evidence indicating the importance of time management in curriculum organisation; that pupils' performance on a topic is likely to improve the more time they spend on it (Bennett, 1988), and not be reluctant to leave topics for secondary education to deal with. However, it should help to release the tensions currently besetting the debate on the primary curriculum and, at the same time, the subject specialisms – including science – would, in the long term, be better served.

Primary teachers would, no doubt, appreciate such a development and would look for clear guidelines and helpful advice and materials to come from it. If the introduction of the National Curriculum in England and Wales is anything to go by, this would be so – as long as sufficient time and flexibility is provided to enable teaching to be adapted to the variety of needs of pupils and the local circumstances of schools.

The role of the teacher has obviously to be carefully looked at in such a development. Although in curriculum terms primary teachers are generalists, they are specialists in the development of young children and teaching methods appropriate for them. They utilise the knowledge and procedures of a variety of subjects, but one cannot expect them to be at a specialist level in each of the areas covered in the curriculum. One does not expect a secondary science teacher to teach social studies or language and yet that, in effect, is what some expect of primary teachers.

Subject Coordination

There is, then, an inevitable balancing act between primary teaching expertise and subject expertise that confronts primary education, and policies to deal with this are required. Obviously traditional in-service courses run external to the school can be of some value, but to achieve a more enduring and self-sustaining benefit arrangements focused more directly on, and in, the school are needed. This, then, leads to my second suggestion.

An approach that appears to offer benefit is the provision of subject coordinators. These are primary school teachers undertaking normal duties but with an allowance of time in which they give help in a subject specialism to other teachers in the school. Possible responsibilities of a science coordinator would be:

- to develop a policy for integrating science into the school curriculum;

- to assist teachers lacking confidence in science, including team teaching;

- to act as a source of science information for other teachers;

- to collect, develop and organise curriculum materials in science;

- to develop the school environment for science teaching;

- to liaise with outside contributors, such as zoos, museums and industry;

- to liaise with secondary school science teachers.
  (based on Harlen, 1993)

There would, of course, need to be a range of subject coordinators in a school, accepting that the term 'subject' is not defined narrowly. Possibly 'curriculum area' would be a better description. The aim is to have a significant number of primary teachers who are both primary specialists and have a special interest and capability in a curriculum area.

Research in Britain suggests that coordinators can have a significant effect, but that this depends on the quality of their training and their ability to detect and satisfy the needs of individual teachers. It appears that, 'within a single school, professional development needs and their solution can seem to lie conveniently close to one another but apparently are unable to connect' (Kinder and Harland, 1991). Merely appointing subject coordinators is not the complete answer. The scheme requires an appropriately encompassing initial teacher education and adequate, continuing support. This support can come from various external sources; advisory teams of the education service and appropriate staff in further and higher education are examples. However, to be effective it has to be intimately structured to meet the needs of individual coordinators and their schools.

The extent that a spread of subject expertise can exist in a school will, of course, depend on its size. It can be a significant problem for small schools in which the number of staff is less than the curriculum areas to be covered. They will inevitably depend on outside support.

One apparently obvious source of such support is the secondary school. Science teachers there have relevant subject expertise and the fact that they provide the next stage in the pupils' education means cooperation is of mutual benefit. Indeed, close liaison between primary and secondary schools is of mutual advantage whatever their size. Unfortunately, due to a variety of reasons – time, finance and professional credibility, for example – to my knowledge it rarely seems to happen; which brings us to a consideration of the relationships between primary and secondary education.

The Primary–Secondary Transition

The relationship between primary and secondary education is perceived in different ways. There are, on the one hand, those who argue for curriculum continuity to aid students' progression to particular learning goals and, on the other, those who see a sufficient difference between the needs of the young child and the adolescent to warrant a discontinuous approach. It is also the case that we are not consistent in defining the age of transition. In Britain, for example, it is generally 11 in the maintained system and 13 in much of the independent sector, but with variations including the insertion of middle schools (8/9–12/13) and junior high schools (11–14). Whilst it is easy to distinguish the 8-year-olds and younger from the 14-year-olds and older, given the variation in development – intellectual, social and physical – it is inevitable that the characteristics and needs of, say, a group of 9- and 10-year-olds and one of 11–12-year-olds will overlap. Indeed, there is a strong element of arbitrariness wherever one draws the line between primary and secondary education.

Nevertheless, however arbitrary the line is it can cause problems. For example, the ORACLE project in Britain found that when some measures of children's attainment in basic subjects were used 30 per cent of children did worse on tests at the end of their first year in secondary school than they did in the last year of primary school (Galton and Willcocks, 1983). Of particular relevance is the evidence that in many countries and for a variety of reasons interest in science declines as pupils pass through secondary school (Harlen, 1993; Husen, 1993). Such findings no doubt reflect the social adjustments pupils have to make with their peers and to differences in school procedures and mores. They are also related, one suspects, to the influence of differences in what is taught and how it is taught, such as those found by research concerned with science (Jarman, 1984) and other subjects. They point to the need, in effect, for the lower secondary school to be more primary-oriented and for the upper primary school to be more secondary-oriented.

In order to smooth the passage from primary to secondary school it is important to deal with the social, contextual and pedagogical aspects, as well as issues of curriculum continuity. For the former I suggest that, as already mentioned, liaison between primary and secondary schools should be encouraged at as close a level as possible. This will, of course, be easier and potentially more effective when the schools are in the same locality. Where they are not, possibly liaison groups established through teachers' professional associations could be utilised. To support this one might also encourage changes in the structure of teacher education. It is, I understand, the policy in many countries to organise the initial and a great deal of in-service teacher education in separate categories of primary and secondary. In Britain, in fact, they have traditionally been in separate institutions although, in recent years, this practice has been on the decline. The division rested on a belief that the needs were different but also it reflected a difference in status.

The question of status will be returned to later. But to deal with the problems of transition, there is a case for suggesting that there be an overlap between the categories. Assuming transition at age 11, teacher education for primary schools should extend to cover pupils up to age 13 and the secondary course should include consideration of pupils down to, say, 8 years. There are examples of such progammes although their effects have not, to my knowledge, been evaluated. Such a reform would lead at least to better informed teachers but it would also encourage fruitful liaison and, incidentally, provide the facility for teachers to move from one sector to the other and thus offer a means of dealing with population bulges as they pass through the school system. A further extension of this idea is the provision of mid-career training for teachers to extend the range of their teaching qualification which, linked to appropriate rewards, would increase the appeal of a teaching career. It could also be allied to previous proposals for enhancing subject coordination.

With curriculum continuity in mind, the importance of having adequate and relevant guidelines cannot be overstated. It is significant that, whilst there have been 'logistical' problems with the introduction of the National Curriculum in England and Wales, the provision of a clear, systematic curriculum structure (now it is less complex and more flexible) has been generally welcomed, especially by primary teachers. At least this enables teachers on both sides of the transition to speak the same curriculum language.

A final proposal on this topic is that primary and secondary teachers should be encouraged to cooperate in practical research on pupils' concept development and other matters that affect learning and teaching. In so doing, it is important to bear in mind a research finding related to geographical education of, 'the gulf that exists between the academic debate on the nature of geography and its pedagogy and the day by day concerns of primary and secondary teachers' (Szpakowski, 1985). It applies, no doubt, to other subjects including science.

To provide an example of what could be envisaged I can refer to the work of a secondary school teacher carried out several years ago. The teacher was concerned with the understanding his pupils had about heredity and evolution before he started teaching the topics (Deadman and Kelly, 1978). Essentially, he was interested in the ideas that the pupils had developed from their primary education (and from the media and other sources, of course) and undertook open-ended interviews with his pupils in the lunch hour and other convenient times.

From this he was able to detect both potential problems and aids to future teaching. He found, for example, that in general terms, his pupils had inadequate understanding of the variety of life and the concept of probability. Their ideas about life in the past were essentially episodic rather than of continuity, and generally they would explain phenomena in Lamarckian terms. On the other hand, they appeared to have much clearer ideas of adaptation and environmental selection and recognised that generations were related.

Although these findings contributed to research the real point of this work was to help the construction of the secondary science curriculum, accepting what had gone before. In the early secondary years work was planned which reinforced the accurate concepts.

Next, steps were taken to introduce the basic, but previously omitted, concepts, and this was followed, in the later years, when heredity and evolution were studied as distinct topics, by a structured approach which deliberately questioned misconceptions.

The key feature of this approach is that it illustrates the value of a two-way vision when attempting to overcome the problems of the primary–secondary transition. The usual perspective tends to ask: what changes to primary education are necessary in order to achieve the aims of secondary education? Equally valid is the question: how can we build on – and, if necessary, correct – what the experience of the primary years has left in the minds of pupils? Extending the argument further, one should recognise the validity of a question already alluded to: given the evidence that interest in science tends to be high when pupils leave primary school and then declines at the secondary stage, what can secondary teachers learn from primary education to avoid this?

A Context for Reform

My concern so far has been with proposals by which science can be appropriately included in the primary curriculum through comprehensive curriculum development, broader responsibilities of the primary teacher and greater concern for the primary–secondary transition. In fact there is little that is really new in these proposals and, indeed, to some extent they are adopted in Britain and, no doubt, in other countries as well. My point is that they need to be more central to policies concerned with the reform of primary education.

At the same time I am aware that cynics will say that there is nothing new in someone proposing that teachers should do more work! That is certainly not my intention, although I recognise that implementing innovation is hard work. However, the comment does signal another dimension to our problem. What policies are needed in order to provide a supportive context for the implementation of the proposals?

In the last two decades or so there has been considerable research into the processes of change involved in educational innovation and the factors that support and inhibit it. This has demonstrated the importance of adequate communication and resources and the complexities of the diffusion processes involved. However, to my mind, the singular feature it highlights is the focal importance of teachers. It is they who interpret and implement change, and it is the extent of their commitment to change which determines its effectiveness.

Central to any reform, then, is the need to provide adequate and relevant support for teachers.

Figure 14.1 represents the findings of a series of case studies of aspects of teachers' thinking when they were considering whether or not to adopt an innovation (Kelly, 1980). It was one of the earlier studies of curriculum change but its general findings appear to have stood the test of time. Essentially it revealed a matching process by which the characteristics of innovation, in this case curriculum development projects, were set against the professional, social and personal characteristics of the teachers' current situation. Two particular features are worth drawing attention to. The first is the prime

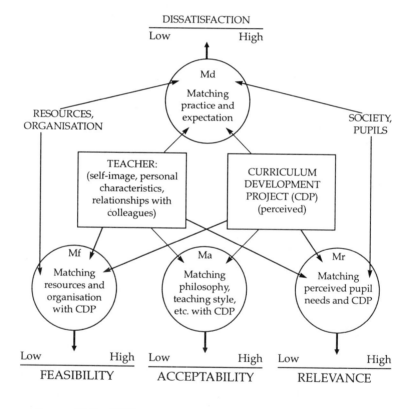

Source: Kelly, 1980

Figure 14.1 The processes of teacher decision-making in relation to curriculum innovations

importance of teachers' relative dissatisfaction with their current practice. The other is that, besides their inevitable concern for ensuring the innovation matches up to the needs and capabilities of their pupils and the resources available to them, there was a particularly personal consideration: whether they felt the innovation – more accurately their perception of it – matched up to their own educational philosophy and that they could cope with any required changes to their teaching style and practice.

Ensuring Conviction

Dissatisfaction can result from a recognition of inadequacies in current practice and/or that an innovation is clearly superior. In other words, for effective adoption and implementation teachers (like most of us?) need to be convinced of the worth of an innovation. This conviction may come purely from personal enquiry and judgement but it can be, at the least, encouraged by respected outside agencies. There are many ways by which this outside support can be engendered, but here I will concentrate on the possible roles of the scientific community in ensuring an appropriate place for science in the primary curriculum.

We can classify these roles as political and communicative. The political roles, particularly, involve negotiating with those controlling the structure and resources of education and stimulating discussion with practitioners, although the value of convincing the general public, especially parents, should not be underestimated. This requires demonstrating that there is social recognition for the innovation, that it is practical, that it is of significant worth to the pupils, and that teachers gain respect from it. Given the case is sound, such an approach can result in a positive climate for innovation and teachers convinced of its worth. Such political roles will need to be conducted mainly by the various associations of scientists although, no doubt, the publicity value of well-known individual scientists can be important.

The importance of communication is reflected in the influence of teachers' perceptions of an innovation. This is not always fully accurate, and this is not so surprising when one appreciates the magnitude of the task of comprehending the statements, curriculum materials and other products associated with a curriculum innovation. It has led some researchers (for example, Kelly, 1980) to distinguish the dissemination of innovations – what is intended to be passed on – from diffusion – what actually happens, i.e. the interaction between dissemination and the complex of influences in the social context in which it occurs.

Of particular significance in communication is the influence of stereotypes and assumptions, and it is in this respect that the scientific professions can help teachers by portraying a balanced view of what is meant by 'Growing up with science' and its implications for primary education. They should make it clear that the aim is to provide understanding and interests of value to the young child *per se* and a balanced, helpful basis for future studies, not merely a device for furthering the professional interests of scientists.

Such a communicative role can be interwoven with the political roles of scientific associations, but of equal, if not greater, importance is the more direct association of scientists with the work of schools. For many years in many countries radio, film and TV, together with visits to museums and other places of scientific interest, have provided a valuable aid to teachers. However, now there is evidence of a growing development of links of a more personal kind. There is the educational work of science museums providing mobile resources which visit schools, and of direct links established through information technology by which scientists can assist, for example, by providing help with understanding scientific information and suggesting class activities. There are examples of associations which organise joint activities between schools and scientists. There are also the often unpublicised but equally valuable activities of individual scientists who provide talks and demonstrations for pupils in a school or from a group of schools, and provide a source of help to their teachers in a variety of ways.

Such personal activities can clearly be of value in terms of communication. Given that they are conducted with respect for the teachers' situation and expertise, they provide also the important additional ingredient of positive motivation which enhances the acceptability of innovation.

Teaching Style and Individuality

When considering innovation we tend to look inwards as well as outwards. A teacher will, no doubt, ask: how does it affect me personally? This introspective attitude which, as already mentioned, has been detected in decision-making associated with the adoption of innovation, applies equally to implementation. Teachers were observed to be successful in implementing teaching strategies – dealing with the overall structure of a course. They dealt adequately with adapting their teaching tactics, such as the form of organisation for practical work in individual lessons, but found greatest difficulty and discomfort in changing their personal style of teaching. This is a phenomenon reflecting the idea of value congruence described as,

'...the personalized versions of curriculum and classroom management which informs primary practitioner's, teaching and how far
these come to coincide with...messages about 'good practice'...'
(Kinder and Harland, 1991, p.138). Research on in-service education
on science for primary teachers indicates that a high level of congruence does not come easily (Kinder and Harland, 1991).

On reflection this is not so surprising. Our teaching style reflects
our personality; a brilliant expositor is not necessarily equally good
at facilitating discussion among pupils or dealing with individual
pupils and, of course, the reverse can be the case. And, whilst it has
to be admitted that, at times, the qualities of the theatre are appropriate in the classroom one cannot act all the time.

What is important is not to judge a teacher by their teaching style
but by the effect their style – whatever it is – produces. As a purely
personal anecdote I recall that one of the most productive teachers of
problem-solving and investigation in a process-based, enquiry science course I have observed succeeded by somewhat didactic
means, ensuring that his pupils had clear, formal instruction and a
systematic routine to follow. He inspired his pupils through his
personality and anecdotes. They had their open discussions after the
lessons, did their thinking on individualised problems and were
successful in their problem-solving and practical exams, and they
remained highly interested in science. And, at the same time, I have
known uninspiring didactic teachers who have not been successful,
and successful teachers who have adopted quite different approaches. Such observations reflect the long-running controversies
over styles of teaching. This is seen particularly in the reaction to
expository teaching by those advocating enquiry methods or, putting it in reverse, of those advocating structured teaching reacting
against permissive styles. The lesson we can learn from all this is that
there is a variety of effective teaching styles and, certainly, no consensus on what is an adequate teaching style.

It is, of course, the responsibility of teacher education to provide
a practical awareness of the variety of teaching styles and their
possible effects, to encourage adaptability and, above all, to provide
an adequate – if necessarily incomplete – understanding of how
youngsters learn. It is then the professional responsibility of individual teachers to use this in adopting teaching styles which they are
comfortable with and which enable them to express their individual
creativity. Surely it is best to encourage teachers to put their own
personal stamp on their teaching rather than to attempt to enforce
prescriptions? If we do this it will certainly remove a major inhibi-
tion to the adoption and implementation of innovation.

Stability for Change

The history of science education of the last four decades has involved a succession of changes reflecting the influence of social change – including at times political and economic influences – and the research and innovatory thinking of what, in effect, has become a new profession, that of science educator. In Britain, for example, this started with the concern of the late 1950s and 1960s for the science taught in schools to be updated and oriented to heighten public awareness of science and enhance recruitment to the scientific professions. It resulted in curriculum development initiatives (Nuffield and Schools Council) which had just about taken off in schools when the social climate changed. Other concerns, some antithetical to science, became dominant. Issues such as environmental pollution and health problems reoriented social attitudes to be less concerned with the nature of science and more with its social implications. New developments were introduced which, again, were just about established when along came another concern. This time it was about the economy and the applications of science. Technology became important. Another major national development was introduced – the Technical and Vocational Education Initiative – and, just as schools were getting used to it, policy changed again. Accountability was now important and in came, for the first time in England and Wales, a detailed National Curriculum coupled with national assessment; which is where we are at present.

Interwoven with these changes were ones concerned with the mode of curriculum development – moving from national projects to school-based development and then to the National Curriculum – and those associated with the introduction of comprehensive education and mixed-ability teaching in a variety of forms. Also, education academics, including science educators, had an impact. This is seen, for example, in the initiatives flowing from the variety of manifestations of the 'Science, technology and society' movement (Solomon and Aikenhead, 1994), and the changes resulting from the influence of discovery learning in the 1960s followed by an emphasis on science process skills, then concept development and, latterly, from the influence of constructivism.

This description, although somewhat superficial, portrays the climate within which schools have operated in recent times. It is one of innovation saturation. The pattern and extent may vary between countries but the consequences are similar for schools. For many there is inevitable difficulty in responding to change, and a subsequent level of frustration which results in lowered morale and even antagonism. It is not surprising that frequently, as research indicates, the aims of innovations are inadequately met and, consequently, we are unable to assess the merits, or otherwise, of individual innovations with any real degree of confidence.

The lesson we can learn from this experience is that in order to obtain effective innovation we need to prioritise and ensure contextual stability over time. Schools should not be continually disturbed by excessive, discontinuous, paradigmatic changes.

It is for this reason, also, that I suggest that the development of science education at the primary level is not conceived as a separate endeavour, as one of several attempted innovations. It should fit into the three-part policy – comprehensive curriculum development, broadening teacher responsibility and increasing liaison between primary and secondary education – as a long-term endeavour. This should be informed by research and the exchange of professional experience. It will need the consistent support of educational administration and relevant agencies external to the school.

Status

My final, but possibly most significant, concern is with the status of primary education *per se*. It is not atypical for the funding of primary schools to be at a relatively lower level than that for secondary schools and, for example, for there to be larger classes in primary education than there are in secondary schools. At the same time the primary teacher is invariably accorded lower professional status, educated separately, and the education and entrance standards for their profession perceived to be of lower quality. In contrast to this we must recognise that primary teaching is as difficult – if not more so – than that for other levels of education. Understanding the individual minds of young children is intellectually complex and calls for a high level of emotional empathy. The breadth of the primary curriculum is equally as demanding as the single-subject specialisms of secondary teachers. And translating all this into relevant teaching and learning activities requires a high-level combination of creative skills.

It is now being accepted that the quality of primary – and earlier – education is a major determinant of performance in later education and that there is significant benefit to be obtained from putting more resources into primary education, enhancing the education of primary teachers and granting primary teaching greater professional respect (National Commission on Education, 1993). One only hopes that this will, at last, accord primary education with the high status it deserves. From it will come the benefits of enhanced quality of provision and, as it is now also being generally accepted that science should be an integral part of the primary curriculum, 'Growing Up with Science' should share in that.

Conclusions

I have been concerned with formulating policy for effectively consolidating science as a component of primary education. Essentially I propose that there be seven strands to that policy. In general terms these can be divided into those focused on arrangements within schools and those concerned with influences external to them.

a) Internal policies

(1) Science in primary education should be fostered as a component of an integrated curriculum, not as a separate, specialist subject.

(2) Some primary teachers should combine the role of subject coordination with their normal generalist roles. Adequate training and support should be provided for this.

(3) Provision should be made in teacher education and other contexts to support greater liaison between primary and lower secondary teaching.

b) External policies

(4) The scientific community should offer collective and personal support for primary teachers.

(5) The individuality of teachers' teaching styles should be respected by agencies attempting to introduce innovation in schools.

(6) Innovation demanded of schools should not be excessive. It should encourage a balanced and confident attitude towards improvement based on relevant research and development.

(7) The status and provision for primary education should be enhanced.

These proposals are based on experience in Britain. I suspect they have a broader relevance.

References

Bennett, S.N. (1988) 'Time to teach: teaching–learning processes in primary schools.' In P. Gordon (ed) *The Study of Education. Volume 3: The Changing Scene*. London: The Woburn Press.

Deadman, J. and Kelly, P. (1978) 'What do secondary schoolboys understand about evolution and heredity before they are taught the topic?' *Journal of Biological Education 12,* 1, 7–15.

Galton, M. and Willcocks, J. (eds) (1983) *Moving from the Primary Classroom*. London: Routledge and Kegan Paul.

Harlen, W. (ed) (1983) *New Trends in Primary School Education*. Paris: UNESCO.

Harlen, W. (1993) *Teaching and Learning Primary Science*. London: Harper and Row.

Husen, T. (1993) 'Factors behind choice of advanced studies and careers in science and technology.' *Working Papers in Education ED-93-1*. Stanford: The Hoover Institution.

Kinder, K. and Harland, J. (1991) *The Impact of INSET: The Case of Primary Science*. Slough: National Foundation for Educational Research.

Jarman, R. (1984) 'Primary science, secondary science: some issues at the interface.' *Secondary Science Curriculum Review, Working paper No.3*. London: SSCR.

Kelly, P. (1980) 'From innovation to adaptability: the changing perspective of curriculum development.' In M. Galton (ed) *Curriculum Change. The Lessons of a Decade*. Leicester: Leicester University Press.

National Commission on Education (1993) *Learning to Succeed*. London: Paul Hamlyn Foundation, William Heinemann.

Solomon, J. and Aikenhead, G. (ed) (1994) *STS Education: International Perspectives on Reform*. New York: Teachers College Press.

Szpakowski, B. (1985) 'Continuity in geography between primary and secondary schools.' In R. Derricott (ed) *Curriculum Continuity: Primary to Secondary*. Windsor: NFER-Nelson.

CHAPTER 15

National Science Education Standards

Science Education Reform in the United States

Janet Tuomi

Introduction

The improvement of science education in the United States has received national attention during the past 15 years as the nation examines its position in a more global economy, experiences a demand upon the workforce and citizenry to become more knowledgeable about science and technology, and is challenged by an increasingly diverse pre-college student population. The rapid growth of scientific knowledge is a further challenge to education reform efforts. A significant milestone in meeting these challenges is the development and publication in 1996 of the *National Science Education Standards* by the National Research Council.

To understand the accomplishments and implications of these Standards, it is useful to examine some basic facts and tenets of American education. Although the Standards refer to science education for children of ages 5 to 18 in the United States, the applications to the primary school level are of special interest the Academia Europaea.

The US Education System

The democratic values inherent in the founding of the nation are retained in the intent to support education for all children from aged 5 to 18 years. Decisions about courses of study are made by the students and parents during these years, based on their interests, their understanding of the prerequisites necessary for future academic study, and the offerings of the local schools. Every state – indeed every local jurisdiction – has control of the curriculum, promotion and graduation standards, and specifies requirements for the education and certification of teachers. Because the local control of schools is a very dearly-held value, any recommendations of the U.S. Department of Education, national standards or government-supported curriculum development must be considered to be resources for informing local decisions. The size of the national education system, summarized in Figure 15.1, further illustrates the magnitude of the challenge to education reform.

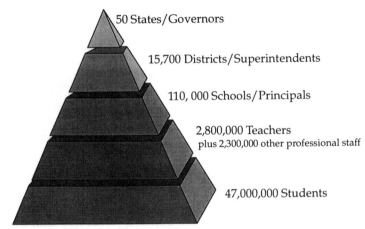

50 States/Governors

15,700 Districts/Superintendents

110, 000 Schools/Principals

2,800,000 Teachers
plus 2,300,000 other professional staff

47,000,000 Students

Figure 15.1 The US Education System

Recent Science Education Reform

In 1983, the U.S. Department of Education published *A Nation At Risk*, a report in which a commission warned that, 'a rising tide of mediocrity...threatens our very future as a Nation and a people'. This report spawned dozens of other reports that expanded on the deficiencies of the current education system. Many of these reports emphasized the need to produce graduates of public schooling with sufficient understanding of science, mathematics and technology to be productive in the workforce, as well as to make informed personal and civic decisions. Two efforts emerged six years after *A Nation at Risk* to point the way to some positive change. The National Council of Teachers of Mathematics (NCTM) produced *Curriculum and Evaluation Standards for School Mathematics* (NCTM, 1989), detailing a new vision of what knowledge and abilities define mathematical literacy, and the American Association for the Advancement of Science (AAAS) published *Science for All Americans*, describing scientific literacy. Both efforts reflected the work of respected professional societies and a consensus effort among practicing academicians, researchers and educators. Attention at the national level to improving science and maths education was further focused in 1989 by an Education Summit meeting of the nation's 50 state governors, convened by the National Governor's Association. Next came a commitment by President George Bush to produce legislation and funding to support the heart of their recommendations; the National Education Goals. Figure 15.2 summarizes those goals.

- ° Ready to Learn
- ° School Completion
- ° Student Achievement and Citizenship
- ° Teacher Education and Professional Development
- ° Mathematics and Science
- ° Adult Literacy and Life-long Learning
- ° Safe, Disciplined and Alcohol-Drug-free Schools
- ° Parental Participation

NATIONAL
EDUCATION
GOALS
P A N E L

Figure 15.2 US Education Goals

In 1991–1993 three further contributions to math and science education reform were published: a companion volume to the national standards for mathematics education from the NCTM (NCTM, 1991), *Benchmarks for Scientific Literacy* (AAAS, 1993), and *The Content Core* for high school science curricula from the National Science Teachers Association (NSTA, 1992). These efforts to guide the reform of science and mathematics education are outlined in Figure 15.3.

Development of the National Science Education Standards

The National Academy of Sciences was chartered by the U.S. congress in the 19th century to advise the nation on scientific and technological issues that frequently pervade policy decisions. This public service, outside the framework of government to ensure independent advice, is accomplished through the efforts of volunteer

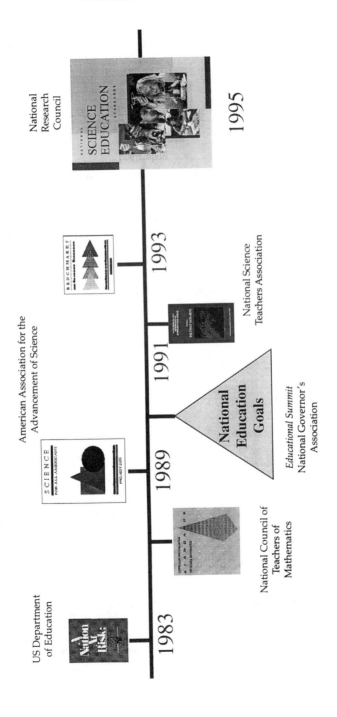

Figure 15.3 Milestones in Science Education Reform

committees of the nation's top scientists, engineers and other experts working through the National Research Council. The committee that was established to develop the National Science Education Standards consisted of scientists, teachers, science educators and other experts; and was directly and continuously advised by other science education agencies represented on the Chair's Advisory Committee.[1]

The credibility of the National Science Education Standards has been enhanced by the inclusive nature of the development team and advisory structure, which served to start building consensus during the process. Many educators and scientists were involved in reviewing the standards during various stages of their development. During 1992 and 1993, working groups on teaching, assessment and content divided up the research and development tasks. Thousands of others were involved in a continuing process to feed critique and consensus information back to those groups. Forty thousand copies of a draft of the standards were distributed in 1994, for a review by 18,000 individuals and 250 groups. These review data were compiled into 11 volumes of collated feedback for the original committee, ensuring that the Standards are grounded in exemplary practice and current research.

Principles of the National Science Education Standards

The Standards describe a vision of the scientifically literate person and present criteria for science education that will allow that vision to become a reality. Scientifically literate students would be able to:

 o experience the richness and excitement of knowing about and understanding the natural world

 o use appropriate scientific processes and principles in making personal decisions

 o engage intelligently in public discourse and debate about matters of scientific and technological concern

---

1   The Chair's Avisory Committee included representatives of The National Science Teachers Association, National Council of Teachers of Mathematics, Earth Science Coalition, National Science Resources Center, National Association of Biology Teachers, Project 2061 of the American Association for the Advancement of Science, Council of State Science Supervisors, New Standards Project, American Association of Physics Teachers and the American Chemical Society.

○ increase their economic productivity through the use of the knowledge, understanding and skills of the scientifically literate person in their careers.

The standards for content define what the scientifically literate person should know, understand and be able to do after 13 years of school science. The standards for assessment, teaching, professional development, programme and system describe the conditions necessary to achieve the goal of scientific literacy described in the content standards for all students:

Schools that implement the Standards will have students learning science by actively engaging in inquiries that are interesting and important to them. Students thereby will establish a knowledge base for understanding science. In these schools, teachers will be empowered to make decisions about what students learn, how they learn it, and how resources are allocated. Teachers and students together will be members of a community focused on learning science while being nurtured by a supportive educational system. (National Research Council, 1996, p.13)

Figure 15.4 presents the various sections of the Standards and the necessity of their use as a whole to accomplish systemic reform of science education.

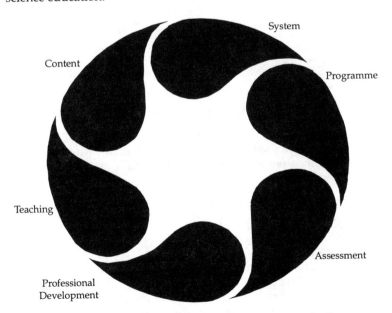

Figure 15.4 Contents of National Science Education Standards

A consistent and sustained effort for decades will be required to make the vision of science education in the Standards become a reality. What has been accomplished to date is the definition of a purpose, which will next require translation into appropriate policies by many decision-making bodies from the national to state to local levels. Further information and an extensive dialogue will be necessary to develop consensus about these policies. The design of actual school programs – and the provisions of the resources to implement them – must become the responsibility of thousands of educators and scientists. Only then will the continuous improvement of practice in the nation's classrooms become a consistent, established reality.

A Focus On the Primary Level

Concurrently with the development of the Standards, the National Research Council has supported primary science leadership development and research on best practices. Through the programs at its National Science Resources Center (a joint project with the Smithsonian Institution), hundreds of school districts have participated in leadership institutes and developed multi-year improvement plans. The key elements present in effective primary science programs have proven to be:

○ a curriculum that engages students at a conceptual level appropriate to their development and includes inquiry

○ professional development to prepare and support primary teachers

○ support systems for supplying materials and equipment to teachers

○ assessment methods for evaluating student performance that are consistent with the goals of the curriculum and instruction methods

○ support of administrators and the community for the primary science program.

Educators and scientists involved in improving science education often advocate beginning reform programs at the primary level. It is efficient to capitalize on the inherent sense of wonder and enthusiasm for exploring the natural world present in young children, and to intervene early to prevent their being discouraged from further studies in science by ineffective or irrelevant instruction. Teachers at the primary level are apt to be frank about how much they need to learn about science, and are quite adept at managing active, discovery-style learning. Many school systems have not invested many resources in supporting primary science education, not having recognized science as a core subject. The surprisingly positive aspect of this deficiency is that there exists less resistance to changing the status quo, especially when science instruction can be demonstrated to assist in developing basic literacy and problem-solving skills.

The Standards provide detailed information about the abilities and understandings appropriate for primary students in performing scientific inquiries and what they should understand about physical science, life science, and earth and space science. Also included is the relationship of science to technology, and to personal, societal and historical perspectives. The Standards themselves are broad statements of concepts, further illustrated by fundamental concepts and principles, as well as by examples of best practice in developing student understanding. Classroom-based vignettes are provided for some concepts, accompanied by examples of student work or student questions.

The Standards are expressed for a range of grades, not each individual grade. Information for the primary level is mostly contained in the standards for kindergarten to grade 4 (ages 5–10 years). The other divisions cover grades 5–8 (corresponding to American middle schools) and grades 9–12 (high school). Table 15.1 outlines the categories contained in the K-4 Content Standards.

To illustrate how the approach to science education envisioned in the Standards differs from current practices, the report contains tables listing changes in emphasis at the end of each chapter. Table 15.2 is an example of this (p.113).

As compelling and convincing as the Standards may be, a monumental effort will be needed to make the vision a reality. A school system in complete accord with the Standards does not exist now; in fact because of countervailing state policies and tests, it could not exist now. Changes in every part of the education system are called for, necessitating the collaborative efforts of all.

It is the systemic approach that separates this call to action from its predecessors. Previous efforts offered new curricula with insufficient teacher education and support, content updates for teachers with no connection to the classroom, innovative programs with no administrative support, and exciting ideas for teachers with no equipment in their classrooms. Tenuous connections between the practising teacher and the educational researcher have ensured that the teachers have been unaware of recent research on learning, while researchers were investigating topics seen as of marginal value to the

Table 15.1 Content Standards, Grades K-4

Unifying Concepts and Processes	Science as Inquiry	Physical Science	Life Science	Earth and Space Science	Science and Technology	Science in Personal and Social Perspectives	History and Nature of Science
Systems, order and organization	Abilities necessary to perform scientific inquiry	Properties of objects and materials	Characteristics of organisms	Properties of Earth materials	Abilities of technological design	Personal health	Science as a human endeavour
Evidence, models and explanation	Understanding about scientific inquiry	Position and motion of objects	Life cycles of organisms	Objects in the sky	Understanding about science and technology	Characteristics and changes in populations	
Change, constancy and measurement		Light, heat, electricity and magnetism	Organisms and environments	Changes in Earth and sky	Abilities to distinguish between natural objects and objects made by humans	Types of resources	
Evolution and equilibrium						Changes in environments	
Form and function						Science and technology in local challenges	

Table 15.2 Changing emphases in science content

LESS EMPHASIS ON	MORE EMPHASIS ON
Knowing scientific facts and information	Understanding scientific concepts and developing abilities of inquiry
Studying subject matter disciplines (physical, life, earth sciences) for their own sake	Learning subject matter disciplines in the context of inquiry, technology science in personal and social perspectives, and history and nature of science
Separating science knowledge and science processes	Integrating all aspects of science content
Covering many science topics	Studying a few fundamental science concepts
Implementing inquiry as a set of processes	Implementing inquiry as instructional strategies, abilities and ideas to be learned

classroom veteran. The school principal has often had to abandon leadership in instruction in favour of discipline, management and public relations concerns. Science teachers are badly undervalued as part of the scientific community. The Standards seek to reverse these conditions – a very ambitious task!

In the primary school, there are many barriers to overcome in order to implement standards-based science education successfully. Four significant areas where change is needed are discussed here. First, science must be seen as a core subject. Second, science teaching and learning must become focused on the development of student understanding. Third, teachers must be adequately educated and supported. Finally, a broader range of community members must become engaged in initiating and sustaining reforms.

Science as a Core Subject

Primary teachers in self-contained classrooms often report that they do not teach science on a regular basis. They are more concerned with reading, writing and mathematics – 'basic skills' which also happen to be thoroughly tested annually. In the U.S. there is considerable pressure from administrators to maintain or raise the reading and mathematics test scores, but science is not routinely tested via standardized tests at the primary level. Science is seen as an elective, or teachers incorporate science content while teaching language, arts or mathematics. When student inquiry, problem-solving and direct experience with scientific phenomena are absent, science learning is relegated to the acquisition of a random collection of facts and explanations.

Aided by the Standards, the content and pedagogy of a science curriculum for each grade must be designed so as to be articulated throughout the grades. Not only the teachers, but the administrators and parents must be aware of what the curriculum is. The assessment, program and system chapters of the Standards outline the basic requirements for policies and practices needed to ensure that science becomes a 'core' subject. What we test students for in science is a key issue. Individual states are now grappling with determining what to count fairly as student achievement, and how and when to make assessments.

A Focus on Developing Student Understanding

A difference between standards-based and other reform efforts in the U.S. can be characterized as a shift of focus from 'inputs' to 'outputs'. Earlier strategies were based on changing only one aspect of the education system – budget, curricula, teachers' content knowledge, graduation requirements – and they failed to produce systemic or lasting change. Instead of targeting an 'input' such as curricula, the Standards focus on developing student understanding of basic content areas and the students' ability to employ scientific problem-solving and thinking skills. This shift of focus to the 'output' of improved student understanding will necessitate the alignment of curriculum, instruction and assessment; and it demands coherent revisions to policies and programs. This approach also asks that we abandon the notion of a 'quick fix' and realize that long-term goals will take a decade or more to achieve.

Supporting the Teachers

In many states, primary teachers have not been required, to complete science coursework during their college program leading to a teaching credential. Therefore, their science preparation consists of a few first-year college science courses or electives, or sometimes solely their high school science courses. Since most of their science classes were based on lectures, reading and memorization of facts – rather than on observation, experimental design and scientific problem-solving – primary teachers can not successfully apply those experiences to facilitating the kind of science learning envisioned in the Standards.

Most primary teachers also teach in what is called a self-contained classroom, which means that they teach all areas of the curriculum. Some schools and almost all school districts have science advisers, but the most generous ratio is about 1 adviser to 25 teachers and the more typical ratio is 1:400. Some districts have even been forced to eliminate science resource teachers entirely in order to ease budget woes. The Professional Development Standards for science education outline a comprehensive design which calls for sweeping changes. Table 15.3 is an excerpt on changing emphases from this chapter of the Standards (p.72).

Table 15.3 Changing emphases in teacher education

LESS EMPHASIS ON	MORE EMPHASIS ON
Individual learning	Collegial and collaborative learning
Learning science by lecture and reading	Learning science through investigation and inquiry
Courses and workshops	A variety of professional development activities
Fragmented, one-shot sessions	Long-term coherent plans
Separation of theory and practice	Integration of theory and practice in school settings
Teacher as technician	Teacher as intellectual, reflective practitioner

One of the biggest challenges to implementing changes in professional development is restructuring the use of time and human resources at the schools to allow a more collegial, reflective environment to coexist with the already intense demands on teachers. Since learning to teach in a new fashion with unfamiliar tools will take 2 to 3 years of practice, the training and support must be implemented in stages. Early in the process the teachers need help with management of materials and new teaching techniques through modelling, encouragement and personalized support. Later, a focus on refining their teaching practices and assessing student learning can be fostered through collegial interactions and deepening their content knowledge in various ways.

It is also a challenge to the school districts to design systems to circulate and maintain the numerous sets of equipment needed to allow the students to be actively involved in experimentation. While 'kits' of materials are available for purchase, most school budgets do not allow each teacher to have a complete set of all materials. Instead, one kit is used two to three times per year. A well-run refurbishment system is necessary to ensure that each teacher begins a unit of study well prepared and confident. Past experience with science kits maintained in the classroom nearly always found half-used kits that would never be used again being stashed away in closets and storerooms.

Broadening the Responsibility

Teachers have a central role in improving science education, but the Standards caution that, 'it would be a massive injustice and complete misunderstanding' to leave teachers with the full responsibility (NSES, NRC 1996, p.244). All of the science education community – from students to state legislators – have a role to play and must proceed collaboratively. Among the many stakeholders, three groups can be much more effectively involved: parents and community members, scientists and engineers, and business and industry. Raising the awareness and understanding of parents about what constitutes a good education in science can help make constructive changes happen in homes, schools and government. When scientists and engineers lend their support in this effort, they contribute their understanding of how scientific inquiry is practised and how important scientific literacy is to leading a productive, intellectually satisfying life. Business and industry can provide guidance in planning and allocating resources to make necessary changes in the educational system, and need to be involved in setting educational goals that meet their needs for a well-prepared workforce.

Scientists and engineers – whether from academic institutions, research and development enterprises, or industry – have unique contributions to make to science education. Their informed support of science education brings a validation of its importance, a certification of its content and design, and a political statement of its worth to society. Teachers can use their support to promote appropriate school district and state policies, as well as to bolster their confidence, help them persist in refining the art of science teaching, and assist in finding interesting new materials and resources. Students and teachers alike can benefit from more exposure to the work and attitudes of scientists and engineers as models of scientific inquiry in everyday life.

Primary science is becoming newly energized, achieving more importance and undergoing unprecedented changes as a result of the vision expressed in the *National Science Education Standards*. Given the unique autonomy given to local school districts in the United States, this process promises to spawn many interesting experiments in primary science education. Many US educators will soon have an array of results to share with our European colleagues.

Science is a global enterprise that is becoming increasingly collaborative. And all over the globe children wonder, explore and seek to explain their world. We share a common goal of improving how we help all children gain better scientific understandings and abilities.

References

American Association of the Advancement of Science (1989) *Science for All Americans*. Oxford: Oxford University Press.

American Association of the Advancement of Science (1993) *Benchmarks for Science Literacy*. Oxford: Oxford University Press.

National Council of Teachers of Mathematics (1989) *Curriculum and Evaluation Standards for School Mathematics*. Reston, VA: National Council of Teachers and Mathematics.

National Council of Teachers of Mathematics (1991) *Professional Standards for Teaching Mathematics*. Reston, VA: National Council of Teachers of Mathematics.

National Research Council (1996) *National Science Education Standards*. Washington, DC: National Academy Press.

National Science Teachers Association (1992) *The Content Core: A Guide for Curriculum Designers*. Arlington, VA: National Science Teachers Association.

US Department of Education (1993) *A Nation at Risk*. Washington, DC: US Government Printing Office.

Further Reading

National Council of Teachers of Mathematics (1995) *Assessment Standards for School Mathematics*. National Council of Teachers of Mathematics.

Useful Addresses

American Association for the Advancement of Science. 1200 New York Avenue, NW, Washington, DC 20005. Fax: 202 371 9849

National Council of Teachers of Mathematics. 1906 Association Drive, Reston VA 22091; fax: 7034762970.

National Research Council, Center for Science, Mathematics and Engineering Education, 2101 Constitution Avenue, N.W., Harris 486, Washington, D.C. 20418. Information on ordering the National Science Education Standards is available from National Academy Press, 2101 Constitution Avenue, N.W., Washington, D.C. 20055; fax 202–334–3313 or Internet at http//:www.nas.edu.

National Science Teachers Association, 1840 Wilson Boulevard, Arlington, VA 22201, fax: 703–522–1698.

United States Department of Education. Current information can be most easily accessed on Internet at http://www.ed.gov/index.html.

The Contributors

Rena Barker has had teaching experience with children ranging from the ages of 4–18. She is currently in primary education and is Deputy Head of Warwick Preparatory School. She has run workshops, both locally and nationally, mostly for non-specialist teachers of primary science and technology.

Paul J. Black OBE is Professor of Science Education at King's College London. He is also currently Chairman of the International Commission on Physics Education and he was a member of the US National Academy of Sciences committee on National Standards for Science Education. He has published research on primary pupils' conceptual understanding and has written on the subject of primary science curriculum materials based on his research.

Kees Both was a primary teacher and a member of project-teams on primary science and world orientation. He is now National Co-ordinator for the development of the Jenaplanschools, editor of the Jenaplan magazine 'Mensen-kindren' and a staff-member of the Expert-Center on World Orientation. He has published work on primary science, world orientation, play, environmental education and Jenaplan education.

Ann Brown is Professor of Education in Mathematics, Science and Technology at the University of California, Berkley. She is a former President of the American Education Research Association (AERA) and has received numerous scientific awards. She has published work on a wide range of topics from memory strategies to reciprocal teaching.

Sir Arnold Burgen was formerly Professor of Pharmacology at Cambridge and Director of the National Institute for Medical Research. He was also the President of Academia Europaea from its founding in 1988 until 1994. He is currently the Editor of the *European Review*.

Goéry Delacôte is Professor of Physics at the University of Paris and Director of the Exploratorium in San Francisco. He was formerly the Director of the Scientific Information Division at the Centre National de la Recherche Scientifique (CNRS) and one of the creators of La Villette, the national science and technology museum in Paris.

Wynne Harlen OBE was formerly Professor of Science Education at the University of Liverpool and is currently Director of the Scottish Council for Research in Education. She has written numerous research reports and journal articles on primary science education. She is a founder member and former President of the British Educational Research Association.

Kjell Härnqvist is Emeritus Professor of Education and Educational Psychology at Göteborg University. He is also the former Dean of Social Sciences and Rector of Göteborg University. He is a member of Academia Europaea and a researcher in differential psychology and longitudinal studies of educational career development.

Gustav Helldén is a Senior Lecturer in the Department of Mathematics and Natural Sciences in Kristianstad University, Sweden.

Peter Kelly is Emeritus Professor in the School of Education at the University of Southampton, where he was previously Dean of Educational Studies.

Anne Lea is Associate Professor in science and education in the Department of Teacher Education at Oslo College, Norway. She has conducted research and curriculum development on activity-based science for primary and secondary school, and developed and taught a series of in-service courses on science topics for teachers. She has also made a series of television programmes for the Norwegian Broadcasting Company (NRK).

Patricia Murphy is Senior Lecturer at the Open University and has written numerous distance courses for professional development as well as master programmes in curriculum, learning, assessment and science education. She conducts research into pupils' problem solving in science and technology and the nature and sources of gender differences in pupils' performances.

Jonathan Osbourne is a Lecturer in Science Education at the School of Education, King's College London. He completed a significant part of the research on young children's understanding of science for the SPACE project and has published work on the teaching of physics and science in both primary and secondary schools.

Ingrid Pramling is Professor of Early Childhood Education at Göteborg University. She has been involved in research into the phenomenographic tradition of the child's conception of learning and the foundations of skills and knowledge.

Naamar Sabar is an Associate Professor at the School of Education in Tel Aviv University. Her specialist subjects are school based curriculum development and qualitative research methods.

Shirley Simon is a Lecturer in science education at King's College London. She provides In Service training for teachers of primary science and is a consultant for TV productions on science education. She has been a member of research teams on primary science, including projects on children's conceptual understanding and perceptions of science. She has written research reports and curriculum materials based on her research.

Janet Tuomi has been an elementary teacher for many years and more recently Director of several R&D projects. She is currently working for the US National Research Council in Washington.

Stella Vosniadou is Professor of Psychology in the Department of Elementary Education at the University of Athens. She has worked with AERA and will be Chair for the next biannual meeting of the European Association for Research on Learning and Instruction (EARLI). She has published work on various aspects of cognitive psychology and its educational applications.

Subject Index

Page numbers in italics indicate figures or tables.

Author Index